KIDS
FIRST

KIDS
FIRST

FIVE BIG IDEAS FOR
TRANSFORMING CHILDREN'S LIVES
AND AMERICA'S FUTURE

DAVID L. KIRP

PUBLICAFFAIRS

NEW YORK

Published in the United States by PublicAffairs™,
a member of the Perseus Books Group.

PublicAffairs books are available at special discounts for bulk purchases in
the U.S. by corporations, institutions, and other organizations. For more
information, please contact the Special Markets Department at the Perseus
Books Group, 2300 Chestnut Street, Suite 200, Philadelphia, PA 19103, call
(800) 810-4145, ext. 5000, or e-mail special.markets@perseusbooks.com.

Text set in 11 point Palatino Light

Library of Congress Cataloging-in-Publication Data

Kirp, David L.
    Five big ideas for transforming children's lives and America's future /
David L. Kirp—1st ed.
        p.   cm.
    Includes bibliographical references and index.
    ISBN: 978-1-58648-947-2 (hardcover : alk. paper) 1. Preschool
teaching—United States—Anecdotes. 2. Early childhool education—
United States—Anecdotes. 3. School children—United States—
Attitudes. I. Title.
    LB1140.23.K55 2011
    371.210973—dc22
                                                        2010041065

First Edition

10 9 8 7 6 5 4 3 2

For the unsung heroes—whose hard work
is changing the arc of children's lives

CONTENTS

A NOTE
FROM THE AUTHOR

THESE DAYS, when public attention turns to kids, the topic is invariably K-12 education, narrowly construed. The only thing that seems to matter is boosting youngsters' reading and math achievement test scores. That's how influential pundits, such as *New York Times* columnist David Brooks and scholars at think tanks across the ideological spectrum, have framed the conversation. It's how the No Child Left Behind Act defines success, and it's where the Obama administration is putting its dollars. The "Race to the Top" Education Department initiative pushed states to compete for $4 billion in 2010, with a promise of more in coming years, by toughening academic standards, holding teachers directly accountable for students' test results, and expanding charter schools, all in the name of making students more literate and numerate.

Tankers of ink have been spilled in toxic debates over the virtues of this approach. "No excuses," its proponents say: The single-minded emphasis on bridging the achievement gap calls schools on the carpet for practicing what former president George W. Bush derided as "the soft bigotry of low expectations."[1] The critics counter that it creates a teach-to-the-test regime, that it gives short shrift to everything from art and music to civics and science, and that it ignores all the other factors—including life outside the school—that mold the lives of children and youth.[2]

It's a false debate. Surely no one would deny that reading and math are keys to the kingdom of success, but it's equally plain that children need more than a 2 R's education. In the late 1960s, when I was the founding director of the Harvard Center for Law and Education, I came to appreciate this problem up close and personal. When parents showed up at legal services clinics with concerns about their kids' health or welfare, the lawyers couldn't do much; only when the problem had to do with school could they swing into action. To these rights-minded attorneys this made sense, because unequal opportunities in education, unlike inequities in health or welfare, could be challenged in court. But viewed from the parents' or children's perspective, it was foolishness. They're right: It's the kids, not just their left brain development between the ages of five and eighteen, we should concentrate on.

What transpires before kindergarten—in the first "school," the family, as well as in preschool—influences everything that happens later in kids' lives. And during their school years youngsters need more than good teachers. Growing up is a journey fraught with challenges. The hours after 3 P.M. and during the summer are critical. Children need to be emotionally and physically healthy. They need reliable and caring adult guidance through the shoals of adolescence and into the world beyond the schoolhouse. They need financial resources for college or vocational training. Most of all they need to feel connected to and part of a larger community and need to be aware of their options for finding their place in it as workers and citizens.

Some people feel that it is a family's—not a government's or a society's—job to meet these needs. But in today's America, in today's economy, fewer and fewer families across the social strata are able to do so without help. If kids' needs go unmet, the consequences for our society, our economy, and our future are enormous. Our children, as the lyric goes, are our future, and their growth into productive and responsible citizens is essential to the public interest.

The value of concentrating on kids, not just on the 2 R's, was drummed into me immediately after the 2008 election, when I served on the Presidential Transition Team. My book *The Sandbox Investment: The Preschool Movement and Kids-First Politics* had been published the previous year, and it had attracted considerable attention among policymakers and politicians, academics and activists. I'd traveled around the country to talk about why early education was of such vital importance, and that visibility likely led to my appointment. There were just a handful of us in the education policy group, which was charged with crafting strategies on issues ranging from parenting to postgraduate education. I worked mainly on developing an early learning and child development agenda.

In the time between the election and the inauguration, seemingly every youth-related organization in the country wanted to meet with us, because they'd felt shut out of the policy conversation during the Bush administration, and so our small gang had to become instant experts on a host of topics. For an hour or so I'd have to bone up on vocational education in order to have plausible questions to pose, and later that day I'd need to be primed to talk about parenting programs. We met with all of them—the nurse home visitors, the vocational education lobby, the pediatricians, the advocates for adolescents who had fallen (or jumped) off the conveyor belt, and lots more.

While everyone we spoke with had the best of intentions, almost all of them suffered from tunnel vision. University leaders didn't connect with community-college supporters, let alone K-12 activists. Early-learning experts distinguished themselves from child-care advocates. Amid the jockeying for primacy of position and competition for scarce public dollars, none of these advocates could step back from the fray to contemplate the full array of needs from cradle to college.

Going from one conversation to the next, absorbing the views and contemplating the concerns of each group, I began to think about pulling the pieces together and devising a coherent system of supports that included, but didn't begin or end with, rigorous K-12 education. What do kids need? How can we as a society have the greatest impact in assisting families to meet those needs? What would a realistic policy agenda look like that puts the needs of kids first? This book emerged from those questions.

Kids First proposes five big ideas for programs that would transform children's lives—and America's future. There's nothing magical or definitive about the number five. It's easy to remember, and we all like best-of lists. Whether it's David Letterman's "Top Ten Ways BP Can Improve Its Image" or *U.S. News & World Report*'s "Top 50 Colleges," the list gives us something to focus on and debate about. So, too, the choice of five big ideas for kids.

When I asked friends and experts what belonged on my "big ideas" inventory, they offered scores of suggestions, ranging from reengaging disaffected youth to giving kids more exposure to the arts. My first cut contained a bakers' dozen of ideas, including greatly expanded child care, a commission to assess the "child impact" of federal policies (just as we look at environmental impact) and a "Berlitz for all" initiative to make American children true citizens of the world.

The five ideas that I've targeted share some key features. They don't single out any particular group, but instead are universal in their reach, offering something of value for every youngster. Rather than tinkering at the margin, they're game-changers that can alter the arc of children's lives. Far from being untested, they've been proven to be effective. They are sturdy enough to be usable across the American landscape. And they're affordable: Think Kia, not Cadillac.

What's most important, these five ideas constitute the building blocks of a solid system of supports from cradle to college. Each of them is designed to reinforce the others, multiplying their impact. Conservative readers, have no fear: I don't have in mind a Bureau of Child Welfare that manages the lives of the young. Quite the contrary—the aim is to make widely available what all parents want for their children, to treat every youngster as well as we'd want our own children to be treated. That's the Golden Rule, and it's sound ethics, whatever your ideology. What's more, it's good for kids and a solid investment for the rest of us.

I don't expect everyone to agree with my choices—indeed, it would be great if people started to generate and mobilize around their own "big ideas" agendas. To be sure, some choices will have to be made and priorities set, because, politically speaking, long wish lists with outsized price-tags are dead on arrival. Kids are politically invisible, and that has to change. Shifting the focus—turning kids' concerns into a widely accepted public priority—is what the kids-first agenda is all about. As the standard disclaimer goes, the buck stops here. If I can prod you, gentle reader, into thinking hard about what kids need and deserve, then I've accomplished precisely what I set out to do.

INTRODUCTION:
FROM CRIB TO COLLEGE

ONE FINE SPRING DAY a few years back, a society matron and prospective donor toured the Salomé Ureña Middle School, a public school at the northernmost tip of Manhattan in Washington Heights, a neighborhood better known for drug deals than good education. She had her twenty-something son in tow, and although he'd gone to the best prep school that money could buy, he marveled at what he saw: classes taught by City University of New York professors; one-on-one tutoring; a clinic that provides everything from eye exams to orthodontia; an after-school program whose riches include dance lessons led by members of the New York City ballet corps, Chinese cooking, and a bike-building class; summer-time explorations; even some evening classes for adults that might appeal to just about anyone.

"I wish I'd had a school like this," the young man said.

He's not the only one. Most of us know what's good for kids when we see it. We know the kinds of support children need if they're going to reach their full potential. And we have created some superb programs that deliver what's needed—not only in the leafy suburbs and the urban Gold Coasts but in seemingly unpromising places like Washington Heights as well.

Whether it's helping young families who are about to have their first child; providing high-quality early education and child care from crib to kindergarten, a time when children's minds are especially malleable; opening dawn-to-dusk, year-round schools that link children and families to the trove of opportunities available in the larger world; finding stable and caring adults who can help teens make their way; or under-writing their long-term dreams for college and a better life, America knows how to do it.

Over the course of the past half-century, literally thousands of experiments across the country have sought ways to raise healthy, happy kids by removing the biggest obstacles to their success. They've focused on everything from improving their reading skills to reducing teen pregnancy, from con-fronting attention deficit disorder to making summer an op-portunity to learn in new ways. Close-grained research has ferreted out which of these ventures really work.

Stable, middle-class families clamor for this kind of help—and rightly so, because such initiatives can change the course of a child's life. The impact is greater still for youngsters from poor and broken families who live in dicey neighborhoods. Without such support, they have only the remotest chance of making it.

FAR FROM NIRVANA

If all families had the option of enrolling their children in pro-grams as good as the best we've devised, America would be Nirvana for the young. But what's available doesn't come close to Nirvana. Although there are oases of top-notch offerings scattered across the country, they can accommodate only a handful of fortunate children. Many families are obliged to settle for mediocrity; many more receive little, if anything, of value. On a single block, sometimes in a single household, great things may be happening for one child, while nothing is being done for the youngsters who live next door or the siblings who've been left out.

Wealthy families can afford to make up the gaps themselves—to blanket their children with support from crib to college. They start off with nannies to assist at home, then spend whatever it takes to get their kids into prestigious preschools, which promise to give toddlers a leg up in the mini-rat-race. These academies of early learning, which charge upward of $20,000 a year, with a generous contribution expected as well, have pupil-teacher ratios rivaling an Oxford tutorial, and some of their teachers possess credentials that could land them university jobs. The most renowned, like the 92nd Street Y in New York City and the Lab School at the University of Chicago, are harder to get into than Harvard. *Nursery University*, a pithy 2008 documentary, detailed the contortions that parents go through in order to secure a coveted place for their three-year-old scions-to-be. There are meetings with "application consultants" who charge $4,000 for seven sessions; heated arguments between parents over whether to say on the application that their child is eager to "engage" or "explore" the richness of the school's activities; and speed-dialing the morning after Labor Day simply to secure an application form.

Preschool is just the start. Well-heeled parents search out private schools with a pipeline to the Ivy League, and hire tennis coaches to turn their children into budding Roger Federers.

They pull strings to secure internships in archaeological digs or their congressman's office, sustaining their kids' interest in academics and more, honing their talents, and impressing their elders. They rely on the best tutors and the finest therapists and pediatricians. They turn to friends, friends of friends, and professionals to make the necessary introductions for their teens or to guide wayward adolescents back on track. And they set up trust funds to pay the college tab, which may run a quarter of a million dollars—and that doesn't count grad school.

Middle-class parents can find themselves spending every spare penny to approximate such advantages for their own kids, while families at the bottom of the economic ladder don't even have pennies to spare. The fate of their children is essentially determined by the luck of the draw. The fact that only a few of them consistently get the assistance that leads to success—assistance that we know perfectly well how to deliver—reflects a failure of leadership and public will.

It's not just the left-out kids who wind up losing—the rest of us also pay dearly. Brainpower has been America's comparative edge, and our fortunes are intertwined within and across the generations. As Harvard economists Claudia Goldin and Lawrence Katz elegantly demonstrated in *The Race Between Education and Technology*, our global economic superiority can largely be explained by the fact that during much of the twentieth century the United States had a thirty-five-year lead, compared to other industrialized nations, in the spread of higher education. But this historic advantage has evaporated during the past forty years. Other countries have sprinted past us, in education as well as in an array of supports that enable youngsters to take full advantage of the education that's available.[1]

Americans are not blind to what is happening. Since the founding of the republic we've prided ourselves on being good stewards who leave the country in better shape for the next generation. No longer. In a 2008 nationwide poll commissioned by the nonpartisan think tank, First Focus, just 27 percent of voters said that the lives of children would be better than their own; more than twice as many said things would be worse.

We know what needs to be done to improve children's capacity for success and with it the future of the nation. What's more, we know how to do it. Yet while we say that we love kids—insert the phrase "for the children" into any policy pitch, the pollsters report, and popular support rises 10 percent—as a nation we fall short.

Youngsters make great photo-ops for politicians, whether at a child-care center or a high-school graduation. But the photo is where this public love-fest ends. Although the United States is the richest nation in the world, a 2009 study of thirty countries that belong to the Organization for Economic Co-operation and Development (essentially the richest countries in the world) reports that the child poverty rate in this country is twice the OECD average. We spend a third less than the OECD average on young children; we rank near the bottom when it comes to infant mortality and child mortality; and the average educational achievement of an American youngster is seventh worst, behind the Slovak Republic.[2]

"We are living in an age of reverse-generativity," with the old taking from the young—taking money, freedom, and opportunity, wrote *New York Times* columnist David Brooks. "In the private sphere, seniors provide wonderful gifts to their grandchildren, loving attention that will linger in young minds, providing support for decades to come. In the public sphere, they take it away." The federal government spends less than $3,000 annually for each child—and seven times more for a senior.[3]

During the past half-century, without anyone paying much attention, Washington has steadily and substantially trimmed the share of the federal budget that's spent on children. Between 1960 and 2008, the nonpartisan think tank First Focus reported in *Children's Budget 2009*, the share of domestic expenditures devoted to youth has fallen a jaw-dropping 22 percent. The kids' share did rise in the first year of the Obama administration, but much of that increase came from the one-time stimulus package—in fact, if it weren't for the stimulus, the percent of the federal budget spent on youth would have been smaller than in 2005.[4]

In 2010, the Obama administration proposed a 10 percent boost—mostly in mandatory programs like the Children's Health Insurance Program, generally known as CHIP. Although that's good news, it doesn't match the increase in the overall budget. In other words, youngsters keep getting an ever-smaller slice of the federal pie.

And the situation for kids is likely to get much worse. In the short term, gridlock in Congress means federal funding for youngsters isn't going to grow, since Republicans have shown little interest in kids' needs. The long-term picture is especially grim. Because of the ever-mounting cost of Medicare and Social Security, by 2019 the share of the gross domestic product that goes to support children is predicted to fall from 2.4 percent to 1.9 percent—a 20 percent decline.[5] "The squeeze between growing entitlements [Medicaid and Social Security] and existing taxes—a squeeze affecting children's programs—is taking place now," a 2008 report by the Urban Institute and the Brookings Institution concluded. "By action and inaction, both political parties bear responsibility for choosing this path and for allowing other priorities to take precedence."

Things are no better in the states, which, unlike Washington, have to balance their budgets and remain awash in red ink. Across the country, the school day is getting smaller, class sizes are getting bigger, and summer programs, health clinics, and after-school activities—the "frills" that can actually spell success or failure—are being eliminated.

Whether you're motivated by social justice or enlightened self-interest, this is policy perversity. The cost to the American economy of a high-school dropout is about a quarter of a million dollars, and a career criminal costs the country $1.5 million. "If the United States had in recent years closed the gap between its achievement levels and those of better-performing nations such as Finland and Korea, the gross domestic product in 2008 could have been between $1.3 and $2.3 trillion higher," a McKinsey report concluded. "This represents 9 to 16 percent of GDP."[6]

A mountain of research by geneticists, neuroscientists, child psychologists, and economists converges on the proposition that investing in the future of children yields handsome long-term gains for youth, in happier and more successful lives, as well as for the rest of us, in greater prosperity and a livelier democracy. Economists calibrate the benefits of a good parent-support program at more than three times higher the cost. For an exemplary preschool, the lifetime benefit/cost ratio can run as high as seventeen-to-one, a figure that Warren Buffett couldn't hope to match on Wall Street.[7]

THE GOLDEN RULE

What's needed is a new paradigm for how we think about youth—a *kids-first* approach. The guiding principle is as simple, and as powerful, as the Golden Rule: *Every child deserves what's good enough for a child you love.*

Making kids a national priority doesn't require breaking the bank by sending every toddler to the equivalent of the 92nd Street Y prekindergarten or every teen on a summer safari to Botswana. Increasing total federal spending on children by about 20 percent, $265.9 billion in 2010, and shifting dollars to where they can do the most good, would make a powerful difference.[8] All children deserve the kind of support that gives them their best chance to learn and to grow—to acquire the skills and resiliency necessary to meet the challenges that life invariably throws at them. This isn't a one-size-fits-all agenda, but support that can meet their particular needs—support that's family-centered, effective, and unwavering. After all, isn't this what you'd want for your own child?

Children's policy generally concentrates on ways to help kids from the wrong side of the tracks. While that's understandable, since in the lottery of life poor children often fare the worst and need the most, it's a mistake to think that a kids-first solution simply requires *us* to do something for *them.* The Golden Rule standard isn't about charity or acts of noblesse oblige: All children, not only those who grow up without money, would prosper if a web of crib-to-college supports were available in every community.

The old joke is that the most important decision any child can make is choosing his or her parents. The point, of course, is that no one exerts more influence on children's lives than their parents. And the conventional wisdom is also true in some important respects: While all families hope to do what's best for their kids, poor parents are less successful than their middle-class counterparts—how much time they spend reading and talking to their children is a good example.[9] But the worst harm to children is done by abusive and neglectful parents; and contrary to common surmise, middle-class youngsters are just as likely to be its victims as poor ones.[10]

As you'd expect, in many ways poor kids *do* fare the worst. Those children, more than one out of five whose family income falls below the poverty line are more likely to do badly in school, become teen parents, and, later on, have a hard time finding a job. Ten percent of them don't have ready access to a doctor; a third rarely, if ever, see a dentist; and one in six can't always count on eating enough to lead an active, healthy life. By the time they enter kindergarten they lag on measures of cognitive skills as well as social and emotional development, and those early differences expand as they progress through school. Matters are only marginally better for the 20 percent of kids whose families earn between 100 and 200 percent of the poverty level, the amount required to cover basic expenses.[11]

These statistics of woe have become so numbingly familiar, the assertions about our public indifference so predictable, that what might be called "child poverty fatigue" has settled in—we know these facts and don't do anything about them. But while middle-class youngsters aren't confronted with all these disadvantages, their situation is hardly cause for complacency.

What's happening in our schools illustrates why middle-class parents should be concerned. In tests of reading and math readiness administered to youngsters when they arrive at kindergarten, the gap between middle-income kids and those born to wealth is just as big as the gap that separates the poor from the middle class. More than 10 percent of middle-class children repeat a grade or drop out before the end of twelfth grade.[12]

A host of factors makes life hard for youngsters across the social spectrum. With mothers and fathers working long hours and dependable child care hard to come by, millions of middle-class youth are left on their own after school, just as those living in tougher circumstances are, often for three or four hours at a stretch. That makes them much more likely to do worse academically and to get in trouble with the law.[13] More than 2 million youngsters have been made homeless by the recent flood of foreclosures; especially hard hit are families striving for a toehold in the middle class, many of them with young children.[14] Rich and middle-income teens are as likely as poor adolescents to be drug-abusers. And regardless of the amount of their parents' paycheck, one youngster in five suffers from a mental disorder such as attention deficit and hyperactivity disorder (ADHD), anxiety, or depression, which often goes undiagnosed and untreated. Whether they're rich, middle class, or poor, such youngsters are likely to arrive at school unprepared to learn. Their reading and math scores suffer, and they are more likely to be left back and to drop out.[15]

Any of these problems can derail a child. The aim of a kids-first approach is to make the availability of cradle-to-college help something that American families take as much for granted as well-baby checkups—to make the array of supports that kids need as commonly available as kindergarten.

A KIDS-FIRST AGENDA—FIVE BIG IDEAS

What does it take to turn the Golden Rule into good policy? What kinds of support produce the biggest results for children, and which can be scaled up to reach millions of them? The chapters that follow combine analyses of state-of-the-art research with on-the-ground accounts of powerful initiatives. Each chapter lays out one of five ideas that make up the kids-first agenda.

Here they are:

1. Give new parents strong support.
2. Provide high-quality early education.
3. Link schools and communities to improve what both offer children.
4. Provide mentors to youngsters who need a stable, caring adult in their lives.
5. Give kids a nest egg that helps pay for college or kick-start a career.

These policies would improve every youngster's chances of success. They would promote fairness as well as efficiency. They've been proven to work in even the grimmest circumstances. They can be put in place on a wide scale. They command widespread popular support. They give concrete meaning to our sense of stewardship for the next generation. They're affordable. And because they represent wise investments, they can keep America competitive.

A kids-first agenda isn't a utopian fantasy. Each aspect of the model is up and running somewhere in the United States, and each has attracted bipartisan support in Congress. If children's advocates and their allies mobilize behind the agenda, understanding that their particular priorities would be enhanced if the whole package were enacted, the system could be operating nationwide within a decade.[16]

"In New York City there are fifty isolated innovations," said Michael Zisser, executive director of University Settlement in New York City, which offers its polyglot Lower East Side constituency everything from nationally renowned Head

Start classes to free meals for seniors, when I spoke with him. "But those innovations aren't changing how the system works." We're habituated to thinking about good *programs* rather than effective *systems*. Yet even the best programs— programs proven to succeed, such as Big Brothers Big Sisters, which mentors adolescents, or the Nurse-Family Partnership, which educates new parents—are overwhelmed by the enor- mity of the challenge to make a difference, not just in one aspect of a child's life, but potentially in transforming lives. Not even the most dedicated Big Sister can do much about the school her "Little" attends or help her pay for college; not even the savviest nurse in the Nurse-Family Partnership can assure parents that there's a good prekindergarten for their three-year-old.

Families live with the consequences of this hit-or-miss approach. When parents search out opportunities for their own children, they often encounter gaps, stretches of time when nothing is available, and so the progress their youngsters have made melts away. Well-to-do parents stress out over who's going to mind their kids during the seemingly endless stretch between the end of summer camp and the start of school. For parents who can't afford summer camp or can't find a decent prekindergarten, those gaps persist for months and even years.[17] It's these holes that the kids-first agenda is meant to fill.

Rallying around a common set of ideas isn't just a political tactic. Each item on the agenda builds on and reinforces all the others—positive family ties, an intimate world of early learning, a good school that's the centerpiece of the neigh- borhood, a caring adult for support, and a stake in the future. Bringing them together strengthens them all. In fact, the kids- first agenda is best conceived not as five separate proposals but as one big, overarching idea—an interlocking system in which home care readies kids for preschool, preschool readies them for school, and school readies them for college. With such a system in place, each initiative would have the opportunity to achieve its fullest potential—and so would each child.

SUCCESS STORIES IN UNLIKELY PLACES

Devising a seamless kids-first system is anything but child's play. There's no call for top-down uniformity—America isn't France, where the famous boast is that, at 10 A.M. on a given day, every fifth grader in the republic is being taught about the Napoleonic Wars. Rather, this agenda is a call for the formation of links among multiple offerings, public and private, each with its own proven competencies. Because the public schools stand as the biggest player on the block, having all but cornered the market on five-to-eighteen-year-olds, they make a natural linchpin. To become an asset and not an obstacle in a kids-first world, though, those schools will have to change, becoming less rule-minded and more limber. That's a tall order, yet there are hopeful signs that it can happen, even in some of the nation's most notoriously bureaucratic school districts.[18]

The point isn't to force every family into lockstep, either, but to enable families to take advantage of whatever is right for their own kids, whether it's a good preschool or a pair of glasses. That's how to make the next generation healthier, wealthier, and wiser.

It's easy to find good examples in the world of youths born to privilege, where the web of support seems to have been fabricated from platinum. We could have an extended look at the Crème de la Crème Preschools—yes, that really is what they are called—where "Disney meets Harvard," as one reporter aptly described it, and where two-year-olds study French and tackle tennis.[19] Another stopover might be IvyWise, an education consulting company that, for $30,000-plus, transforms students' hobbies into internships and summer adventures that leap off their college application forms. And so on and so on.

We're fascinated by the lives of the rich and famous, and their children's lives as well, but it's not just in such rarefied habitats that we can find models for the rest of us. The real news is that all of the working parts for a kids-first America can be found—and are thriving—not only in the most privileged neighborhoods but in some of the most unlikely corners of the republic. In a dirt-poor barrio on the Rio Grande, the high desert near Los Alamos, a backwater town in Maine, or a Chicago neighborhood where gunshots are as common as birdsong, you can come across remarkable parenting programs, child development centers, preschools, community schools, mentoring initiatives, and scholarship opportunities. All of these ventures easily pass the Golden Rule test, for they're as good as anything you'd choose for your own children. Bring them together and bring them to scale—then you have a system of support for kids as inclusive as what we unblinkingly provide to the elderly, a great improvement over the now-you-see-one-now-you-don't hodge-podge that currently passes for children's policy in America.

"I WISH I'D HAD A SCHOOL LIKE THIS"

What would a kids-first America look like? You can get an idea at schools like Salomé Ureña Middle School, which so impressed the wealthy young man we met earlier. It's one of twenty-one schools in impoverished Washington Heights and nearby neighborhoods that are run by the Children's Aid Society, a 150-year-old nonprofit, in tandem with the New York City public school system. These schools offer help to expectant mothers and new parents. They sustain families and engage kids from the time they're infants through high-school graduation. They're the country's finest example of a kids-first model.

The Children's Aid Society provides doulas to help mothers during childbirth and in the first months afterward. At the Children's Aid–run schools, parents can enroll in a course that hones their parenting skills and makes them more savvy job-seekers as well as more knowledgeable participants in the life of the schools. There are Early Head Start classes for infants and toddlers. Transitions are apple-pie easy, since preschool and kindergarten are housed in the same building. The children who go through the full progression are usually at the top of their elementary-school classes.

Children's Aid delivers health care and social services, high-power programs for developmentally delayed youngsters, and a packed calendar of activities before and after school as well as on Saturdays and holidays. It recruits partners such as the Alvin Ailey Dance Company and the New York Public Library to share their talents and resources. Companies such as LensCrafters contribute; and Legal Aid offers free counsel. There are buzzing summer programs as well as tutoring that sharpens academic skills, field trips, and sports.

Students help out in the community, volunteering in local clinics, spending time with shut-ins, and tutoring younger kids. An after-school class for preteens situates a discussion of sexuality in the big picture of life prospects; it's one of the few documented success stories in this field, cutting pregnancy rates by two-thirds.[20] Because there's a social worker on the premises, kids have someone to turn to with their problems. Their parents can also solicit advice; and, because teachers can rely on a professional who understands troubled youngsters, there are fewer of those dreaded trips to the principal's office, and fewer suspensions as well.

Parents are encouraged to meet with their kids' teachers, not just on designated parents' nights, but whenever they think it might be helpful. They can take advantage of a range of classes—everything from cooking and computers to conversational English and citizenship education—and this day-and-night bustle of adults helps to keep the gangs away.

Although most of the students in these schools come from poor families, many of them are defying the odds by beating the citywide averages in reading and math. Children's Aid's engagement extends through high school, as trips to scout out colleges, help with college applications, and one-on-one conversations about future plans make higher education a realistic option for students who, discouraged by their lack of prospects, might otherwise have dropped out.

Here, education for parents of infants and toddlers segues into good preschools, which in turn segue into public schools with an array of health and social services, with summer and after-school programs matched to the ages and needs of the students. Not surprisingly, evaluations of the Children's Aid schools report impressive results, including everything from higher grades to fewer pregnancies.[21]

The best way to appreciate what this means is by honing in on the particulars—say, watching teenagers build a bicycle, learning some math and reading along the way, or seeing adolescents dance with the ease of young professionals. A visitor might listen in as an eighth-grader talks about a writing project with a college professor, or as this same student, in turn, helps a third-grader who's struggling with a reading assignment; see the grin on the face of a child who has just had a painful cavity filled; or sit in with students who are taking courses at Columbia and City College, where, amid the Gothic spires, they can glimpse a future entirely different from what they might otherwise have contemplated. These are high-ambition schools that embed youngsters in an expanding network of community connections, building social capital by creating a daisy-chain of successes, tying that support to schools that increase youngsters' skills and knowledge. If this strategy works, young adults will emerge from the experience ready to take on the world. And in some of these schools, it *is* working.

No one is declaring "mission accomplished." For one thing, the doulas and Early Head Start classes reach only a fraction of the families—as ever, money is the constraint. What's more, the model depends on a solid academic core, with talented teachers and a well-tested curriculum, but the quality of education in these Washington Heights schools varies from excellent to mediocre. And the final element of the kids-first agenda—a nest egg—is missing, so some kids will graduate from high school with all the skills and motivation you'd want but without the money they need for college tuition. Still, what's happening in these schools represents a kids-first system geared to helping youngsters achieve their potential— the kind of system that ought to be available to all our children.

WHY SHOULDN'T EVERY CHILD BE SO LUCKY?

With public dollars tight, it makes sense to start with poor youngsters, since their needs are most acute and the payoff is likely to be most impressive. This is what social scientists call "progressive universalism." But if the kids-first solution never transcends the poverty divide it will almost surely fail. When he headed Head Start in the 1970s, Edward Zigler, a Yale psychology professor and a patriarch of child development research, predicted that unless these classes for three- and four-year-olds were made available to middle-class as well as poor kids, the program would be perennially starved for funds. He was right—since its inception, Head Start has never had a big enough budget to enroll more than half of all eligible youngsters. That experience persuaded Zigler that prekindergarten should be open to all, and history backs him up. Even as the 1960s' War on Poverty has receded into history, with Head Start as its lone survivor, the big-ticket social initiatives that endure are those, like Social Security and Medicare, which reach everyone. "Programs for the poor," Zigler bluntly told me when we spoke of his experiences, "are poor programs."

Beacons of excellence can be found in every state in the union, and we'll look at some of them in this book. They include parent education that has transformed the lives of thousands of South Carolina families; a Washington, D.C., preschool that enrolls the children of both indigent immigrants and K-Street lobbyists; community-linked schools in Chicago with top-flight art courses and health services on the premises; mentoring in Portland, Oregon, that salvages kids who, by the time they are five, have been pronounced doomed to failure; and a money-in-the-bank nest-egg scheme in Maine that is convincing parents to rethink what lies ahead for their children.

You walk out of one of these special places awed by what is happening there, seeing how children for whom the society has such modest expectations can come alive with possibility.

At the same time, you come away troubled that so few young-sters, whatever their background, are lucky enough to have such experiences. It's as if they've won the lottery. Why shouldn't every child be so fortunate?

CHAPTER I

THE LITTLEST SCHOOLHOUSE
TEACHING PARENTS TO TEACH THEIR KIDS

IN 1923, A FORTY-TWO-YEAR-OLD woman named Mary Breckinridge—a Kentuckian born to privilege, the granddaughter of a U.S. vice president, and the daughter of an ambassador to Russia; a widow at twenty-five, and later, daringly for those times, a divorcee; and a nurse who had served in France following World War I—journeyed to the desolate Kentucky hollows. Her two children had died before the age of five, and those tragedies had motivated her to look for ways of giving Appalachian youngsters a shot at a decent life.

The odds against her were long. There were few roads in the region, doctors and nurses were rarities, and hospitals nonexistent. Most women gave birth at home attended by self-taught midwives, whose harsh ministrations exacted a terrible toll. One woman in a hundred died during labor, and a tenth of the children died before their first birthday.

Observing nurse-midwives in Europe, Breckinridge had been struck by the idea that nurse-midwifery was something America needed: "It grew upon me," she said, "that nurse-midwifery was the logical response to the needs of the young child in rural America." She went to England for training, since the practice of nurse-midwifery was then unknown in the United States. Back in the States, she crisscrossed remote Kentucky terrain on horseback to see for herself the kind of help that pregnant women and young mothers needed. She recruited nurses, founding the Frontier Nursing Service in 1925. Not only did the nurses deliver babies expertly, they also helped those mothers navigate the first years of the children's lives.[1]

The Frontier Nursing Service, which Breckinridge ran until she died in 1965, is still going strong (instead of riding on horseback, the nurses now drive SUVs). It has radically reduced infant and maternal mortality in the region, and it has become a worldwide model, not just for serving rural areas but for offering help to parents—the first big idea on the kids-first agenda.[2]

THE IMPRIMATUR OF SCIENCE

Four decades of research in neuroscience and genetics have given the imprimatur of science to Breckinridge's intuition that helping families do a better job of raising their babies can recast the fortunes of the next generation.[3]

Studies of how the brain functions show that at no other time in a person's life does the brain develop as rapidly as during the first years—with 100 billion neurons at birth, a baby's brain creates and discards neural synapses at an astonishing rate. At a 1997 White House conference on brain development, then–First Lady Hillary Clinton proclaimed a scientific revolution of Copernican dimensions: "Fifteen years ago we thought a baby's brain structure was virtually complete at birth. Now we understand that everything we do with a child has some kind of potential physical influence on that rapidly-forming brain"—and, by implication, on an individual's entire life.[4]

"Birth-to-five" advocates appropriated this evidence to argue that what happens during the first years of life is an irreversible "use it or lose it" proposition. While this claim badly distorted the data—and terrified parents—the key finding, that early brain development forms the scaffolding on which later refinements can be built, was right.

Geneticists were long skeptical of these claims. Drawing on hundreds of IQ studies, they argued that the fate of children was lodged in their genes, and their position was widely accepted.[5] *The Bell Curve*, a book by Richard J. Herrnstein and Charles Murray that recycled and popularized this claim, has sold more than half a million copies. If these geneticists were right, then Mary Breckinridge was on a fool's errand when she sent nurses to coach new families—if the die was cast, childrearing wouldn't much matter. A new generation of studies, however, decimates the "nature, not nurture," paradigm.

Research conducted by University of Montpellier psychologist Michel Duyme found that when four- and five-year-old French children who had been abused and neglected as infants were adopted by caring families, their IQs increased by as much as 25 points. So much for the idea of immutable intelligence. What's more, the youngsters who were raised in well-to-do homes, where parents presumably took fuller advantage of the teachable moments, gained the most.[6]

Even more startling were the results of a study of thousands of twins carried out by University of Virginia psychologist Eric Turkheimer.[7] Quantitative geneticists have rested their case on the consistent finding that identical twins, who share all their genes, are far more alike in intelligence than fraternal twins, who share only half of their genes. But those researchers had a fatal blind-spot—until Turkheimer came along, they had studied only middle-class twins.

Among twins with well-off parents, Turkheimer found, virtually all the variation in IQ could be attributed to genes. But the story was exactly the opposite for twins from poor families: The IQs of identical twins didn't vary any less than the IQs of fraternal twins. Heredity explained almost *none* of the IQ variation for these children. The impact of growing up impoverished, with little social or economic capital, overwhelmed the genetic capacities of these children. "If you have a chaotic environment, kids' genetic potential doesn't have a chance to be expressed," explained Turkheimer when we discussed his findings. "Well-off families can provide the mental stimulation needed for genes to build the brain circuitry for intelligence." If that's the case, then less-well-off families could be taught to do the same.

Molecular geneticists, who open up this genetic black box to specify biological causes, have come to the same conclusion—nurture makes all the difference. Recent studies have identified instances in which variations in a child's home life determine what's called "gene expression"—the form, or allele, that the gene takes. The gene linked to aggressive and potentially violent behavior, for instance, is effectively deactivated when an individual grows up in a caring and intimate family; and a relatively stress-free environment has the same benign effect on the gene that regulates the brain's production of serotonin, a neurotransmitter thought to play a major role in the biochemistry of depression.[8]

Genetics and neuroscience have converged on a paradigm-changing model of human development, one that emphasizes the interplay of genes and the environment. This new frame looks at nature *through* nurture, not nature *versus* nurture. It is the "nurture" part of that equation that Mary Breckinridge and her successors have sought to affect.

"AMERICA'S SMALLEST SCHOOL"

To child development researchers, these reports from the laboratory are stunningly obvious.[9] The discipline grew out of the insight, based on close observation of behavior at home and in the nursery, that what transpires between pregnancy and the start of school can mold a child's destiny. Prenatal health care, nutrition, exposure to toxic environments, poverty, race, psychological state—all these factors contribute to stress for expectant mothers.[10] Stress leads, in turn, to more premature and low-birth-weight babies as well as more problematic childrearing, all of which can subvert the futures of children.

"We have been desperate to treat anxious, pregnant women, to see if making them less anxious will have an effect on the kid," University of Rochester psychologist Thomas O'Connor told me. "If responses to stress are tied to the immune function, psychological outcomes, maybe intelligence, then all bets are off. We could save the world by making moms less stressed in pregnancy."

Better parenting would break the un-virtuous cycle of generation after generation of abuse and neglect in middle-class homes as well as poor ones. Children are more likely to grow up smarter and more caring when, during the earliest years, their parents are warm and positive, authoritative rather than authoritarian, mindful of the dangers they run, attentive to signs of ill health, and prone to reading, playing, and talking with them. "The infant brain is hardwired for relationships," noted New York University psychology professor Lawrence Aber, "and the optimal growth and development of the human brain in the early years is largely dependent on the nature and quality of a child's few and most important human relationships."[11]

The young are often resilient—they must be in order to survive.[12] They devise ways of coping when their parents are distant and unaffectionate, or when they are disciplined harshly and arbitrarily, but those coping strategies often do not bode well for their futures. "Better parenting results in children's better behavior," wrote Yale psychology professor Edward Zigler and his colleagues, delivering a message that most mothers and fathers intuitively understand.[13] That's why offering families the buttressing that enables them to do the best they can for their kids matters so much.

Some people are natural-born parents, and others aren't, but most of us have a great deal to learn about how to raise a child. (If you're skeptical, check out the curriculum of the Nurse-Family Partnership and see how much you know about, say, decoding an infant's wide repertoire of facial expressions.) Yet it's been poor families—who can potentially gain the most—who have had the least help. Even as middle-class mothers stock the nursery with Baby Einstein and Baby Mozart, treating these gadgets as if they were Baby Lourdes, mothers making Burger King wages must scrimp to purchase a second-hand crib. "Infant-development strategies, like other forms of social capital, are perversely distributed in America," *New Yorker* writer Katherine Boo pointed out, "fetishized in places where babies are fundamentally secure and likely to prosper, undervalued in places where babies are not."[14]

Having more money surely makes things easier, for being poor often means having to live in a chancy and insecure world where simply surviving can become a consuming pre-occupation. But poverty isn't the only explanation for the infant-development gap. Poor children whose parents find the time to read to them and play mind-stimulating games with them do much better on IQ tests than those growing up in a home barren of books—in fact, the home learning environment explains *half* of the relationship between poverty and achievement-test scores.[15]

"Biological motherhood needs at least three links with social experience," psychologist Erik Erikson observed nearly half a century ago. "Mother's past experience of being mothered; a conception of motherhood shared with trustworthy contemporary surroundings; and an all-enveloping world-image tying past, present and future into a convincing pattern of providence."[16] Many poor mothers can't draw upon even one of those experiences.

By the time they are four years old, a much-cited study concludes, the typical child of professional parents will have heard *32 million* more words than the youngster whose parents are on welfare; and the vocabulary of well-positioned youngsters is often bigger than that of the welfare mothers. Moreover, while many poor youngsters hear "no" a lot, because that's the style of parenting their parents were exposed to and pass on, well-educated parents, brought up on a diet of parenting guru T. Berry Brazelton, love-bomb their young.[17] Those differences endow most middle-class children with a big edge even before kindergarten.

NO MAGIC BULLET

How can we close this cognitive gap as well as the parallel gaps in health and social and emotional development that

✳ emerge during the first years? It's one thing to appreciate that
the quality of parenting deeply informs children's lives, another and altogether harder task to influence the ways parents
raise their children. This is the test for any parent-education
initiative, and often the promise has gone unrealized.[18]

Why so? Many parents are working long hours and irregular
schedules, and they can't devote as much time to their offspring as they'd like. Moreover, for all new parents, the transition from being a childless adult to becoming a caring parent
generates profound, developmentally sequenced changes in
how the brain is wired. "The period surrounding birth, and
especially the birth of a first child, is likely to require the greatest transformation of [parents'] brain-based neural circuitry,"
said University of Colorado developmental psychologist
David Olds, whose home-visiting program, the Nurse-Family
Partnership, is the leader in this field. "Parents' earlier experiences, their current behavioral dispositions and genetic
makeup can have profound impacts on the care they provide
to their offspring." That's not a process easily tampered with.[19]

Policymakers, who habitually hunt for quick answers, have
long hoped that parenting programs would be the magic bullet, the single intervention that could change the trajectory of
kids' lives. Thirty years ago the American Academy of Pediatrics hailed home visiting, one kind of support, as the single
best remedy for family meltdown. A decade later the U.S. Advisory Board on Child Abuse and Neglect, urged by Louis
Sullivan, who headed the Department of Health and Human
Services under President George H.W. Bush, to "think big,"
proposed home visits for every new mother.[20]

Although those efforts had little immediate impact, they
did get the ball rolling, and parenting is now high on the policy
agenda. Until recently the states have led the initiative, with
thirty states investing $250 million in 2008.[21] In 2010 the fed-

eral government enacted the first major parenting program, budgeted at $1.5 billion over a five-year period.

Each year an estimated half a million American families sign up for one of more than 4,000 programs variously labeled "parent education," "parent support," or "home visiting"—catchall terms for multiple strategies. There's even a wide variation among the efforts dubbed "home visiting," Jeanne Brooks-Gunn, professor of child development at Columbia University, has pointed out. "Who is visiting whom, for what purpose, at what point in a baby's life, with what intensity? Who is spending time with the family (and how much time)? Which families are eligible?"[22]

In this "let a thousand flowers bloom" world, it's essential to figure out which models live up to their billing. As with each item on the kids-first agenda, quality is the key. Rigorous evaluations have shown that the best initiatives can generate the kind of powerful long-term impact that satisfies policy-makers' and parents' hopes. It is possible to counteract the baleful influences associated with growing up poor, or being raised by a single parent or a depressed or drug-using parent, or living in a troubled neighborhood—the array of risks that can derail lives at the start. Altering the dynamics of family life can foster a more loving home. Both parents and children are better off—and when *that* happens in enough families, the social script about childrearing gets rewritten.

"THE WHITE COAT EFFECT": THE NURSE-FAMILY PARTNERSHIP

David Olds launched the Nurse-Family Partnership more than thirty years ago, and his name has become synonymous with that highly touted model. But at the outset of his career

Olds didn't see himself as a paradigm-builder. His hopes were more modest—he wanted to help a handful of kids—and in 1970, straight out of Johns Hopkins University, he took a job at a day-care center in a down-and-out West Baltimore neighborhood.[23]

The experience was a revelation. Olds's college professors were adamant that children's futures were not fixed at birth, that how they were raised made all the difference. Now he found himself teaching eighteen three- and four-year-olds in a cramped church basement. The prospects looked bleak for these youngsters—some of his fellow teachers regarded their job as mere babysitting—and Olds wanted to kick-start their minds. He started using a rigorous new curriculum called High/Scope that was being tried out on similar kids at the Perry Preschool in Ypsilanti, Michigan.

Many of Olds's children flourished. (So did the Ypsilanti children. As we'll see in the next chapter, the studies that demonstrated Perry Preschool's lifelong impact have been critical in the campaign to make prekindergarten universally available.) Yet when Olds reviewed the records of the kids who *weren't* making it—the boy who could only bark, not talk, or the three-year-old who swore a blue streak—the explanation was to be found much earlier in life, in infancy or in the womb. The mother of the first child had beaten her infant son when he wet himself; the other mother had been using drugs when she was pregnant.

Two years later, Olds headed to Cornell University to study psychology. His mentor, developmental psychologist Urie Bronfenbrenner, was a contrarian. Rather than concentrating entirely on the behavior of individual children, like his colleagues, Bronfenbrenner studied what he called the "ecology" of human development. Children aren't autonomous, he pointed out. They grow up in "systems." The intimate world of the family, and, later, the classroom, is linked to the surrounding community, which is in turn embedded in the larger society. These environments mesh to form life histories.[24]

"The mother-child dyad is an interactive system," Bronfenbrenner wrote, and, "since the participants remain together after the interaction ceases, the momentum of the system assures some degree of continuity." This way of thinking influenced Olds. In his model, nurses frequently go to the homes of first-time parents from early in pregnancy until a child's second birthday. Olds's theory was that a bond would form between the nurse and the mother—and the father as well, whenever he was a part of this process—and that this bond would enhance what Bronfenbrenner termed the "microsystem." The number of low-birth-weight and premature babies would drop, and parents would be better able to bring up their children.

In 1978, the U.S. Public Health Service funded Olds to do a random-assignment study—the research gold standard—in Elmira, New York, a hardscrabble community located in the region that had the state's highest rates of child abuse and neglect. Four hundred women, almost all of them poor and white, were enrolled. Nurses made visits to families every week during the first months of pregnancy and during the six months after birth; later on the frequency of the visits tapered off. The nurses were told what to cover during each visit, with the lessons matched to the stage of an infant's development. Encouraging parents to get their lives in order—returning to school and finding work—was also part of the nurses' assignment.

Only a few projects that are intended to change the way people behave meet the researcher's strictest test of statistical significance—a bet, made with 99 percent confidence, that the findings don't result from chance. The initial findings from the Elmira study satisfied that test. When the babies were two years old, the incidence of child neglect or abuse was 19 percent among mothers who weren't in the program and just 4 percent among those who did participate. When their youngsters were four, these women were more likely to be in a stable relationship, off welfare, and holding down a steady job; they were also waiting longer before having a second child.[25]

Federal officials urged Olds to expand the program immediately, but he resisted, believing that more evidence was needed before going big. In social experiments, as in natural science, replication is the critical test. When Olds repeated the Elmira study—first with 1,139 black families in Memphis, and later with 735 Hispanic and black families in Denver—the results were positive, though not as dramatic as in Elmira. Still, the model had been shown to have sizable and sustained effects for mothers and children, in cities as well as in rural areas, and for blacks and Hispanics as well as whites. Compared with those who weren't in the program, child abuse and neglect rates were reduced at all three sites, and children born to mothers with low IQs or lacking in self-confidence fared better in school. But some of the effects differed depending on the locales: Welfare rates fell in two trials, for instance, but not in the third.[26]

The Denver study incorporated a new wrinkle by comparing the effect of relying on paraprofessionals rather than nurses. Paraprofessionals—laypeople who receive limited training— are far cheaper than nurses; and because they usually live in the community where they are working, they may have an easier time connecting with parents. On some criteria the paraprofessionals were more effective than the nurses: There were more positive interactions between mothers and children, and mothers were more likely to enroll their youngsters in preschool and to have found jobs. But by age six the children whose mothers had nurse visitors were faring better in school and were less likely to act out.[27] Olds attributes the nurses' success to the "white-coat effect"—because nurses are held in high esteem, mothers paid closer attention to their advice than to the paraprofessionals'—and he has stuck with his original model.

Most studies end after a few years, because the government agencies and foundations that pay for the research demand quick answers, but Olds was able to track the Elmira youth to age fifteen. By then their IQ advantage had evaporated, but there were 48 percent fewer reports of parental abuse and neglect among those who received nurse visits than among those in the control group. The big news was that the adolescents whose mothers had participated in the program were much less likely to have gotten into trouble with the law than those whose mothers had not participated.[28]

The U.S. Justice Department reviewed the data and saw a crime preventer. Economists studying human capital saw dollar signs. The Project for America's Economic Success estimated that every dollar invested in the Nurse-Family Partnership would generate a $2.90 return—$5.70 for high-risk families—and the Coalition for Evidence-Based Policy pronounced it the most effective parenting program ever devised.[29]

If you're a social engineer, like David Olds, the first step is to show that your model works, and the findings from Elmira, Memphis, and Denver accomplished that. The next step is to make the model widely available. It's a perilous stage, because the fact that an approach works in the carefully controlled conditions of a study doesn't guarantee that it will succeed when others, perhaps less well trained and less committed to the model, are running the show. Olds worried that without strict controls the training might not be as good and the protocols not as faithfully followed as in the pilot programs.

Top-down management was his solution. By training all the nurses at his Denver headquarters, as well as gathering data from all the sites and making each site responsible for its results, the organization has done a remarkable job of keeping the model intact—maintaining "fidelity to model," as researchers say. The Nurse-Family Partnership has been scaled up successfully. In 2009, it was operating in 350 counties in twenty-eight states, including most of the nation's major metropolitan areas, and was poised to expand with the anticipated influx of federal dollars.

"GOD PUT ME IN THIS JOB"

Most New Yorkers know Jamaica only as the place to change trains on the way to Manhattan. But in Jamaica's battered blocks, and other down-and-out neighborhoods, a corps of nurses, the vanguard of the Nurse-Family Partnership, gives first-time parents the tools that will help them do better by their babies.

"God put me in this job for a reason," said Carol Coleman, who has been with the program since it started operating in New York in 2003. Carol is a warm African American woman with lots of experience, the kind of nurse you'd want for yourself. She has twenty-three clients, many of them Haitian and Jamaican immigrants, mostly single women. "I love empowering people who look like me," she told me. "I get rewarded when the lightbulb goes on."

I went with her to visit a seventeen-year-old mother we'll call Jackie, who opened the door and hurried us into her cramped third-floor walkup.[30] Her neighborhood is Archie Bunker–land gone to seed, block after block pockmarked with boarded-up houses. Young men with time on their hands hung out on street corners. A few blocks away is the seedy strip club where, in 2006, Shawn Bell, an unarmed groom-to-be, went down in a hail of police gunfire, an event that shocked the city.[31] "It's the concrete jungle," said Carol. "I won't come here at night." She began to visit Jackie when she was four months pregnant. Now the baby, Cherie, was two and a half months old, and Carol had become a fixture in Jackie's home. This was her twenty-first visit, and it had taken almost that long for Jackie to trust her.

"She lied about being in school, lied about the fact that she'd been in prison because she'd beaten up the school safety guard when she was high," Carol had told me before we arrived. But the months Jackie had spent in prison seemed to have shifted her perspective. "I'm tired of that life," Jackie had told her. The father—Kevin, who was also seventeen— had stayed in the picture. He was out of jail—he'd been sent away for jumping a subway turnstile—and going to catering school. "That the father's around is pretty rare in my experience," said Carol.

"These are private people, and the fact they're okay with me coming to their apartment is a big deal," Carol pointed out as we approached Jackie's door. Once we were inside, Jackie's mother, Marcie, joined us for the conversation. The discussion turned to birth control, about which Jackie knew little. Getting her to adopt some sort of birth control and educating her about the options was one of Carol's priorities for this visit. "What do you think about the IUD?" Jackie asked her mother.

It was September, school was starting soon, and the conversation turned to Jackie's plans. Carol had looked into a local high school that offered a life education program. It was a good deal, since Jackie could attend classes while Cherie stayed in the child-care center at the school. Jackie was curious about the program, but it was far from certain that she would follow through.

"The teens are my toughest clients," Carol said later. "They're with you and then they're not. You may lose them for a while, but months later they'll complain 'you didn't call me.'" Lisa Landau, who directs the citywide Nurse-Family Partnership, made the same point in more general terms. "By building trusting relationships with these women, the nurses help to build their confidence. As they learn to take good care of themselves and their babies, they discover that they can share a healthy future."

Baby cues were another focus of this visit: What does it mean when Cherie arches her back, or turns away, or even fans out her toes? The idea, said Carol, was to pick up on the early warning signs, avoiding meltdown, and recognize the positive cues. "What can she show you?" Carol asked. "She is happy, talk and stuff," said Jackie. "Also when she is mad—she frowns, she whines." "Those are all engagement cues," said Carol, showing photos of babies and asking Jackie what she thought they were trying to communicate.

"I went to the social services place. Baby was agitated. I tried to do paperwork and hold baby. She was good, went to sleep," said Jackie, and Carol nodded. "She's learning more things, has more control over her hands and legs," she told Jackie. "She's gone from 'I'm just a blob' to 'I am my own person.'"

"We're still learning," Jackie's mother said, and Jackie agreed. "Me, too," said Carol. "I learn from clients all the time." For women like Jackie and Marcie, for whom many of the concepts are new, this kind of learning is sometimes a "two steps forward, one step back" kind of process; the hope is that they gradually move forward.

The Nurse-Family Partnership finds its clients at hospitals, through pediatricians and social workers, and more and more through word of mouth. Only first-time expectant mothers in their first or second trimester are eligible. Those strict criteria, like every key aspect of the program, from the number of nurse visits to the sequence of the lessons, are based on the long-term research.

Thomas Frieden, New York City's health commissioner when the program was implemented, had a reputation as a stickler for solid evidence.[32] When he was selecting a home visiting model for adoption by the city, he had asked Landau to comb the literature and determine which one had been shown to work best. The Nurse-Family Partnership had the most powerful results, and Jamaica was chosen as the first New York City site. Nurses began seeing families there in 2003, and over the next few years the program gradually grew. By the end of 2008 the program had doubled in size and expanded to all five boroughs in the city. Nurses were visiting 2,600 families, making it the largest such enterprise in the country. Still, the Nurse-Family Partnership can reach only a fraction of the eligible mothers.

"We know this program makes a difference," Frieden said in 2008 when, standing alongside Mayor Michael Bloomberg, he announced the expansion. "It has already helped more than a thousand New York City families to achieve better health and better lives." The Mayor's Commission for Economic Opportunity, charged with identifying ways to reduce poverty and improve prospects for poor children, made its expansion a top recommendation.

During the time I spent with Carol Coleman and other nurses in New York and Philadelphia, joining them on their rounds, I watched young mothers make room during drama-filled days—boyfriends coming and going, part-time jobs disappearing, gang trouble in the streets, drug deals going down, eviction pending—to talk candidly about the most intimate aspects of their lives. "Trust is the key," Philadelphia nurse Sue Browning told one of her clients. "When you're comforting him, when you're holding him close to you, you're winning his trust, and that's how he'll learn to love as he's growing up."

David Olds is continuing his research and fine-tuning the approach, having turned over day-to-day operations to a professional staff. Thomas Jenkins, who directs the national organization, spoke to me about his years working in welfare, juvenile justice, and prisons as "having to deal with the effects of *not* intervening early." Jenkins's dream is to implement the same program nationwide, reaching the 575,000 first-time mothers eligible for Medicare every year. The price tag would be $2.5 billion annually. He and Olds have been promoting a Nurse-Family Partnership training track in nursing schools to educate the 25,000 nurses that such an expansion would require.

Olds and Jenkins spent countless hours pinning down how the model should be replicated, and out of those conversations there emerged a thick guide that specifies what "fidelity to the model" requires. Every nurse is trained at the Denver national headquarters, which Jenkins calls "the mother ship," and the recruits, their jitters abated, come away enthusiastic. Olds has no problem with additions to the model, such as organizing get-togethers for parents, as long those sessions don't cut into the number of home visits. "Our big concern," Olds told me, "is that nurses spend the right kind of time, one on one, with the mother—that relationship is the core."

"Now we're doing a hard-core look at practice," said Jenkins. "Is Chicago the same as Philadelphia?" With better information comes greater accountability. Every nurse is monitored: How many parents are on her client list? How healthy are the newborns? Are they making progress? How many parents miss appointments and how many drop out (the bugaboo of all parenting initiatives)? Each nurse's record is compared with all the others, enabling the field staff to pinpoint who could use additional coaching. The sites are monitored similarly. This feedback loop sets the Nurse-Family Partnership apart, not only from other parenting programs, but from other ventures aiming to alter behavior.[33]

If you were manufacturing Jaguars, you'd want absolute fidelity to the model. But helping new parents isn't like manufacturing cars, and when people's lives are involved, such strict fidelity is neither doable nor desirable. Even the most carefully worked out approach must ultimately rely on the judgment of the professionals on the ground. The nurses spend time with many parents who are teenagers, like Jackie—children themselves. They need to learn how to design and carry through with a plan for the future that will bring them back to school or help them find a job, that stiffens them against the temptations of the street and the violence that often lies close at hand. To help their clients, the nurses must possess the skills of educators, parent-substitutes, coaches, mentors, psychologists, and social workers as well as nurses. None of those roles is spelled out in the multivolume Nurse-Family Partnership curriculum.[34]

Meanwhile, the model keeps evolving. Reports from the field describe family situations almost unheard-of when David

Olds began his research nearly forty years ago; and the long-term evaluations have pinpointed areas where the approach has to change. The latest data from the Elmira study reveals that many of the women have been abused by the men in their lives, and nurses are now spending more time teaching women how to combat domestic violence. "We've come a long way from Elmira," said Olds. "Some of the problems have changed. . . . The world has changed. There will never be a point when we say, 'We've got it.'"

TEACHING PARENTS TO TEACH THEIR CHILDREN

In the early 1970s, when David Olds was pondering how best to reach the children for whom preschool came too late, Mildred Winter, a veteran kindergarten teacher in St. Louis, was seeking out ways to help youngsters who started kindergarten far behind their classmates.

"They all came to kindergarten eager, but pretty quickly they learned that school would be more fun for some kids than for others," Winter told me. "The reason was how these children were raised. Some parents had taught youngsters the alphabet and how to count, but I remember a father telling me, 'You'll like having Jimmy in your class 'cause I ain't taught him nothing.'"

To reach kids like Jimmy, Winter realized she needed to reach not only the children themselves, but also their parents. With a few thousand dollars from the state, she started a Saturday school for four-year-olds—and their parents had to come, too. When those youngsters posted higher test scores than kids who had gone to Head Start or private nursery schools, the *St. Louis Post-Dispatch* hailed it as a "quiet revolution."

In the 1960s, psychologists were beginning to assert that education should begin, not in kindergarten, but even earlier. Winter looked to Harvard psychologist Burton White, the director of the Harvard Preschool Project, who had concluded that one could predict by age three how a child would perform in school three years later.[35] It was essential, he argued, to engage parents from the moment their children were born. When Urie Bronfenbrenner, David Olds's mentor, evaluated early education projects, he found that all the successful models brought parents into the picture.[36] Inspired by those findings, Winter expanded her Saturday schools throughout her community. After she was named the state's first director of early education, in 1971, she set about designing a birth-to-three home-visiting approach.

Not everyone was happy with these changes. Missouri has a richly deserved reputation for social conservatism, and right-wing lawmakers fulminated about a Soviet-style plot to take over the family. Televangelist Pat Robertson spread fear among parents with a phony story about a "government worker" who barged in on a family and had the child removed by the state. Those tactics slowed Winter's effort to expand early education, but she had a key political ally in Republican governor Kit Bond. The personal touch did the trick—when Bond had his first child in 1981, at the age of forty-one, Winter regularly stopped by the governor's mansion with materials on parenting, and the Bond family was won over. Lawmakers balked until Bond threatened to freeze their salaries, and with that unsubtle prod, they voted, in 1984, to require that all 525 school districts in Missouri offer a home-based parenting program.

Educators from across the country learned about Parents as Teachers when the *New York Times* reported on the positive results of a pilot study.[37] "We never imagined the program would grow so quickly," Winter recalled; now the program operates in every state, reaching over a quarter of a million families. Its "Born to Learn" curriculum, developed in collaboration with neuroscientists at Washington University, gives parents useful research-based information on child rearing, incorporating everything from developmental milestones (the time when an infant bats at objects overhead, for example) to an understanding of the "sensitive periods" when parents can help their infant's brain develop.

Although Mildred Winter and David Olds had similar objectives and similar understandings of the stages of child development, they adopted very different approaches. Whereas Olds looked to nurses based in public health departments, ex-schoolteacher Winter saw the school district as the natural hub. "He was using nurses, I was in education," she told me, explaining why their paths never crossed. For Olds, the critical success factor was the "white-coat effect," the special bond between a nurse and a mother. Winter saw teachers and social workers as the best people to convey the message.

The biggest difference is which parents are eligible to participate. David Olds concentrates exclusively on poor, first-time expectant mothers, because his findings indicate that these are the women with whom his approach can work best. He acknowledges that some middle-class parents would gain from a concentrated dose of nurse visits—and that, because second- and third-time parents confront new challenges with each child, they could learn a thing or two as well. But Olds believes that the impact on these families would not be as great and that the cost—$4,000 to $8,000 annually—wouldn't be recouped. By this calculus, making the Nurse-Family Partnership open to all would not be a prudent investment.

Winter's Parents as Teachers program has an entirely different philosophy—its aim is to help *all* parents. This approach has an advocate in Edward Zigler, a Yale psychology professor. "I'm supposed to be a world authority on child development," Zigler said, "but when we brought my son home from the hospital, I didn't know what to do." Many new parents would agree with that sentiment. An open-door policy reassures mothers and fathers, who might otherwise worry that signing up means, as Zigler put it, they're "somehow deficient in the mom-and-dad department." Making the program available to everyone also expands the base of political support—it becomes *our* program, not *theirs*.[38]

But can a "one-size" model like Parents as Teachers really "fit all"? Even though the essence of being a responsive mother or father may be the same for the Mexican immigrant and the Maine Yankee, as Karen Guskin, the organization's research director, has pointed out, the variations still matter. The training regime is supposed to make parent educators aware of their own cultural blindspots so they can relate to, say, ultraorthodox Jews or gay couples. But can these paraprofessionals, who receive just thirty hours of training, be effective with families who can seem so alien to them? Can they help a mother living in a fog of depression, or anxious about being deported, or fearful of being beaten up by her partner?[39] And by the same token, is every parent best reached by the same pedagogy? That's a problem that all of the visiting programs, including the Nurse-Family Partnership, confront.

"In 1990 we thought we had all the answers, but our optimism was premature," said Deborah Daro, a senior scholar at the University of Chicago's Chapin Hall. The influential Washington, D.C.–based Invest in Kids Working Group, in a 2005 review of the research drafted by Deanna Gomby, was lukewarm in its overall appraisal. Although the Nurse-Family Partnership had made a marked difference in the lives of

children and their parents, the report concluded, no other program, including Parents as Teachers, was consistently effective.
The problem had less to do with the models themselves—
there isn't much disagreement about the milestones of child
development or brain formation—than with how the models
were put in place. In some instances the visitors came as in-
frequently as four times a year. Half of the visits were cancel-
lations or no-shows, and half of the families dropped out.
Even when the results were positive, the effects were small.[40]

Encouragingly, the newest evaluations are considerably
more positive. One study of Parents as Teachers, conducted
in multiple sites in Missouri, tracked a representative sample
of 5,721 children. It found that the school-readiness scores
of youngsters whose parents participated in the program were
notably higher, whatever their income level; and while such
gains often fade out over time, these kids remained ahead of
the curve in third grade.[41] Since every Missouri family can participate in Parents as Teachers, it was impossible to carry out
a random-assignment study like the ones conducted by David
Olds. But because this is large-scale evaluation over an eight-
year period of a model that's being widely used, the results
give reason to believe that Parents as Teachers can have a
real impact.

The likeliest explanation for the documented improvements, not just for Parents as Teachers but for other home-
visiting models as well, is that closer attention is being paid

to what's actually happening in the field, as the effectiveness
of individual home visitors is being more carefully scrutinized.
Parents as Teachers, and other popular models are learning
from Nurse-Family Partnership's success in bringing its model
to scale without sacrificing quality—they have to, if they're
going to receive the federal money they need for expansion,

since they're expected to show evidence of their success. It looks like home visiting is finally proving its worth.

NO STAY-AT-HOME MOMS (OR DADS)

Newly minted mothers and fathers can learn a lot from adroit home visitors—and they could use that knowledge to even greater effect if they had the time to lavish lots of attention on their infant. In the typical family, however, both parents are back in the workforce before their baby is six months old.

David Olds thinks that this demographic shift may explain why the results in the later trials of his model weren't as powerful as in Elmira. In the 1970s, when the first study was done, stay-at-home moms were still the norm. In most families, a good chunk of child care has now become someone else's responsibility—kith or kin, perhaps a neighbor—and that can stir anxiety for the parents. "Managing and maintaining these various child care arrangements can be exhausting and stressful, and are vulnerable to changes in work schedules, illness, and changes in adult relationships," Berkeley public policy professor Rucker Johnson has pointed out. "It would not be surprising if the constant stress took an emotional toll on mothers and children."[42]

One of the basic insights of developmental psychology is the pivotal importance of babies forming secure ties with loving adults.[43] "It provides a sense of basic trust and a foundation for the infant to explore the world and form attachments with others," said Columbia social work professor Jane Waldfogel in her book *What Children Need*.[44] The ideal person to fill that role is usually a parent. "Children tend to do better if they have a parent—mother or father—home at least part-time in the first year of life," she added, summarizing half a century of research.[45]

The dynamics of intimacy are complex, and so the balance between staying at home and going to work that fits one household isn't necessarily right for another. Still, the evidence shows that when a parent stays home for a year after childbirth, the rate of death during the first six weeks of an infant's life declines by 25 percent, and the death rate for children between ages one and five falls by 11 percent. Extending paid leave by just two and a half months, a multinational study concluded, causes infant mortality rates to drop by as much as 2.6 percent and child mortality rates to fall by 3 percent. What's more, three-year-olds whose mothers stayed home during their infancy do better on cognitive tests, and at age eight, fewer of those children pose behavior problems.[46]

Since 1993 federal law has required companies with more than fifty employees to allow parents to stay home for a combined twenty-four weeks after childbirth without risking their jobs, yet because the leave is unpaid, most families cannot afford to take advantage of this opportunity. And although a handful of states offer new parents paid time off, their jobs aren't protected while they are absent—another worker can replace them, leaving them stranded when the paid leave is over. It's no wonder that so few parents opt to take this time off.

Paid parental leave would have been on the books years ago in the United States, as it is in almost all other well-off nations, if politics ran according to logic.[47] Liberals like the notion of paid leave because it's good for kids and offers parents a genuine choice between being a stay-at-home parent and going to work. By rights, conservatives should favor it as well, because it reinforces family values. But they've been scared silly by fears, stoked by the mercantile lobby, that such beneficence would wreak economic havoc. The fact that federal legislation isn't likely to pass anytime soon underscores the value of making parenting education widely available, enabling mothers and fathers to make the best use of the time they do spend with their babies.

N.J.

CHANGING THE CULTURE OF PARENTING

If giving *all* new parents the support they need is to become more than a slogan, what's required is a system of family support that's as affordable, commonplace, and widely accepted as well-baby check-ups.

New Jersey has started down this road by bringing the biggest home-visiting programs together under a single organizational roof. The model, launched in 2009, calls for every expectant mother to be screened when she visits her obstetrician for a prenatal check-up. Doctors complete a form that includes all the information—everything from alcohol and drug abuse to homelessness—needed to match mothers and programs.

"Universal screening is the key," Sunday Gustin at the New Jersey Department of Children and Families, who pioneered this model, told me. "That's the moment when mothers are most receptive to someone they can connect with. And because everyone is being screened no one is singled out as a bad parent."

As director of the Children's Futures Initiative in the city of Trenton's Public Health Department, Gustin had seen too many new mothers go without the help they needed because they didn't know where to turn. The answer, she decided, was to get the city's parenting programs to work together rather than scrapping for clients. When she became the state's home-visiting program manager, she took this idea statewide.

Gustin's vision is to link all new mothers to a system of care capable of responding to problems that range from maternal depression to developmental delay. Expectant mothers who meet David Olds's stringent criteria learn about the Nurse-Family Partnership, and everyone is told about Parents as Teachers. (The third participating home-visiting program, Healthy Families America, which is similar in approach to Parents as Teachers, is open to mothers whose babies are three months or younger). New Jersey also has scores of locally based parenting organizations, and mothers are informed about them as well.

"Initially there was a lot of in-fighting and distrust," said Gustin, "and it was hard to get everyone to the table. Because funding is so scarce, these programs are used to competing for dollars, and the advocates aren't above badmouthing one another. We told them: 'There are plenty of families who need support. There's no room for competition in this state.' Now all the groups have bought into accountability for evidence-based outcomes, and there's less fragmentation."

New Jersey's strategy of coordination represents a substantial improvement over the parenting program bazaar that's in place in most states. Yet, together, these programs can enroll only 3,300 mothers a year. To put that figure in context, in 2008 there were 115,443 births in New Jersey: Nearly 7 percent of the new mothers were teenagers, 30 percent were single, and a third were living below the poverty line. The scarcity of home visitors means that only a fraction of parents will receive the kind of assistance that can make a decisive difference in their kids' lives.

"We're open to expanding the collaboration by bringing in Early Head Start [the federally funded program that offers home-visiting and center-based education programs for poor families with infants and toddlers] and locally based parenting programs," said Gustin. Yet that's a partial solution.

New Jersey, and other states as well, ought to add the Positive Parenting Program—Triple P—to their kitbag of approaches. That model relies on an entirely different strategy, one that's new to the United States but widely accepted elsewhere in the world. It doesn't aim at altering individual behavior but, far more boldly, at changing the norms about parenting across entire communities. It's also far less expensive than the one-parent-at-a-time models like the Nurse-Family Partnership or Parents as Teachers. If Triple P were to be adopted widely, then universal support for mothers and fathers could become a reality

"CURING THOUSANDS AT A TIME"

A new generation of reformers dreams of rewriting the American cultural script about parenting. The boast in public health is that doctors cure one patient at a time while public health cures thousands at a time, and over the years public health advocates have learned a lot from Madison Avenue. By relying on advertising maxims to meet public health goals, they have persuaded millions of people to get vaccinated, quit smoking, and eat healthier foods. Social marketing is what this strategy is called, and the bet that these paradigm-smashers are making is that a population-based approach can have an equally dramatic impact on how parents bring up their children.[48]

Triple P, the exemplar of this strategy, is in place across the state of South Carolina.[49] Although the model is little known in this country, since the early 1980s it has been used in seventeen nations, from Singapore to Switzerland. In twenty experimental studies, the regimen has been shown to reduce children's problem behavior as well as abuse by parents while improving school performance. The results of a recent South Carolina study are stunning—across entire counties, among whites and blacks, rich and poor alike, parents are doing a better job of raising their children.[50]

The passion to help children must be lodged in Matt Sanders's genes. The man who developed Triple P grew up in placid 1950s New Zealand, the son of a teacher and a principal who helped start the play-center movement for young kids. He studied psychology in New Zealand and later in Australia, where he spent more than a decade training clinical psychologists.

A visit in 1983 to the Laboratory for the Study of Behavioral Medicine at Stanford University introduced Sanders to the public health approach. Rather than treating individual heart patients, the Stanford project was designed to change behavior. Similar campaigns—to convince people to buckle up, stay out of the sun, or drive sober, for example—were in the works. Sanders's "aha" moment came, he told me, when he realized that, "even if all the psychologists I've been training successfully applied the best therapeutic techniques to all the parents they ever see, their impact will be nil—the number of psychologists is tiny and the problems are vast."

During his time in Palo Alto, Sanders started thinking about how he could apply these techniques to parenting, and he spent the next twenty years designing, testing, and modifying his approach. "We had to bring in the media, the health system, the education system—everything that could influence parents," he said. While reducing child abuse was one of his biggest concerns, the message emphasized the positive—building healthy relationships in families and positive parenting in communities. "We don't want Triple P to be associated with child abuse," Sanders noted, since that would scare away parents.

"Everything needs to be in the parents' hands—whether they participate, what kind of help they want. We created different access points—social workers, teachers, pediatricians, nurses, ministers—and developed programs that respond to what they said they needed." For many parents, a TV show, a handout, or a one-hour group session—"a lighter touch," Sanders called it—gives them all the information they can absorb. Others go to group gatherings or sign up for one-on-one sessions. "They have to see this as healthy and normal, not 'this is what you do to prevent abusing your children.'"

Word-of-mouth is the main source of referrals to Triple P. When the program is in full swing, mothers talk about it with one another across the back fence and in the beauty parlor, and parents discuss it over the kitchen table. "The idea is to create social momentum," Sanders said, "the understanding that this is an okay thing to do."

Classic home-visiting models deliver a crash course in developmental psychology and neuroscience. Sanders's focus is more pragmatic—he wants to improve family dynamics in order to preempt children's behavioral and emotional problems. "Triple P concentrates on the *parents'* responses—increasing positive interactions, reducing coercive and inconsistent behavior," Sanders said. The goal is to help parents build the confidence and skill they need to do their job well. "When parents feel more competent and work better together, there is less conflict in the family," he added, citing Triple P research to back up each assertion. "Mothers are less likely to get depressed. And you reduce some of the key risk factors associated with kids' behavioral and emotional problems— they behave better and they do better in school."

Sanders has relied on focus groups to find out how parents want to connect with Triple P, and he's given them what they want: face-to-face, one-on-one meetings, group sessions, radio and TV shows, self-paced Internet programs, and workplace-based sessions. Sanders produced a popular TV series, *Driving Mum and Dad Mad*, for British TV, and another for New Zealand television. There's a Triple P specifically tailored for parents of disruptive preschoolers and another for parents of premature babies; others for parents of children who are developmentally delayed or can't get to sleep, who have lots of headaches, or who suffer from attention deficit disorder. Sanders tested each of these iterations, refining as he went along, always looking for the minimum intervention required—often one or two sessions—to address the parents' concerns.

In 2002, the Centers for Disease Control and Prevention (CDC) gave Sanders a $2 million grant to test whether Triple P could reduce the incidence of maltreatment and foster-care placement for children from birth to age twelve. The study took place across eighteen counties in South Carolina, a state where poverty and child abuse rates are high. Nine counties were randomly assigned to receive Triple P; the other nine served as controls. The initial findings, published in *Prevention Science* in 2009, have attracted considerable notice, for they showed that Triple P had fulfilled its promise—reducing the prevalence of child abuse as well as the unhappy consequence of foster care.[51]

STRAIGHT TALK IN JIM AND
TAMMY FAYE BAKKER COUNTRY

The town of Fort Mill, South Carolina, pop. 10,032, brushes up against the North Carolina border in York County, one of the counties picked to participate in the Triple P study. It's a bedroom community for Charlotte—a Triple A baseball team, the Charlotte Knights, plays in Fort Mill—and by South Carolina standards it is well-off. It is also conservative, even by South Carolina standards. During the 1970s and 1980s it was home to Jim and Tammy Faye Bakker's Praise the Lord (PTL) Ministry as well as their 2,000-acre Pentecostal theme park, which drew a million visitors a year. Now it's the headquarters of the Inspiration Network, which broadcasts "family-oriented Christian television and Biblically-based entertainment."

Fort Mill seems like the kind of place where Triple P might incite angry talk about a "communistic" plot to take over families, but things haven't played out that way. Triple P's publicist, Candace Challew, vividly remembers her appearance on the "Straight Talk" radio chat show. Everyone tunes in—it's an institution in York County, having been on the air for nearly a quarter of a century, the kind of show that features a local doctor talking about the canine epilepsy trial he's conducting, or the Catawba riverkeeper describing the current condition of the river. The show airs live daily from Harry and Jean's Restaurant in Rock Hill, the only city in York County (pop. 60,000). The restaurant's slogan is "Passionate American Food," and as Candace fielded questions about the kinds of problems that any parent might encounter, in the background you could hear the sound of

diners polishing off a wedge of iceberg lettuce or the signa-
ture dish, smothered chicken.

This "Straight Talk" appearance was one of many ways
that Triple P reached out to parents; a Q&A column in the
local paper was another. Mary Echols, the staffer assigned to
York County, came to every local health fair. "It gave us a
chance to connect with fathers," she said, but it took a while
to get the practitioners to pay attention. She had come to
town with the blessing of the state agencies that serve kids
and the credibility of having the endorsement of the CDC.
"Sometimes I felt like a drug rep. Sometimes people would
listen and sometimes they weren't interested."

Home visiting programs like Parents as Teachers were already in place in the county, and Triple P has never promoted
itself as a better option. "We can complement what they're
doing," Echols said. "There's no need to replace anything."
The fact that the Triple P model was based on research helped
to convince people that it was worth their time, though, as
did the fact that training was free.

Any initiative needs a champion if it's going to take off, and
Echols found one in Karen Helms, the principal of Riverview
Elementary School. "She got it immediately," Echols said, and
helped to spread the word. Twenty people came to the first
training, including the guidance counselors and assistant principal from Riverview Elementary and administrators from the
Department of Mental Health. By the last training course nearly
a hundred people had been certified. They were drawn from
the county social services department and mental health centers,
the Head Start program, local elementary schools, St. John's
Methodist Church, a family literacy project, a day-care center,
and the Catawba Indian Nation. Sara Costillo, a psychologist
working in the Department of Mental Health, was another

champion, and for a while that department was active in promoting Triple P. When Costillo and her fellow enthusiasts moved on, they brought the model with them to new jobs in the local battered women's shelter and the Fort Mill school district.

At the schools, at pediatricians' offices, and in the mental health clinic—wherever parents went to talk about their kids—they were likely to hear about Triple P. "If they try one strategy, it's the hook that gets them in the door. They go to one seminar and that whets the whistle," Echols said. The seminars attracted well-off and poor parents alike. "There wasn't a stigma," she told me. "It doesn't matter how much money you have, children do whine and have trouble doing their homework." Some parents came because they'd been ordered to do so by a judge. That's the antithesis of Triple P's philosophy, which stresses parent empowerment. Parents ordered to attend are not labeled as potential child abusers by the Triple P staff; they attend the same meetings as everyone else.

Testimonials posted on Triple P's website suggest how parents get hooked.[52] Take the Padillo family. Angie Padillo, forty-three years old, had been teaching at Riverview Elementary School for fifteen years. She was comfortable being around special needs kids, since they were mainstreamed into her class, so when Triple P was recruiting local trainers, she signed up. But Padillo was having problems coping with her own five-year-olds, triplets born premature and with developmental disabilities.

Triple P taught Padillo a variety of parenting strategies, but giving her children clear directions was the first one she put into practice. "I remember thinking during training that I already do that—I don't ask my kids to come to the dinner table. But when I got home I caught myself asking, 'Guys, are you ready to take a bath?' instead of 'It's time for a bath now.'"

Those "baby steps" have made a big difference. "Before Triple P, I used time-out and I did a lot of talking. It made me feel better but it did not change the behavior. I also did the counting—'by the time I count to three'—but I was really teaching them that they didn't have to change their behavior until I get to three."

Triple P encourages parents to use whichever approach proves the most helpful in handling difficult situations—like mini-tirades. As Padillo has discovered, the approach some-times needs to be tailored not only to the individual family but to the individual child. "My children are completely dif-ferent," said Padillo. "Quiet time works for Isabella and Amanda. We usually go straight to time-out for Anthony, but it doesn't always work. One thing that does work for him is taking away a toy for a short period of time. I don't have to do that for the girls."

Things have improved a lot in the Padillo household. "Whenever I'm talking I get more eye contact. Before, I didn't think about yelling out instructions, but now I know I need to come to their level, look them in the eye and give an in-struction. They are starting to listen. Do they always make the best choices? No. But, at least now they are making eye contact with me. Before I felt like they were just tuning out."

Riverview Elementary holds Triple P seminars and intro-duces the program to families on parenting nights. "Give Triple P a try," Padillo tells them. "It's working for us. We are by no means perfect and we've got a long way to go. It's reaf-firming and it makes me feel more at peace knowing that I have some strategies and skills that I can use as a resource."

Sara Castillo, the psychologist who moved from the health department to the Fort Mill school district, sees the effects in the classroom as well—the youngsters she's working with are doing better academically and their parents are more engaged.

"Triple P is helping parents feel more confident in their ability to parent their child," she said. "And parents are seeing how much their ability to parent impacts their child's ability to be successful in school."[53]

This multipronged strategy has been remarkably successful. Over the course of two years, the nine Triple P counties had significantly lower rates of confirmed child abuse, fewer foster-care placements and adoptions, and fewer hospitalizations or emergency-room visits related to child abuse injuries than the counties without the program. The South Carolina study is the first in the nation to show that providing all families—not just families thought to be at risk—with reliable access to solid information and support can substantially reduce rates of child maltreatment.

In a community with 100,000 children under eight years of age, the effect of implementing Triple P translates into 688 fewer cases of child maltreatment, 240 fewer out-of-home placements, and 60 fewer children with injuries requiring hospitalization or emergency-room treatment. These are astonishing figures. The South Carolina project collected data on child maltreatment because that is of particular interest to the Centers for Disease Control and Prevention, which funded the research. If you make the plausible assumption that benefits identified in other trials of Triple P, like greater success in school and healthier psyches, are also being realized in South Carolina, then the scope of the program's impact on parenting—and on children—looks even more striking.

WHAT'S NEXT?

Politicians are natural credit-claimers—they have to be if they're going to be reelected—and they're inclined to look for quick fixes. That's why some officials are hailing the Nurse-Family Partnership as the sure path to bright futures, and why Triple P may well be the next model to be treated as a panacea.

A nanosecond's reflection reveals the foolishness of this. No single strategy can be a "magic bullet." What parents would dream of sending their three-year-old into the dark forest that lies beyond the front door—the realm of time-wasting and sometimes dangerous child care, learning-deprived preschools (or no early education at all), hard-to-find health care, and skill-and-drill public schools—with any confidence that he or she would flourish? The kind of parenting that can be fostered by home-visiting programs like the Nurse-Family Partnership and public health strategies like Triple P contribute to a child's storehouse of social capital. These programs help to create an intimate, powerful bond between parents and children, which in turn helps youngsters form relationships with others—friends, neighbors, teachers, mentors, and partners. It prepares them emotionally and intellectually for the next step, the intimate community of preschool.

In the 2008 study of the Parents as Teachers program in Missouri, Edward Zigler and his colleagues found, as we've seen, that by the third grade, children whose families enrolled in the program were doing better than those who hadn't participated. What's more, the youngsters who were enrolled in Parents as Teachers *as well as* a good preschool did still better.[54]

The lesson should be plain. Parents as Teachers—or any solid support for good parenting—is valuable for children. High-quality early education—idea number two on the kids-first agenda—will amplify its impact. Isn't that what you'd want for your own child?

CHAPTER 2

A GARDEN OF
EARTHLY DELIGHTS
DELIVERING BRAINY EDUCATION TO TOTS

WALKING INTO THE EDUCARE CENTER on Chicago's South
Side, you might hear a group of four-year-olds doing
a song-and-dance routine—or, just as likely, an infant bawl-
ing her head off. Some parents bring their babies to Educare
when they're just six weeks old—there's a row of bassinets—
and many continue to participate until kindergarten. There,
these 158 children, all of them poor, many from splintered
families and broken neighborhoods, are immersed in a stable
and loving world.

To avoid the problems that can come with transitions, they
have the same teacher for three years. They then move from
the intimate enclave of the infants and toddlers to a preschool
classroom that's just across the way. Language is the key to
the magic kingdom of school success, and from the day these
children arrive they're flooded with words. Artists-in-residence
bring in modern dance and mobile-making to ignite their cre-
ativity. By keeping families close and maintaining regularity

and continuity of care, Educare smoothes the journey from home to school.[1]

Although Educare enrolls only poor youngsters, its approach to child development would also suit the needs of middle-class families. Many parents return to work just a few weeks after their baby is born, and in the typical household they are back on the job before their infant is six months old. They would pay a queen's ransom for a place as good as Educare.

When Irving Harris, the godfather of early education in Chicago and the founder of Educare, went searching for the model most worth emulating in his hometown, he selected the Abecedarian Project, one of the most renowned demonstrations of the long-term impact of early learning. In the early 1970s, in a center located near the University of North Carolina campus, fifty-seven infants, all of them poor and nearly all of them African American, participated in a full-day, year-round child development program, where most of them remained until they were five years old. When researchers tracked these youngsters into their mid-twenties, they found that, compared with a matched group of children who were not in the program, the Abecedarian youngsters had higher IQs. They were three times more likely to attend college, more likely to have good jobs, and half as likely to have been teen parents.[2]

Those results were good enough for Harris. In 1986, the Ounce of Prevention Fund, the nonprofit that he set up to help disadvantaged youth, started the Beethoven Project. Beethoven was located in the infamous Robert Taylor Homes— the South Side high-rise housing project notorious for its lawlessness, poverty, and violent youth gangs. (Lafayette and Pharaoh, the boys whose struggles were chronicled in the best-selling book *There Are No Children Here*, were among the 50,000 people warehoused there.) Beethoven's site wasn't much—the playground was a breezeway, and the blinds were kept closed over bulletproof glass—but it was an oasis in a neighborhood where drive-by shootings were more common than birdsong. The project won national renown for combining Head Start, child care, and support services for adults, and in the mid-1990s it became a model for Early Head Start, the federal initiative for infants and toddlers.[3]

Gang violence made the Robert Taylor Homes a no-go zone in the late 1990s, and Beethoven was forced to shut down. But the menacing towers were torn down a few years later and replaced by a long grassy expanse and mixed-income residences. In 2000 the spanking-new Educare Center opened its doors a few blocks away. The award-winning building, a whimsical row of connected one-room schoolhouses painted in pastel hues, was designed for the pleasure of children and built on a budget that a typical school district could afford.

I stopped by to see the center and talk with Harriet Meyer, who runs Ounce of Prevention. "The infants and toddlers are the heart and soul of Educare," she said. We were walking past the enclosed play area, where a sign read, "Toddlers on the Move." A teacher passed by, cradling a two-month-old infant in her arms. In a nearby room, a three-year-old was tending to a younger toddler. Around the corner, a class of four-year-olds was snaking around a classroom while dancing to a tune ("Plant the seed. Rain comes in the ground, the sun comes up . . .") played by a jazz pro.

"We want the teachers to follow the children's lead," said Ann Kirwan, who is responsible for strategic direction at Ounce of Prevention. "That's how they learn." What most startled her, Meyer said, was "seeing the transformation of the kids, how they blossom over time. That's what I love best about this setting."

Educare has leveraged every available public dollar, including federal child-care money, Early Head Start and Head Start funds, and state prekindergarten dollars. That money pays for a substantial chunk of the $20,000 per pupil cost, and donors chip in the rest. Educare maintains a one-to-six teacher-child ratio for three- and four-year-olds, far lower than most preschools. For infants and toddlers, the ratio is one to three, which is about the same as in a hospital intensive care unit.

Twenty thousand dollars may sound extravagant, but it's considerably less than the tuition at many private preschools in large cities. What's more, the investment appears to be paying off. A 2008 study showed that Educare children were doing substantially better than similar youngsters who were in Head Start. The continuity that Educare emphasizes also seems to make a difference: The longer these children were in the program, the better they did. Youngsters who started before they were two years old scored well above the national average on a reading-readiness test and came close to the national average on a vocabulary test—eyebrow-raising results, especially considering the often-fraught circumstances of the children's lives.[4]

At the start of the 2007–2008 school year, when kindergarten teachers in Chicago were asked to assess the Educare children in their classes, three-quarters were rated as likely headed for success. Those kids must have proved themselves during the year: By spring 2008, nearly nine out of ten were regarded as solid bets for first grade. These youngsters had also learned how to work and play well with others, how to take turns, and how to manage their feelings. According to the teachers, almost nine out of ten had social and emotional skills on par with or better than the national average.

What's more, the effort put into easing the transition from preschool to kindergarten paid off. The Educare graduates were less than half as likely as their non-Educare classmates—15 percent versus 34 percent—to have had a hard time adjusting to kindergarten.

A FOOT IN THE DOOR OF POLICY

When it came to children's welfare issues, Irving Harris, the moving force behind Educare, was the go-to guy. Harriet Meyer recalled him saying, with a dollop of Hebrew, "If only we can build a place where kids from chaotic communities can have a predictable, responsive place for their first five years, then *dayenu*—it would be enough."

Harris was a master of persuasion—when he spoke, philanthropists and foundations wrote seven-figure checks—and he inspired other benefactors to open similar centers in their hometowns. Susan Buffett, the daughter of financial legend Warren Buffett, started one in Omaha; her brother Peter followed suit in Milwaukee; and George Kaiser, ranked by *Business Week* as the twenty-seventh richest man in America, did the same in Tulsa. By 2009 nine centers were up and running, and more were in the works.

In the world of the super-rich, connections beget connections. George Kaiser won over a private foundation in Oklahoma City. The Buffetts recruited Bill Gates, whose foundation, together with the Packard Foundation, has plans to open several centers on the West Coast.

The total enrollment of the nine Educare centers that are up and running is less than 1,000. That's not even the tip of the tip of the iceberg of need, of course, but because of its high cost, Educare isn't perceived as a viable national model. Still, it's a foot in the door of policy, proof that the best crib-to-kindergarten education can put children from poor families on an almost-even footing with those born to privilege. Two federal programs, Early Head Start and Head Start, enroll nearly <u>1 million poor children annual</u>ly. Though they do not rely on billionaire backers, if they even approximated the caliber of Educare they would work wonders.

Educare's benefactors haven't been shy about prodding their home states to do more for young children, and the success of the model gives them a platform from which to make their pitch. In Oklahoma, George Kaiser hired two lobbyists, a Republican and a Democrat, to massage the state legislators, and Susan Buffett convinced the Omaha school superintendent to invest public school dollars in education for infants and toddlers.[5] In 2009, they turned their sights on Washington. When the billionaire funders of Educare centers around the country descended on the capital, more than fifty members of Congress, Republicans and Democrats alike, as well as key figures from the Obama administration, came to a reception.

During the 2008 presidential campaign, Democratic front-runners frequently brought up the topic of early education. This was unprecedented: A subject that had rarely, if ever, been mentioned by a presidential candidate in previous elections became a staple on the campaign trail. Hillary Clinton, a long-time advocate for children's causes, proposed a $10 billion program to underwrite pre-k for every three- and four-year-old. Barack Obama took a different approach. As a freshman state senator, he'd been won over by the ever-persuasive Irving Harris, and he proposed making a $10 billion investment in crafting a birth-to-five system. During the presidential debates he singled out early education as a domestic priority.[6]

Obama and Clinton understood the educational value of giving kids an early boost as well as the political gains that could be harvested from promoting the idea. During the previous decade the preschool movement had taken off, with thirty-eight states and the District of Columbia underwriting pre-k, and governors emerged as champions even in Republican redoubts such as South Dakota and Mississippi.[7] Though Republican presidential candidates remained mute on the issue, shifting demographic realities had changed many people's minds about the value of early education. In the 1970s, in families with small children, the stay-at-home mom was the norm, and early education programs were frowned upon by right-wingers as feminist or communist plots. Economic necessity has pushed more and more women into the working world since then. Liberal or conservative, many families depend on the paychecks of working mothers, even when their babies are still in their cribs. Child development initiatives have taken hold even in socially conservative states like Oklahoma and Nebraska. Seemingly overnight, early education has become a motherhood-and-apple-pie idea, a textbook example of how to do well politically by doing good.

THE ICON: DEMONSTRATING THE LIFELONG IMPACT OF PRESCHOOL

The case for early education rests on the bedrock of research. Genetics and neuroscience, as we've seen, have proven the lifelong impact of brain development during the earliest years, and that finding has been underscored by long-term studies of model early education projects.[8] In designing Educare, Irving Harris relied on one of these well-tested models, the

Abecedarian Project. Another such study, of Perry Preschool, has traced the effects of a good preschool over four decades, and that experiment inspired a nationwide movement. That study came about almost by happenstance. It was conducted not by a well-known team of researchers, like the Abecedarian study, but by a freshly minted Michigan State Ph.D., David Weikart, who also ran the preschool. That makes its prominence especially remarkable.[9]

In the fall of 1961, and without any fanfare, thirteen three- and four-year-olds entered prekindergarten at Perry Elementary School in the blue-collar town of Ypsilanti, Michigan. All of them, as well as the forty-five other children who enrolled during the next three years, were poor and black. Based on past experience, it was a near certainty that most of these youngsters would fail in school. During the previous decade, not a single class at Perry Elementary had ever scored above the 10th percentile on national achievement tests, while across town, in the primary school that served the children of well-off professionals, no class ever performed below the 90th percentile.

The hope was that a good early education could change all that. That is just what happened, to an extent that exceeded anyone's wildest imaginings. These youngsters' lives were so dramatically altered that they have become what David Ellwood, a professor at Harvard's Kennedy School of Government and the architect of the Clinton administration's welfare plan, calls "the most powerfully influential group in the recent history of social science."

When David Weikart first contemplated opening a preschool for poor kids in the late 1950s, the psychologists with whom he conferred were discouraging. "I was working in a context where most people felt that IQ was God-given,"

Weikart said, "and, unfortunately, low-IQ people were just born that way." The reigning experts argued that an intellectually rigorous regime might actually harm poor children by demanding too much of them.[10]

These were just claims, not proof, and Weikart, although trained in special education and not evaluation, was brash enough to test them. From a group of 123 applicants, 58 were randomly assigned to Perry Preschool. Most of them attended for two years, going to class for three hours a day. High/Scope, the curriculum that Weikart devised, treated children as active learners, not sponges. (These were the materials that David Olds, who would later found the Nurse-Family Partnership, used when he taught preschool in Baltimore.)

The High/Scope model invites youngsters to plan their own projects each day, then carry them out and review what they have learned. The Perry teachers, one for every six youngsters, most of them with master's degrees in child development, received salaries equivalent to those of public school teachers. In addition to their classroom duties they made weekly visits to the children's homes, showing parents how everyday activities, like clipping coupons, reading the sports pages, and going shopping, could be used as teachable moments.

The initial findings from the Perry study were mixed. Although the participants had higher achievement scores in fourth grade, their IQ scores, which had spiked earlier, were no better than the control group's. Did the effects of preschool fade out, as a damning 1969 evaluation of the federal Head Start program had concluded?[11] But Weikart and his colleagues cared less about IQ scores than about how the youngsters actually fared in school. They kept collecting data, publishing a series of studies beginning when the Perry children were eight years old and continuing until they were in their forties. Such an extended time frame, which has no precedent in education research, is what has given these findings such cachet.

As the Perry youngsters progressed through school, the enduring—and statistically significant—benefits of their early experience began to emerge. They were less likely than students in the control group to skip school, be assigned to a special education class, or have to repeat a grade. By age nineteen, 66 percent of them had graduated from high school, as compared to 45 percent of those who hadn't gone to Perry.[12]

Presciently, David Weikart recognized that his findings would make a bigger splash if they were converted into the language of economics. With the publication of a series of cost-benefit analyses beginning in the early 1980s, early education came of age, politically speaking. The research showed that the youngsters' success in school had saved taxpayers dollars. Compared to those in the control group, they earned more as adults (and paid more taxes). They were less likely to be on welfare, and fewer of them had been incarcerated. These benefits, to the Perry participants as well as society, outstripped the costs of the preschool education.

As this pattern of accomplishments persisted, the benefit-cost ratio grew ever more favorable. In 1996, when the Perry alumni were twenty-seven years old, they were significantly more likely to have stayed out of prison, to be earning more money, and to own a home and a second car. Steven Barnett, the economist who began the research as a graduate student at the University of Michigan and now directs the National Institute for Early Education Research, estimated that for every dollar spent at Perry Preschool, the return was $7.16. The savings in prison costs alone more than recouped the cost of their early education.[13]

→ bring up in class.   (con____)

The reverberations of what happened to these three- and four-year-olds continued to be felt as they reached middle age. Whatever the yardstick—schooling, income, crime, or family stability—the contrast between the Perry children and the control group, shown in a 2005 follow-up study, is striking. Two findings have drawn the most attention. In their forties, the Perry graduates were earning 25 percent more—$20,800 versus $15,300—and this difference pushed them above the poverty line. What's more, significantly fewer of them had been arrested for violent crimes, drug-related crimes, or property crimes; only about half as many, 28 percent versus 52 percent, had ever spent time in jail or prison.[14]

Because Perry Preschool was a multipronged initiative, there is no way to determine exactly why it was so effective. Was the critical factor the caliber of the teachers, the hands-on curriculum, the one-to-six ratio of teachers to children, the home visits, or David Weikart's leadership?[15] Steven Barnett believes that "the creative ferment" was crucial. "You had great teachers working with these youngsters half a day, then going to their homes and tutoring them, getting to know them and their families really well." Lawrence Schweinhart, who succeeded Weikart as High/Scope's president, perceives a cycle of reinforcement. The children's preschool experience provided the tools to do well in kindergarten. When they succeeded, their teachers became more attentive. That positive attention made them more committed to education, they did better, and so they chose to stay on, rather than dropping out. Because a high-school diploma brought decent job prospects, they were less inclined to turn to crime.

The 2005 study calculated the benefit-cost ratio to be an astronomical seventeen-to-one, and the annual return on the initial investment exceeded 11 percent. Over the course of three decades, Perry Preschool had outperformed the stock market by nearly two-to-one.[16]

James Heckman, a Nobel Prize–winning economist at the University of Chicago, seized on these results. With his trade-mark audacity, Heckman wanted to build an econometric model that explained how individuals acquire skills. Every study he laid his hands on converged on the same conclusion—spending on early education yields the biggest social return. "Because those children are more highly motivated to succeed they will do better in school, even though their IQ scores don't improve," Heckman argued. "Skill begets skill and learning begets learning."[17] With the blessing of Heckman and other prominent economists, early education came to be seen as being not just good for kids but also vital to the effort to main-tain America's position in the world market—an "investment" in "human capital" that promised "exceptional returns."[18]

The long-term evaluations of Perry Preschool and the Abecedarian Project, the findings of the neuroscientists, the economic calculations—taken together, those results provided ammunition for a sustained drive to expand pre-kindergarten nationwide. The Pew Charitable Trusts, an un-characteristically venturesome foundation, orchestrated a decade-long, fifteen-state campaign that in its political so-phistication resembled a run for national office, and the Packard Foundation mounted a similar, though studiously apolitical, initiative in California. The foundations recruited astute advocates, prepared media blitzes, and conducted state-by-state economic analyses showing the returns that preschool could generate.

These tactics paid off handsomely. Between 2002 and 2008, a time when Washington was disinvesting in children, the National Institute for Early Education Research reported that the percentage of four-year-olds in state prekindergarten classrooms grew from 14 to 24 percent; 80 percent of all four-year-olds were enrolled in a public or private preschool or a child-care center. In 2008 the states spent $4.6 billion on pre-k, an increase of 23 percent in a single year, and although the recession forced some budget-challenged states to trim their support, an infusion of federal stimulus dollars partly made up the difference.

Just as the Elmira study put David Olds's Nurse-Family Partnership on the map, the Perry Preschool study made early education a hot topic.[19] But the world has changed a lot since 1961. Perry Preschool was the only game in town, and so the Ypsilanti kids who drew the short straws likely stayed home with their mothers, many of whom were on welfare. Now more than half of the four-year-olds from poor families attend Head Start, and skeptics wondered whether publicly funded pre-k was needed.[20]

Two well-crafted studies—one that included five states with prekindergarten programs, the other focused on Tulsa, Oklahoma—have answered that question with a resounding yes. In the multistate assessment, children who attended state pre-k scored 31 percent higher on vocabulary tests than a similar group of youngsters who weren't enrolled—that's the equivalent of three months of school—and did even better on early math skills, outscoring their peers by 41 percent. Most of the youngsters who didn't go to pre-k didn't stay at home, as had been the case in the Perry Preschool study, but were in Head Start or child-care centers. That makes the effectiveness of the state-run prekindergartens all the more remarkable.

The state-financed prekindergartens aren't nearly as good as Perry Preschool. The classes are bigger, few teachers have master's degrees, and home visits are rarities. Nonetheless, these preschools have a substantial impact on how kids do in school. And while the benefits are greatest for poor children, middle-class youngsters are helped as well.

GROWING A SYSTEM

The belief that a well-designed preschool yields powerful long-term benefits rests heavily on the findings from the Perry Preschool and Abecedarian studies. Yet those studies were carried out in hothouse conditions. Each involved just a handful of youngsters: 121 at Perry Preschool and 112 at Abecedarian. What happens when the models are widely used—"scaled up," as the researchers say? As generations of reformers have learned to their sorrow, unless a model is hardy enough to weather less-than-ideal circumstances, scaling up is doomed to fail.

Quantity versus quality—the equation is simple, the debate complicated. Every dollar spent on improving preschool—for instance, by paying higher salaries to attract better-educated teachers—is a dollar that isn't spent to expand the number of pre-k slots. In almost every community the demand for early education far outstrips the supply. But a shoddy program where television is the palliative doesn't give children an educational leg up. Indeed, enrolling kids in an overcrowded preschool with an inept teacher can make their lives worse.

Politicians welcome the chance to boast about increasing enrollment, since it offers a tangible measure of accomplishment. Quality is harder to explain—why should preschool teachers have bachelor's degrees? why does using an evidence-based curriculum matter?—and so it generally gets short shrift. In 2008, as preschool enrollment continued to climb, the states spent an average of $4,586 per child. That's less than they spent per child in 2002, about $3,000 less than Head Start spent, and a quarter of the cost of Educare.[21]

Is high-quality pre-k for all within the realm of the feasible? Florida offers a cautionary tale. Prekindergarten advocates cheered in 2002, when the citizens of the Sunshine State amended their constitution to mandate universal "high-quality" prekindergarten. But the legislators coughed up a miserly sum, just $2,500 for each preschooler, and the law allowed anybody who'd taken a few college courses and didn't have a prison record to set up shop as a preschool entrepreneur.[22]

Although the Florida story is worrying, it is not the norm. I've crisscrossed the country, crouching in scores of pre-k classes, and what I've observed, coupled with the evaluations I've combed through, give reason for cautious cheer. Preschool systems that reach thousands of youngsters, middle class and poor alike, held in church basements, converted living rooms, redesigned elementary-school classrooms, and state-of-the art centers, confirm that good early education can be delivered on a wide scale without breaking the bank. And while these success stories have important similarities—each has well-trained teachers, an evidence-driven curriculum, engaged parents, and savvy managers—what works best depends on the particulars of the community. There's no one right way to scale up preschool education while maintaining quality, and in a nation allergic to top-down decision-making, that's excellent news.

POOR, CROWDED, LATINO—AND EXCELLENT: UNION CITY, NEW JERSEY

Public schools are routinely assailed as Kafkaesque bureaucracies, staffed by incompetents, that batch-process children rather than educating them.[23] Why should preschoolers be subjected to the un-tender mercies of the public schools, the critics ask, when the schools have performed so miserably?

Like most caricatures, this one contains more than a grain of truth. But some of the best early education is happening in school systems that come freighted with disadvantage. Case in point: Union City, New Jersey, which sits directly across the Hudson River from Manhattan.[24]

Interesting

Although Union City is only five miles from Times Square, it might as well be on Pluto.[25] It's a community of dubious distinctions—one of the ninety-two poorest cities in the nation, according to a Brookings Institution survey, and among the most distressed in the state. Succeeding waves of immigrants have passed through on their way to better lives—Germans and Dutch, who at the turn of the twentieth century made Union City the nation's embroidery capital; Irish and Italians; Cubans fleeing the Castro regime, who created "Havana on the Hudson," the second-largest Cuban enclave in the country. Now most of the residents are Ecuadoran, Dominican, and Mexican immigrants: "Proud of Our Ethnic Heritage," reads a sign on Bergenline Avenue, the main shopping street. This latest wave of newcomers is crammed into run-down triple-deckers, three and four families to an apartment—so tightly packed that Union City has become the nation's most densely populated city, 67,088 souls sardined into little more than a square mile.

Three-quarters of the children have grown up hearing only Spanish spoken at home, and they come to school speaking little, if any, English. Eighty-seven percent are poor enough for free and reduced-price school lunches—a figure that would be considerably higher if some families didn't fear that signing up could mean being deported—and half of them have been diagnosed as having "special needs."

These are society's disposable kids, and they're not expected to make it. The "prison track" is what some educators privately call them, because, as teenagers, many of them will get in trouble with the law. But someone forgot to tell Union City. Their kids *are* making it.

For the past several years, Union City's third-graders have been doing as well as the statewide average on the New Jersey reading- and math-readiness tests. That's impressive. Here's the headline news—the *eighth-grade* students are close to the statewide average in math and reading. Nearly 70 percent are scoring at the proficient or advanced-proficient levels, a jump of 30 percentage points in the span of a decade. It's a feat even more remarkable than what Perry Preschool accomplished, because while the Perry youngsters fared well in school, they didn't do this well.[26] This once failing school district has evolved into a national model.

As soon as I walked into Celia Rojas's prekindergarten class in Room 114 of the Hostos Center for Early Childhood Education, a building jam-packed with three- and four-year-olds, I was sucked into the hum and buzz of activity. Some kids were doing cutouts for paper clothing; others were painting. Signs around the room in the children's own handwriting were in English and Spanish: "Make a Man Out of Spagetty," "Girafo Como El Tail." A group of kids built a pink cardboard chair and called it "A Chair for My Mother."

Fingerpainting, circle time, letter-drills—those are the preschool commonplaces, but classes as good as Rojas's are rarities. You come across them at the University of Chicago's Lab School, founded by John Dewey, where MacArthur "genius award"–winner Vivian Paley taught for years. There, well-off and hyper-ambitious parents register their children soon after they're born. Once in a while you'll find treasure troves in far meaner neighborhoods, like gang-ridden South LA, where Para Los Niños holds forth, or Chicago Commons, a preschool where young artists bloom in a Chicago neighborhood so scary that the playground is surrounded by barbed wire.

Four-year-olds, Alison Gopnik wrote in *The Philosophical Baby*, are in some ways "smarter, more imaginative, more caring and even more conscious than adults are."[27] The French psychologist Jean Piaget, whose ideas held sway half a century ago, viewed little children as irrational and immoral. But if you think of them as Gopnik does—as little Lewises and Clarks, explorers with open-ended and seemingly unlimited intellectual curiosity—then it's a breath-catching moment to enter a classroom like Maria Rojas's prekindergarten that invites such explorations.

Art plastered the walls, plants were hanging from the ceiling, and in every classroom nook there was something to seize a child's imagination. Angel, Neville, and Alex were peering at insects through a microscope, explaining to me what they were seeing. "Remember when we went to the museum and the butterfly landed on my arm?" Angel asked his friends. "Are these *all* insects?" asked Rojas. "How do you know?" "That one has eight legs," Neville responded, "and that means it's not an insect." Rojas brought over a prism. "What do you see when you look through it?" she asked, and Alex looked up to say that he couldn't tell the insects apart, that they looked like leaves. "Why do you think so?" she wondered aloud. The boys had already learned about lenses, and she told them the prism was a special kind of lens.

There was more to be learned about the insects. "How about an insect salad—would you want to eat it?" she inquired, and when the boys chorused "ugh," Rojas asked, "How come?" They stared once more at the insects. "How many parts does an insect body have? Do you remember what they're called?" Neville knew the answer: "Three parts—the antenna, abdomen, and legs." Rojas walked over to talk with a group of kids who were solving a puzzle on a computer, but she returned when Neville and Alex started fighting over who got to look next at the insects. "Use your words," she said—familiar teacher-talk —but then she said something that teachers often don't say. "What can we do?" The boys thought about it. "How about adding another container for insects—that way you can all take turns," Rojas suggested.

In the reading nook a girl was sitting on a cushy pillow, learning about how, when the wasp larva hatches, it eats the spider. Three of her classmates were playing dress-up, trying on old felt hats and checking themselves out in the mirror. In the poets' corner, the teacher's aide, Luz Otero, was reading *Churros y Chocolate* aloud, asking the kids questions as she turned the pages. Five minutes later, Rojas was getting her hair done in the "beauty salon." "What's hanging on my head?" she asked. "A roller," the juvenile hairdresser told her. Alex was shaving her arm, using real shaving cream.

Although Maria Rojas is an especially gifted teacher, she doesn't have a glittering resume—she grew up in Union City, like many of the other teachers, and went to a local college. But unlike teachers in most school districts, she gets lots of support from the school system, including coaching by master instructors, time to share classroom successes and failures with other teachers, and frequent evaluations, coupled with detailed, what-to-do-in-the-future feedback.

The same curriculum is used in every prekindergarten classroom in Union City. Several nationally known pre-k curricula that boast a solid record of success take the same project-driven approach that Union City's teachers rely on, among them the materials developed at Perry Preschool. But rather than having a "curriculum specialist" make the call, as most school systems would, Union City is confident enough in its own staff to hire several of its teachers to spend a summer to custom-design what will be taught.

The prekindergarten program resulted from a 1998 state Supreme Court decision that ordered the legislature to underwrite high-quality prekindergarten for all three- and four-year-olds in the state's poorest school districts.[28] Those districts received a sizable infusion of pre-k dollars, an average of $12,000 for each pre-k student, coupled with stiff new requirements. Every prekindergarten teacher had to have or be on track to obtain a bachelor's degree, the student-teacher ratio could not exceed 7.5 to 1, and the curriculum had to be aligned with a statewide framework.

Sandy Sanger, who became Union City's school superintendent in 2003, grabbed the opportunity. The district delivers preschool to three-quarters of the three- and four-year-olds in the city, six hours a day, 245 days a year. It also offers, among other things, four additional hours of wrap-around child care daily, a doctor who does health screenings and vaccinations in the preschools, parenting classes, and a parent liaison, employed by the district, who links the worlds of home and school, helping families find their way around the state's byzantine bureaucracy.

Sanger makes an unlikely reformer. He's a Union City native with a master's degree in education administration from Seton Hall who has spent his entire career in the district. Unlike nationally known school leaders, Sanger has never summered at Harvard, and when an interviewer asked him to name his hero, Jesus Christ was his answer.[29]

"Many people have gone through our school system and lived in the city. There's a lot of personal and professional pride," Sanger told me. Until the 1998 court ruling, prekindergarten for four-year-olds was a rarity, and private child care was the only place parents could send their three-year-olds. "What some of those providers did was sinful. There was no stimulation—kids were left in cribs all days," said Adriana Birne, the principal of the Hostos Center.

Because the public schools didn't have the space to house all the preschool classes, those child-care centers had to be transformed. State funds paid for major renovations and covered the cost of tuition for child-care providers who returned to college for their B.A.s. Sanger deployed his pre-k standouts to serve as mentors to these newly minted teachers—"twenty straight days someone from our schools would work with them"—and monitored their progress. "We had to change the paradigm," he said. "Instead of being just places for play, they would be centers for learning."

"Preschool without quality is just high-cost day care," said Gordon MacInnes, the state official who was responsible for implementing the judicial decree. "It is not a simple matter of buying colorful alphabetic rugs, supplying age-appropriate toys, and finding two adults to supervise play." What's happening in all of Union City's preschools is essentially the same, whether the sign on the door reads child-care center, private preschool, or public school. I spent time in four pre-k classes, all of them funded with state money, housed in the basement of St. Anthony's Church. Two of them were outposts of the public schools, taught by regular preschool teachers; the other two were sponsored by a nonprofit learning center affiliated with the church. I couldn't tell which was which.

There aren't many teachers as inspiring as Maria Rojas. But one takeaway from Union City is that there are lots of good teachers who don't have advanced degrees from high-power universities. With skillful coaching, helpful feedback, and the chance to work together, many more could become a great deal better.

FRANCHISING PRE-K IN LOS ANGELES

How do you design and build a good early education system from the ground up with less than $5,000 a child? How do you convince a cadre of women who have been earning their living as glorified babysitters that they should return to college in order to learn about the nuances of child development? Los Angeles is showing the way.

Sprawling Los Angeles County is a planner's nightmare. Its landmass is as big as Connecticut; its population, which is bigger than Michigan's, speaks more than a hundred tongues; and it's notoriously ungovernable. Yet LA County has done remarkably well in building a prekindergarten system. Despite limited funding, it has melded 317 separate public, private, and home-based programs into a system and pushed them to improve. This system has brought prekindergarten to more than 10,000 four-year-olds in greatest need; and, money permitting, it can be expanded to reach every preschooler in the county. Despite having limited resources to work with, the evidence suggests that it is offering something of real value.

From the outside, the Graciela Montes Ceja Family Child Care Center in South Los Angeles looks just like the other modest bungalows on the block. This neighborhood used to be called South Central LA, a name tainted by race riots and gang violence, and its official rebranding in 2003 marked a failed attempt to airbrush its image. Inside the center, though, it's another story. The living-room-turned-classroom is buzzing with activity. Two teachers, one with a college degree, and twelve four-year-olds, many of whom speak little English, are engaged in the kind of learn-and-play puzzle-solving that will smooth the way for these kids to kindergarten and beyond.

One year after South Central LA was proclaimed South Los Angeles, LA began a $600 million effort to expand access to preschools. The prime mover was Rob Reiner, the actor, director, and social activist, who has done more than anyone else in the country to popularize the brain research behind the preschool movement.

Reiner is no more than one degree of separation from any opinion-shaper in the country. Beginning in the mid-1990s, when the needs of young children became his consuming passion, he used his Rolodex to great advantage. He enlisted Hollywood stars, White House staffers, foundation officials, early childhood researchers, and public relations experts, all to great effect, helping to secure cover stories in *Time* and *Newsweek*, extensive coverage on "Good Morning, America," and a 1997 White House conference on early brain development.

In 1998 Reiner pulled together a California coalition, which included the American Cancer Society and the American Heart Association, to back a statewide initiative earmarking tobacco tax revenues for birth-to-five programs.[30] In many California communities, these funds have been spent on a potpourri of initiatives that are too scattered to have much of an impact, but Reiner cajoled LA officials into focusing on prekindergarten. From his conversations with neuroscientists he'd learned about the importance of the earliest years, the period of greatest brain plasticity, and he regarded preschool as a politically salable first step down the path of a birth-to-five program.

Rather than relying on the problem-plagued school district, Los Angeles launched a nonprofit Los Angeles Universal

Preschool (LAUP). Because there wasn't enough money to meet the aspiration of universalism, LAUP has concentrated on "hot zones," neighborhoods where preschool is hard to find and school performance is abysmal. The goal is to assure that every youngster enrolled in an LAUP-certified pre-k receives a good early education.

A 2006 California initiative, also backed by Reiner, would have guaranteed a Cadillac preschool program for all four-year-olds, but when the state's voters turned thumbs-down, LAUP had to figure out how to do better with less. The challenge was to construct a first-rate system out of a hodge-podge of public and private prekindergartens and mom-and-pop child-care centers. LAUP had just $4,950 to spend on each preschooler—slightly more than the nationwide average, but $3,000 less than Head Start and less than a quarter of the cost of Educare.

Incentives became the LAUP answer—give the best preschools more money for each child and other preschools will be motivated to improve. A "quality rating system," a rubric that's used nationwide, takes into account whether the teacher has a college degree and the size of the class, since in every study that has shown that prekindergarten can make a lasting difference, the teachers have college degrees and the classes are small. The rating system also incorporates what's happening in the classroom. Are the children talking to their teachers, or are they passive listeners? Are mind-engaging books and projects on hand? What about the parents—are they given the information they need to be smart decision-makers?[31]

The preschools in Los Angeles have steadily improved, and that makes everyone better off. Teachers with community-college degrees are returning to college to obtain bachelor's degrees. That's good for them, since they will know more about kids and take home bigger paychecks. It's good for the prekindergartens, because having more college-educated teachers means better teaching, a higher quality rating, and more dollars for each pupil. The parents, who have learned that having a "nice" teacher isn't enough, are migrating to the more highly rated programs.[32] What's most important, the youngsters are getting a superior education.

Some public schools were already operating prekindergartens when LAUP set up shop, and those classes have garnered the highest quality ratings. One of them, Edison Center, is located in a strip-mall neighborhood on the wrong side of the tracks from classy Redondo Beach. The classroom is stuffed with picture books and art supplies, animals and blocks, and the makings of science experiments. The two teachers, Nancy Pekarek and Nancy Sandavol, freely dispense ideas and hugs to their sixteen charges. When I was there, a cockatoo named Edison ruled the roost and salsa tunes hung in the air. If you were a kid, you'd be thrilled to spend time there.

Many of these kids were from immigrant families, and while they were in class their parents were in school, studying English as a second language. Some children had never spoken English before arriving at Edison. "Sometimes they won't say a word for five or six months," said Pekarek. That's why she had used some of her LAUP money to bring in an American Sign Language instructor, "so that they can have a common language."

"Anybody can rate a program, but that doesn't tell teachers how to do it better," said Gary Mangiofico, who ran LAUP until 2010. That's why 10 percent of the budget is spent to hire veteran preschool teachers as coaches. These mentors give pointers to less experienced and less well trained teachers. Instead of having to depend on question-and-answer scripts, for instance, teachers learn to devise projects that will spark kids' thinking. They also spend time observing at top-notch preschools, where they can see for themselves what happens when lightbulbs switch on.

The day I visited Para Los Niños Child Development Center, an unprepossessing building on a skuzzy block in South LA, several preschool teachers were there as observers. That's understandable, for this prekindergarten is one of LAUP's best.[33]

There are only so many ways to teach calculus or history, but when it comes to preschool the choices seem endless. The best teachers pull ideas from everywhere and engage the kids in art, hands-on experiments, and improvisational theater. Carmela Santiago is one of them. Like all the teachers at Para Los Niños, Santiago has adopted an educational approach that was developed in the Italian city of Reggio Emilia. To simplify a complex pedagogy, respect for the child is the central theme. "Authentic learning" comes from children's own curiosity and the ways they collaborate with their classmates. Teachers lend their expertise, provoking and stimulating learning while also documenting what the children are doing. And at every step parents are enlisted as participants. It's brilliant when done well, but easily messed up.[34]

The Reggio Emilia philosophy emphasizes the natural over the artificial. The tables and chairs in Santiago's class were made of wood, not plastic; the dishes were pottery; and the couch could have come from grandma's house. Japanese banners were hanging from the ceiling, plants were blooming, and scores of photos chronicled what was happening in the classroom. Four adults, Santiago and three aides, were constantly talking with nineteen four-year-olds. Art plays a big part in the Reggio model. Few preschools allow children to venture beyond fingerpainting; here, a precocious artist, his hands covered in paint, was pushing black and white paint rollers across a large sheet of construction paper on the floor. In the kitchen nook, Arturo and Felicia were engrossed in gluing their collages; Susana and Hector were using look-alike money to buy a pretend pizza, counting out the change. The class swung back and forth between Spanish and English. Almost all the children at Para Los Niños are Latino, as are two-thirds of the children in LAUP and 61 percent of the children in the school district, and many of them come from families where Spanish was the exclusive language.

Each teacher had adapted the Reggio pedagogy to make it work for her. Consistency resides not in the specific activities but in the approach—the grownups (a teacher, an aide, and a parent or two) talking with the children; kids working on their own or in small groups; and an endless variety of things to do, whether it's sculpting a zebra out of clay or manipulating a model of the human body. Reggio isn't something you can pick up from a book. That's why many of the teachers at Para Los Niños have made the pilgrimage to Italy, and it's why so many LAUP teachers spend time at this preschool. What's happening in these classes easily passes the Golden Rule test.

The most impressive accomplishment of LAUP, and the one most worthy of emulation, is the transformation of family-based child-care centers into preschools, not just in name but in fact. The fact that these centers still label themselves "child care" hints at the difficulty of the task. The stereotype of family-based care is *Abuela* Julia, Grandma Julia, a maternal figure who might have finished high school, rummaging among half a dozen toddlers in a living room scattered with coloring books, a few games, a couple of dolls, discarded milk cartons, and a big TV—in other words, the antithesis of good prekindergarten.[35]

Because many home-based child-care programs are simply child-minders, only six states fund them with pre-k dollars. In Los Angeles, though, there wasn't any other option. The neighborhoods that LAUP targeted had few public school or center-based early education programs—that, together with the poor school performance of children who live there, is why they were selected—and building a spanking new preschool center costs a bundle. Besides, said Karen Hill Scott, a public policy professor at UCLA and onetime preschool teacher who shaped LAUP's approach, "many parents favor an intimate, homey setting for their four-year-olds." That's especially true of Latino families. When Los Angeles parents were polled about early education, three-quarters of the Latinos, far more than any other group, believed that the best place for a four-year-old was at home. Sending them to a school was out of the question, but they were reassured when their children spent time with a teacher who lived in their neighborhood, spoke their language, and knew their culture firsthand.

To glimpse how the plan has worked—how these *abuelas* are transforming themselves into *maestras* (teachers)— consider how Graciela Montes Ceja changed her life and turned her South Los Angeles child-care center into a top-rated pre-k. For years Montes had wanted to get her B.A., and now it made financial sense to do so. Her mother-in-law also enrolled in college, studying for the child development certificate she needed to become a licensed teacher's aide. Those courses have made a big difference. "For instance, when I started teaching, I used a lot of coloring books. I learned that children learn more when they are being creative, not when they are just staying within the lines, and now they draw beautiful pictures."

After breakfast and the ritual tooth-brushing, the children split up and picked an activity. Everything here, including the computer with learning games and the listening center, where the kids tune into books and music—both paid for by LAUP—had been chosen by Montes with the advice of her coach, Laura Jimenez, because it invited the kids to pursue their natural curiosity. Jimenez checks in about once a month. "It's really just about setting up the environment and letting them go with it," said Jimenez. "Graciela and Maria [Montes's mother-in-law] are meeting the kids where they are—we've set developmental goals for each child—and working with them." Montes said she had learned a lot from Para Los Niños, where she spent time both observing and doing her practice teaching.[36]

With support from an LAUP "parenting coach," Montes has found new ways to connect with the parents. Every month she organizes a workshop, which might be an introduction to "Ages and Stages," a low-cost screening tool parents can use to see how their children are developing, or a session on "positive discipline" ("raising children who are responsible, respectful and resourceful"). Latino parents often defer to figures of authority, but when Montes took them on a kindergarten visit, she was preparing them to become advocates for their own kids. Her pre-k, judged as only adequate when she joined LAUP, now earns the highest quality rating.

In a host of settings—state-of-the-art privately run preschools, classrooms tucked away in public schools, and jam-packed living rooms—LAUP is pushing the "quality" agenda. These impressive quality-rating scores are reason for optimism, as such scores are usually reliable predictors of success for children as they move on to school and beyond.

On the nationally used quality-rating scale that LAUP deploys, preschools like Para Los Niños scored an average of

5.62 out of 7 points—that's nearly 2 points higher than the schools in a 2005 study rating 240 programs in five states, and nearly a point higher than the typical Head Start. Home-based preschools like Graciela Montes's averaged 6.25 points out of 7; that's a whopping 3 points higher than a random two-state sample of family child-care homes.

LAUP has adopted a novel strategy, a decentralized and mixed-market model that relies heavily on family child-care preschools, to accomplish what it set out to do. It's delivering good preschool to 10,000 of the kids in LA who can gain the most—and it's doing so without breaking the bank. When California is no longer a financial basket case, it may reach its goal of serving 60 percent of four-year-olds, and the Los Angeles preschool model should be up to the task.

MANAGEMENT 101

When searching out why a venture has succeeded, it's tempting to credit the charisma of a single individual like Geoffrey Canada, the moving force behind the renowned Harlem Children's Zone. The reality, however, is usually less dramatic. Reinventing Union City's public schools or devising a pre-kindergarten system in Los Angeles wasn't the work of giants. Although Sandy Sanger in Union City and Gary Mangiofico at LAUP are talented managers, both would cringe at the "genius" label. Their big accomplishment—and it *is* a big accomplishment—is to have figured out how to sculpt a system that ultimately doesn't depend on their being on hand. The formula for a first-rate early education program—indeed, for any first-rate kids' initiative—is about 2 percent personality and 98 percent system engineering.

Every few months, Sanger meets with the leaders at each school. The agenda, he told me, is always the same: What are you doing for all your kids? What's the blueprint for sustained academic achievement? His management approach is straight-forward: "Have a plan, make sure everyone understands and follows it, and don't let anyone fall through the cracks." Improvement is a continuous process. "Once there's a plan, well-structured and well-organized, and people see they'll be supported every step of the way, everyone becomes part of the movement —administration, teachers, parents, students are on board."

During his tenure in New Jersey state government, Gordon MacInnes came to know Union City well. In his 2009 book, *In Plain Sight: Simple, Difficult Lessons from New Jersey's Expensive Effort to Close the Achievement Gap,* he examined why the district had done so well, and his explanation was straight-forward. "Union City focuses on academic achievement and uses performance on state and district assessments as its principal accountability measures," he wrote. "It stresses early literacy. It analyzes the probable reasons that students fall behind and spends *whatever time is required* to bring them up to standard. It continuously measures the progress of all students. It *enlists teachers* to help solve pedagogical problems. It sees *literacy as the doorway to deeper and more rigorous learning*. It knows how to teach English to immigrant Latinos."[37]

What makes Union City's pre-k program hum so smoothly is the meticulousness with which it has been put in place. This is Management 101: "Plan-Do-Study-Act" is how successful organizations evolve. The same lesson can be drawn from the Perry Preschool chapbook—"plan, do, review" is how three-year-olds learn to solve problems there—or, for that matter, from the fable of the tortoise and the hare. In the business world, it's called "continuous process improvement," a constant effort to figure out and then eliminate the main causes of problems—not with some flamboyant gesture but step by step, making sure to engage everyone in the process. "Make sure nobody, student or teacher, is left out," Sanger said.

Educators and politicians take notice when the Los Angeles preschools score high on the quality-rating scales, or Union City's students match the statewide average in reading and math. But unless people like Graciela Montes are thinking about how to excite her four-year-olds, the LAUP model will fizzle. The same holds true of the teachers who are engaging their kids in the basement of St. Anthony's Church in Union City.

facts

WHAT'S WRONG WITH HEAD START? (*important*)

Two federal programs for children from poor families—Head Start, which enrolls three- and four-year-olds, and Early Head Start, which combines home visiting, parent education, and center-based classes for infants and toddlers—represent the biggest public investment in early education to date, more than $7 billion a year. This seems like the logical starting point for the seamless, high-quality, birth-to-five system of early education that is being pushed by the Obama administration. But—and it's a big "but"—after nearly half a century, the jury is still out on Head Start.

A national Head Start study published in 2010, the latest installment in a multiyear research project and the most recent of a bookshelf's-worth of evaluations, concluded that most of the edge in learning that children gain as three- and four-year-olds disappears by the time they finish first grade.[38]

What about the children who attended Early Head Start and then went on to preschool, either Head Start or state prekindergarten? A 2009 assessment found that, although these youngsters do better than similar youngsters who didn't go to pre-k, "better" doesn't come close to being good enough. Those kids came to kindergarten well behind the national average—and well behind the poor children in Educare and Union City.

The research confirms just how much quality counts. In the Early Head Start study, the babies who received a good early education and whose parents got help with childrearing were better off—on some measures, almost five times better off—than those who'd gotten less attention. John Love, a senior fellow at Mathematica, who coauthored the study, summarized the findings: "We need programs that are of the highest possible quality and intensity, begin at birth (or before), and provide for continuity from birth to school."[39] But that isn't happening.

To Craig Ramey, a health studies professor at Georgetown University who developed the Abecedarian Project in the early 1970s, the latest Head Start report only confirms what researchers already knew. "They see Head Start as a great idea, but it must hold its feet to the quality fire."[40] Education Secretary Arne Duncan read the report as a wake-up call. "We need to build a more coordinated system of early care and education, and to focus on key improvements to teaching and learning in the early grades. We have begun to tackle this challenge by identifying the key elements of high quality early learning programs, and studying what works to improve and sustain outcomes once children reach school."[41] Almost half a century after the first Head Start center opened its doors, it's disheartening to hear a cabinet official talk about "beginning" to take quality concerns seriously.

cost $

A lack of money partly accounts for Head Start's checkered track record. Union City spends about $12,000 for each preschool student and Educare runs about $20,000. Head Start costs about $8,000, and in early education, as in life, you often get what you pay for. Because most Head Start centers can't pay their teachers decent wages, many of the most talented earn their bachelor's degrees and migrate to the public schools, where the salaries are typically more than 30 percent higher. But money isn't everything. Even though Union City has opted to spend fewer dollars per pupil than other impoverished New Jersey school districts, its youngsters do much better; and LAUP, which spends considerably less than Head Start, looks to be on the right track as well.

what teachers usually do with their jobs

Head Start is a big program, enrolling nearly a million kids, and size can bring headaches. Yet size doesn't fully explain why these children don't do better. Many states enroll a substantial number of youngsters; as we've seen, rigorous appraisals show that youngsters in state-financed universal preschools have a leg up over their peers, including those in Head Start, and that this advantage persists during elementary school.

Unlike state-funded prekindergartens, Head Start isn't so much a program as a loose, and at times unruly, confederation. As Congress designed Head Start, federal funds bypass the states, going straight to each center—1,604 at last count—and that creates a managerial nightmare. Although Washington has issued scads of directives on quality, it lacks the clout to make its standards stick. Federal officials haven't been able to coax centers into changing their ways because, unlike the Los Angeles pre-k system, it doesn't have the funds to reward Head Start centers that hire teachers with college degrees or use evidence-based curricula, and shutting a center risks a political firestorm.[42] Nor has Head Start relied on regular evaluations and feedback to teachers as a way of improving classroom practice, a strategy that's critical to Union City's success.

Some Head Start centers are good enough to pass the Golden Rule test. University Settlement, in Manhattan's Lower East Side, is a fine example. The program for three- and four-year-olds is embedded in a nonprofit that, true to its settlement-house roots, delivers something for everyone, from toddlers to seniors. The Head Start classes use imaginative materials, such as "Big Math for Little Kids," developed with National Science Foundation funding, which have proven their worth. All the teachers at University Settlement's pre-k have bachelor's degrees, and several majored in child development. Parents regularly help out in the classroom, working with small groups of kids, a critical strategy in places where the families, many of them immigrants, speak half a dozen different languages.

A national evaluation team lauded University Settlement as one of the best Head Start programs in the country, but among other Head Start centers it's largely unknown. That's bad management. But there's another reason why Head Start isn't doing well in many communities. The only children who are permitted to enroll are those whose family earnings fall below the poverty line (in 2009, that was $22,050 for a family of four). Middle-class parents wouldn't put up with such mediocrity. Poor parents have no option—and that's the problem.

From the New Deal to the present, programs earmarked for the poor haven't fared well in the competition for federal dollars. Initiatives aimed at *them* are less popular with taxpayers and politicians than programs meant for *us*. That's why Social Security, Medicare, and the federal highway system, which belong to everyone, are politically untouchable, while Medicaid, welfare, and housing subsidies, with few friends in high places, barely scrape by.[43] At a town-hall meeting in Simpsonville, South Carolina, in the summer of 2009, when health reform was the hot topic, a constituent hollered at GOP Congressman Robert Inglis: "Keep your government hands off my Medicare." Ingalls recalled that he "had to politely explain that, 'Actually, sir, your health care is being provided by the government.' But he wasn't having any of it."[44]

No comparable claim of ownership can be made when it comes to the poverty agenda. "We declared war on poverty, and poverty won," Ronald Reagan announced in the 1988 State of the Union Address, and the Great Communicator had it right.[45] Head Start belongs in the have-not category, and Early Head Start has it worse—its budget covers only 3 *percent* of poor infants and toddlers, the very kids who could benefit most.

Families hoping to enroll their children must prove repeatedly that their income falls below the poverty line. Consider the plight of a mother of a prospective Head Start student in Alexandria, Virginia, recounted by Lisa Guernsey, who directs the early education project at the New America Foundation:

> This woman I met was excited to sign her child up for Head Start. Her son, climbing over and under chairs in the registration room, kept asking when he would start. But it wasn't completely clear that her family would actually qualify in the first place. Yes, she was unemployed for the moment, and so her income was clearly low enough to make her son eligible. But what was to happen, she asked me, when she got a job? What if the job paid too much? Where else could she go? And would she be able to find a place to enroll her son that would enable her to work full-time, until 5 or 6 P.M.? Would it be as

good as Head Start at preparing her child for school? How expensive would it be? If she got a childcare subsidy to help her with the tuition payments, would she still be eligible for those discounts if she lost her job or her hours were reduced?[46]

Yet when Edward Zigler, director of Head Start during the 1960s, proposed opening up the program to middle-class families, who would pay on a sliding scale, he was hammered as an elitist. The idea went nowhere. "I've been troubled from day one that we came up with a system that segregated kids," said Zigler. "Does anybody think that that is a moral society?"[47]

PRESCHOOL FOR ALL?

Because poor youngsters gain the most from early education, it's right to focus on them first, as Los Angeles is doing.[48] Should the ultimate goal be publicly subsidized preschool for all?

James Heckman, the Nobel laureate in the preschool firmament, says no. He makes the economist's case for offering good, state-supported prekindergarten to disadvantaged youngsters, but "children from advantaged environments receive substantial early investment [from their parents]. There is little basis for providing universal programs at zero cost."[49]

Efficiency—bang for the buck—is the economists' usual starting point, and concentrating public dollars on poor kids seems self-evidently efficient. No one has ever studied the long-term effects of the University of Chicago's Lab School. What would be the point, since most of the four-year-olds lucky enough to have gone there are children of privilege? Because youngsters from fraught backgrounds begin so far back in the intellectual and cultural capital derby, they are likely to gain more from pre-k, narrowing the social-class gap in education. Preschool for the disadvantaged, James Heckman has written, represents one of those rare instances of a policy "that promotes fairness and social justice and at the same time, promotes productivity in the economy and in society at large."[50] In short, targeting looks to be fairer and more efficient. For most economists, that's case closed.

Not so fast, say others. "This bias against universalism collides with planet reality," countered Steven Barnett, head of the National Institute for Early Education Reform and one of the few dissenters in the trade. Although the direct cost of targeted programs is lower, he argued, in practice its benefits are likely to be fewer as well, because targeting has never led to a Perry Preschool–caliber education.[51] In theory, concentrating entirely on poor children will reduce the educational gap, but a study by two World Bank economists concluded that, when the voters effectively set tax levels, the poor are in fact *worse* off when a program is targeted, because the citizenry is willing to pony up much less money.[52]

Universal preschool can help poor youngsters in other ways. Forty years ago, the *Equal Educational Opportunity Survey*, a mammoth study of American public schools, concluded that the most valuable thing that schools could offer to poor children—far more significant, in terms of its impact on achievement, than smaller classes, more up-to-date textbooks, or well-equipped labs—was the chance to attend school with classmates from better-off families.[53] In 1966 this was big news, but in retrospect it sounds exactly right. Although teachers and curricula are important, children learn a lot from one another. Cultural capital rubs off, and so do vocabulary words.

gray

area financially

What's true of school-age children is probably even truer for three- and four-year-olds, whose etiquette about who's in and who's out is less race-or class-conscious. A nationwide study in Britain found that youngsters from poor families who went to preschool with middle-class kids did better than those who were educated in social and economic isolation. The result was the same for children enrolled in Georgia's universal preschool program: On reading and math tests, poor kids did best in socially mixed classes.[54] Middle-class youngsters can also gain from going to an economically heterogeneous pre-k. When it comes to the skills they bring to the classroom, no bright line separates poor and not-so-poor children, but as things stand, many families earn too much to be eligible for Head Start but not enough to afford high-quality pre-k. As a result, their children often wind up in threadbare child-care centers.[55]

No one is talking about putting three-year-olds on buses to desegregate the nurseries. Yet, while parents typically send their children to pre-k in their own neighborhoods, some do look elsewhere— for, say, a Reggio Emilia preschool, which can attract a mix of students because of its educational philosophy, or a prekindergarten with a sterling reputation. Universal prekindergarten may be the last and best, if limited, hope for bridging social divides among the young. That hope disappears if only poor and working-class children can enroll in state-sponsored preschools, since economic segregation will have been codified into law.

The quarrel over the merits of universalism has a long history in American education. Not so long ago, public kindergarten was a rarity except for the poor; now, it's taken for granted as part of the common school system, and no one regards it as a giveaway. What makes five-year-olds different from four-year-olds?[56] In the late nineteenth century a similar fight was waged over free public high schools. Let the government pay only for so-called pauper schools, the opponents argued, while the well-to-do can educate their offspring on their own. That idea now seems quaint. The concept of equality of educational opportunity has dramatically expanded, but preschool remains on the policy border between "pauper schools" and universalism.

The Rosemount Center in Washington, D.C., embodies Ed Zigler's dream for a Head Start open to all.[57] On first sight you might think you had stumbled into the trophy house of a K-Street lobbyist. Then you encounter a gaggle of kids playing in an *Alice in Wonderland* garden, clambering over the rocks, slithering down the slides, and you know, in more ways than one, that you've come to the right place.

The century-old California Mission–style mansion that Rosemount calls home was initially run by the Association for Works of Mercy, an Episcopalian organization, as a "voluntary retreat for fallen women and girls." By the 1940s it cared for young mothers and their infants, with a nursery and a kindergarten on the premises, and in the 1970s it became a Head Start center. An Early Head Start program was added in 1996. Now the center enrolls 170 youngsters, ranging from a few months of age to preschoolers.

Many of the homes in the Mount Pleasant neighborhood where Rosemount is located sell in the seven-figure range, but only a few blocks away, a decrepit housing project is home to hundreds of immigrant families, crowded into the most densely populated quarter of D.C. Rosemount serves both communities. Two-thirds of its children live in those projects, and their education is partly paid for by Head Start and Early Head Start. The rest reside in the stately mansions, and their parents pay $12,000 a year—a bargain by elite preschool standards—which supplements the Head Start money. The waiting list hovers at 500, half of the hopefuls coming from the projects and half from the mansions. The center's director, Jacques Rondeau, has a background that's unique in the preschool world—he's a retired air force colonel who used to work for Senator Daniel Patrick Moynihan—and by assiduously mining public dollars and cultivating private donors, he has kept the program on firm financial footing. "We could easily open two more Rosemount Centers," he told me.

Harriet Meyer at Educare is a fan of Rosemount, and the way children spend their days at Rosemount is much the same as at Educare. In the "Chicks" room, three teachers, all of whom have studied child development, were attending to six babies when I visited. The lesson plan hanging on the wall offered a reminder that even here—perhaps *especially* here—children were learning. As at Educare, the children stay with their teacher for three years. In all the classrooms family photos festooned the walls. Parents can tune in from home or work to watch the class via webcast, and they become part of the life of the school in all sorts of ways—a carpenter-dad might build a stage set or coach a soccer game, a mom might bring in chocolate cookies or tamales, or show the tots how to use the computers.

Many of these children come from immigrant Latino families, and conversation in the classrooms flowed back and forth between Spanish and English. *"Vamos a leer un libro,"* Benedicta Lenis told her two-year-old "Pandas," opening a picture book. *"Que es eso?"* she asked, pointing to a pig. On the wall, the horse on Old MacDonald's farm was also labeled *caballo,* and the children's *cumpleanos* (birthday) celebrations were remembered in photos.

Watching these children chirruping in English and Spanish, I found it hard to distinguish the poor kids from the junior plutocrats. They were teaching one other, and that's exactly the point. At the beginning and end of the preschool day, said Rondeau, "the blond mommies and the brown mommies meet when they drop off and pick up their children."

IS GOOD PRESCHOOL GOOD ENOUGH?

When the youngsters at Rosemount turn five, this classless world abruptly ends. Most of the families that live in the projects send their kids to the low-performing neighborhood public school, and the well-to-do families use their pull to get their sons and daughters into charter schools with track records of high achievement, or send them to private schools. The achievement gap, which has narrowed considerably during the five years these children have been together, will widen because of those divergent experiences.[58]

Art Rolnick, an economist with the Federal Reserve Bank in Minneapolis, wants to find out whether combining two evidence-based initiatives—parenting programs and preschool, the first two items on the kids-first agenda—can close the achievement gap. It's astonishing that a Federal Reserve economist would immerse himself so deeply in such matters, but as Rolnick sees things, this is economics for dummies. "Look at it through an economic development lens," he told me. "Cities always think that they can promote economic growth by building a stadium, but that's a terrible investment. The best way to promote growth is to invest in kids."

Not content with churning out journal articles, Rolnick has become a social entrepreneur, raising $20 million in private funds to launch the Minnesota Early Learning Foundation.[59] Its mission is to improve the prospects of poor youngsters, especially those who are, as he put it, "super-risk." In the fall of 2008, the enterprise began to enroll families in St. Paul, Minnesota. The parenting program, step one, is an adaptation of the Nurse-Family Partnership. In Rolnick's version, an expectant mother meets with a teacher as well as a nurse, who together figure out what kind of support will be most beneficial. The home visitor—in this model she is called a mentor—sticks with the family until the child is ready to go to kindergarten. The children also receive a scholarship that covers two years in a thoroughly vetted preschool. That's when the program ends and the family is on its own.[60]

It's not so hard to forecast the outcome of Art Rolnick's experiment. In the short term, the "parenting-plus-preschool" combination will give these children an edge   that's what the Educare research suggests —and some of those gains are likely to stick. The children in this program are likely to do better than those who didn't have the same experience, both in school and after they graduate—that's the lesson from Abecedarian and Perry Preschool.

But only a handful of the Perry and Abecedarian kids were lifted into the middle class. There's no reason to anticipate that the St. Paul youngsters will fare any better, unless the schools they attend next offer, at a minimum, the caliber of education and the consistency of support that public school systems typically provide to middle-class children.

Poor families, left to their own devices, will likely have to send their kids to their neighborhood public school, and that isn't a comforting thought. As Steven Barnett, director of the National Institute for Early Education Research, has pointed out, most poor children receive a markedly worse education than middle-class children; and poor black children, like almost all the youngsters in Rolnick's study, fare worst of all. Thirteen years of inferior schooling can only dampen children's prospects. Would you want any child you cared about to be treated so cavalierly?[61]

In a 2010 paper, Berkeley public policy professor Rucker Johnson examined the life histories of several thousand children who attended Head Start in the 1970s. By the time they were in their thirties, those who went to well-funded elementary and secondary schools were more likely than non–Head Start graduates attending the same kinds of schools to have graduated from high school. They also had higher earnings and were in better health—for them, Head Start mattered. But for those who attended poor schools, Head Start made absolutely no difference. Whatever advantage they acquired as three- and four-year-olds had been erased. The conclusion is straightforward—in early education, as in parenting support, there are no quick fixes, no birth-to-five "solutions." Continuity, from the earliest years onward, is the key to success.[62]

• • •

AT EDUCARE, Harriet Meyer witnessed the unhappy fate that befell many of the youngsters who enrolled in the nearby elementary schools. In a neighborhood where most students drop out, failure is not only acceptable but anticipated. That's why Educare has started to search out better schools for its kids.

Meyer fears, and rightly so, that these efforts will undermine the random-assignment experiment that Educare has embarked upon to provide a scientifically rigorous demonstration of its effectiveness. Once the "treatment" extends beyond age five, there's no way to disentangle the effects of Educare from what happens afterward.

But what might be called "Educare-plus" is testing a different, and more important, proposition: *If you give poor children the kind of nurturing throughout their school years that well-off families regard as their children's birthright, then the achievement gap, and perhaps the success-in-life gap as well, will disappear.*

Skill begets skill, in economist James Heckman's memorable phrase, and success begets success. The kids-first agenda builds a system around that idea. Start with a well-supported family and then continue with a top-drawer early education. The next step, item number three on the kids-first agenda, is an academically rigorous school, closely linked to the community, that extends from kindergarten through high school.

CHAPTER 3

ALL TOGETHER NOW
CREATING ACADEMIES OF
LEARNING AND LIFE

J UST MONTHS AFTER being named secretary of education, Arne Duncan was handed a pot of gold. The $4 billion Race to the Top initiative, part of the 2009 federal stimulus package, is a bigger investment in public education reform than all his predecessors combined ever had at their disposal. Duncan has taken advantage of this unique opportunity to advance what sounds like a tough-love agenda—reversing the dumbing down of academic standards; holding teachers accountable for students' performance, rewarding those who are effective and replacing those who aren't up to the job; and transforming the culture of low-performing schools.[1]

Critics have attacked this strategy as imposing a teach-to-the-test regime on the schools—"No Child Left Behind" on steroids—and the relentless emphasis on reading and math test scores gives them ammunition for that characterization of the federal agenda. Yet Duncan's understanding of what's required to reinvent the schools also includes breaking the lock step of the traditional school calendar; linking academics to youngsters' cultural, social, and health needs; offering one-stop shopping for harried parents who lack the time to ferry their children to pediatricians, psychologists, sculpture classes, and baseball practice; introducing students to the resources available in their neighborhood; and bringing parents into the schools as learners and collaborators in their children's education. The effect is to boost literacy, numeracy, and critical thinking, the tools of human capital that are the classic purview of schools, as well as to enhance students' social capital, giving them the skills they need to navigate in a networked world.

When he was CEO of Chicago's public schools, Duncan converted 150 schools—more than in any other city—into hubs for their neighborhoods, and the community schools approach is built into his agenda for change. "I don't know how schools and districts [think innovatively about reform] without thinking about the concept of community schools," he said in a 2009 keynote address.[2]

In the kids-first agenda, the community school is the logical third step, after support for parenting and good early education, because it is animated by the same philosophy as the best preschools—it pays attention to the physical and emotional as well as the intellectual needs of kids, building networks, expanding horizons, and drawing parents close. It applies these ideas to the evolving needs of youth, from kindergarten through high-school graduation, readying them for what comes next.[3]

"Community connectedness is not just about warm fuzzy tales of civic triumph," wrote Harvard political scientist Robert Putnam in *Bowling Alone*, the best-seller that popularized the concept. "In measurable and well-documented ways, social capital makes an enormous difference to our lives"—and that,

Putnam pointed out, includes how well youngsters do in school.[4] The kids-first agenda helps parents lay the ground-work by forging *bonding* social capital that ties infants to their families. Early education fosters *bridging* social capital on an intimate scale, as toddlers and preschoolers bond with caring adults outside the home and learn how to work and play well with other kids their own age. Community schools widen the aperture by generating the *linking* social capital that helps youngsters navigate the wider world.[5]

"COMMUNITY" VERSUS THE THREE R'S?

School officials have historically defined their responsibility in narrow terms, as expanding students' storehouse of knowl-edge, sharpening the tools of problem-solving so they can thrive academically. Community school advocates aim to pre-pare students not only for further education but for life more generally.

This expansion of the schools' mission makes sense for all students. "Youth of all descriptions—not just so-called dis-advantaged youth—find insufficient supports in their com-munities to be able to move confidently and safely to adulthood," observed Stanford Education School professor Milbrey McLaughlin. "Many schools lock up tightly at 3 P.M., sending children and youth into empty houses, barren neigh-borhoods, street corners, or malls. Youth interpret a local landscape void of engaging things for them to do as adult in-difference."[6] Community schools are designed to fill this void.

Since principals and teachers have enough on their plates in trying to raise the academic bar, a school system that is interested in opening community schools usually forms an alliance with a high-asset city agency or community organization, a partner with the know-how to bring together services provided by an array of groups, each with its own distinct contribution to make.[7] Medical care, social services, tutoring, after-school activities, and summer camp—that's generally the core offer, but no two community schools look exactly the same. The particulars vary according to what is needed and wanted in each community and depend on the resources at hand. When the partnerships are humming, the line blurs between the school day and the rest of the day, with real-world problems injected into the curriculum and academics continuing well into the evening and weekends.[8]

With little fanfare, this model has grown into a national movement during the past decade, with community schools up and running in forty-nine states and the District of Columbia. A host of school systems, among them Chicago, Baltimore, Portland (Oregon), Cincinnati, Tulsa, Lincoln (Nebraska), and San Mateo (California), have bought into the concept. One version—called Schools of the 21st Century, and devised by Yale psychologist Edward Zigler—combines prekindergarten and elementary school with after-school child care and health care. This model has been adopted by 1,400 schools nationwide, and studies conducted in Arkansas, where Schools of the 21st Century has operated the longest, show that it promotes academic achievement.[9]

Thanks in considerable part to the efforts of a big-tent research and lobbying organization, the National Coalition for Community Schools, the movement has acquired a host of allies. It can count on support from the two big teachers unions, the National Education Association and the American Federation of Teachers; the National Governors' Association and the National League of Cities; the federal Centers for Disease Control and Prevention; major foundations such as the Carnegie Corporation; and such prominent national organizations as Big Brothers Big Sisters, the Boys and Girls Clubs, United Way, the YMCA, the American Public Health Association, and the Education Alliance.

This reimagining of the responsibilities of the public schools might sound obvious, almost platitudinous, but it rankles some prominent educators. Joel Klein, the no-nonsense chancellor of New York City's public schools, insists that to emphasize anything other than literacy and numeracy promotes the "culture of excuse"—the contention that "schools cannot really be held accountable for student achievement because disadvantaged students bear multiple burdens of poverty."

No single impediment to closing the nation's achievement gap looms larger than the culture of excuse," Klein wrote in a 2009 column for the *U.S. News & World Report*.[10]

Klein mocked "the favored solution du jour . . . reducing the handicap of being poor by establishing full service health clinics at schools . . . expanding preschool programs, and offering after-school services"—that is, community schools. The only ingredients for success, he wrote, are "good teachers, effective principals and great schools." And Klein has done more than opine. He has forged an unlikely alliance with the civil rights activist and political provocateur Rev. Al Sharpton, launching the Education Equality Project to highlight his "3 R's" agenda, and he has conscripted some of the biggest names in education to his cause.

There should be "one measuring stick," Klein contended. "Does a policy advance student learning?" As practiced in New York City, this means trying to whip the schools into shape by using reading and math scores as the yardstick of success or failure.

Klein's vocal critics, foremost among them Diane Ravitch, author of the 2010 best-seller *The Life and Death of the Great American School System*, swiftly countered with what they called the Broader, Bolder Approach to Education, gathering their own A-list of supporters. The purpose, said Ravitch, is to advance the conversation about good education beyond the confines of test scores, embracing "student engagement in a broad range of academic subjects, as well as students' health, well-being and civic behavior." Ravitch dismissed Klein and his ilk as poseurs—"edu-pundits" who know little about what's involved in educating children.[11]

This thrust and parry makes good fodder for reporters, who live for controversy, but it's a spurious debate. There's no reason to choose between promoting intellectual rigor and giving students a solid prekindergarten experience, and there's no contradiction between attending to academics and caring about children's health and well-being. "Will it help or harm children's academic achievement if they have access to good pre-K programs?" Ravitch asked rhetorically. "Will it help or harm children's academic achievement—most especially the neediest children—if they have access to good medical care, with dental treatment, vision screening, and the like? Will it help or harm children's academic achievement to have access to high-quality after-school programs?"

Administrators in school districts that Klein admires—communities where poor kids are beating the odds by closing the achievement gap—don't denigrate preschool or health clinics. On the contrary, these data-driven leaders have adopted the community schools approach for a very pragmatic reason—it works.

In Montgomery County, Maryland, just outside Washington, D.C., poor and minority students, many of them first-generation immigrants, are graduating from high school at the same rate as the national average—and graduating from college at higher-than-national-average rates. That achievement is so special, and its national implications so consequential, that it prompted a team of Harvard Business School professors to write an adulatory account of the school district's strategy, *Leading for Equity*.[12]

Superintendent Jerry Weast's driving ambition is to shrink the gap between schools in the impoverished "red zone" and well-to-do "green zone" neighborhoods in his district. He relies on hard evidence in determining which reading and math curricula to use, how to measure teacher performance, and how to increase the number of students taking Advanced Placement courses. Evidence, not trendiness, prompted Weast to introduce preschool, after-school, and summer programs in every red zone school. (Parents in the leafier precincts then successfully lobbied for comparable summer and after-school opportunities, since rich and poor youngsters alike flock to Judo or Indian cooking classes.) A staffer at each red zone school is assigned to reach out to parents, helping them locate the help they need, whether it's finding housing, getting medical treatment, or lining up job training, while also engaging them in their kids' education. The teachers have shown more than lip-service regard for this work—during a recent budget crunch they accepted a pay cut to keep those employees on the job.

The same evidence-based approach is on display in Union City, New Jersey. As we saw in the previous chapter, Union City's students, most of them first-generation immigrant kids whose families speak only Spanish, are—astonishingly—doing as well on the state's third- and eighth-grade reading and math tests as the average youngster in the state. In Union

City, frequent student evaluations, lunch-hour tutoring in reading and math, feedback and coaching for the teachers, and a curriculum tightly aligned with state standards—everything that Joel Klein admires—is in place. So, too, is full-day prekindergarten for all three- and four-year olds, child care, health clinics and social workers, parenting classes for parents, schools that remain open fourteen hours a day—everything that the community schools movement stands for.

For Union City superintendent Sandy Sanger, it's a no-brainer. "We have to bring the parents in and give the kids what they can't get at home. Otherwise we're sunk."[13]

As the National Coalition for Community Schools pointed out, in a report bristling with scholarly citations, all the initiatives that Klein has derided as frills are vital to academic success.[14] The amount of time youngsters spend hanging out on street corners with their friends after school is actually a more reliable predictor of failing in school than family income or race. Students who spend time on after-school and summer projects have higher math and reading scores than their gone-at-3-P.M. classmates.[15] Their attendance records are better, and so is their behavior.[16]

What's more, when teachers take the time to talk with parents about what their kids need in order to make it, the parents realize they can make a useful contribution to their children's education. Children whose parents take an interest in their homework and push them to succeed do better in school—indeed, parents' involvement is a better predictor of student performance than family income.[17] As sociologists Esther Ho Sui-Chu and Douglas Willms have reported, growing up in a "school-like family," where parents take an active interest in their children's schoolwork, has a sizable effect on achievement. "Big gains could be realized through programs that give parents concrete information about parenting styles, teaching methods and school curricula."[18] In short, when parents become knowledgeably involved, the achievement gap can markedly shrink.

A host of studies have concluded that, on an array of measures, good community schools do a better job than conventional institutions on an array of measures. Immunization rates are higher and more kids come to kindergarten prepared to do the work. There are fewer suspensions and dropouts. Students come to trust their schools and teachers. The achievement gap narrows and more youngsters attend college.[19]

It's important not to overstate the significance of these findings, for the research isn't nearly as compelling as the studies of early parenting and prekindergarten. Most evaluations of community schools have been small in scale and short in duration, and few have been rigorously designed. What makes them interesting isn't the reliability of any single study, but the consistency of the results—*when done right*, the research says, community schools can make a powerful difference in the lives of children.[20]

GETTING IT RIGHT

Quality is the make-or-break factor for community schools, as it is for every kids-first initiative. As we've repeatedly seen, well-designed programs can work wonders, while bad ones are worthless and sometimes even harmful.[21]

Relentless replication of successes, as with the Nurse-Family Partnership, is the researcher's aspiration. Yet because community schools, situated in diverse neighborhoods with differing needs and resources, cannot hew to a precisely defined model, it's a challenge to maintain consistently high standards. Community schools can fulfill their potential only if they rest on a solid academic foundation, and many public schools are flunking that test.

In November 2008, Secretary of Education Arne Duncan ventured to the Harlem Children's Zone—the nation's best-known community schools model, a "conveyor belt," as founder Geoffrey Canada calls it, that's intended to carry Harlem's youth from birth though high-school graduation and beyond.[22] There, Duncan laid out his vision of the Promise Neighborhoods program, an initiative designed to seed the country with twenty versions of the Harlem Children's Zone.[23] Because of his experience as chief executive officer of Chicago's public schools, he knows this topic well. Nearly half a century earlier, his mother had started an after-school tutoring program in a poor South Chicago neighborhood under siege from the notorious Blackstone Rangers, and that personal history makes him a fan—but hardly an uncritical one.

Much of what Duncan had to say was catnip to this audience, many of whom had journeyed to Harlem in hopes of securing a chunk of those federal dollars. "I am a big believer in full-service community schools," he asserted. "We need to move beyond the agrarian-era calendar of a 9:00 to 3:00 school day, five days a week, nine months a year. Schools don't belong to you or me—they belong to the community." Duncan rattled off a list of things he'd like to see going on in the schools—eye exams, tutoring, and chess clubs for the students; English as a second language and GED classes for the adults; and lots more.

Yet interlarded with this boosterish talk were admonitions about the checkered reality of community school partnerships. The 21st Century Community Learning Centers, a $1.1

billion federal investment in after-school activities, continued to show disappointing results.[24] There were too many "patchwork" after-school ventures, Duncan scolded, that couldn't muster evidence that they were effective. The department would commit $10 million in Promise Neighborhood planning grants only to projects that were "much more rigorous about managing for outcomes, sustainability and regional scalability."

Three weeks earlier, Duncan had journeyed to Manhattan to deliver another speech on the same topic. "*Making every school a community school*—that's got to be our collective vision. This is what it has to be about, not just the isolated islands of extended time, but really the norm for every single student."[25] But this time the speech was a love-note, not a lecture. It was the audience that made all the difference. Duncan was speaking before the Children's Aid Society— "a remarkable group," he called it—which runs the best community schools in the country.

THE ICON: CHILDREN'S AID SOCIETY COMMUNITY SCHOOLS

The twenty-one community schools in New York City, twelve in Manhattan and the others in nearby South Bronx, run by the Children's Aid Society in collaboration with the public school system are among Gotham's best-kept secrets. But educators from around the country and across the globe know all about them, and a constant stream of visitors makes the pilgrimage to spend time there.[26]

Children's Aid has been lending a hand to New York's youngsters for more than a century and a half—hence its antique name.[27] It ran the city's first free kindergarten and the first nursery for the infants of working mothers; a generation ago it made public education a priority. "If Andrew Carnegie were alive today, he'd build schools, not libraries," said Pete Moses, who led the organization until 2009. "The public schools don't understand the marketplace they control because they have the kids."

The Children's Aid schools in Washington Heights, on the northern tip of Manhattan, epitomize its work. "We didn't want an easy neighborhood," said Moses, and in the late 1980s, when the program started, Washington Heights was the biggest drug distribution center in the Northeast. Its streets were run by the local crack gang, the Wild Cowboys, and one local public housing project was dubbed Crack City. But even in its worst days, Washington Heights stood for more than a string of negatives. It has been the heart of the city's Dominican community, and immigrants from that Caribbean nation have made their mark in business, politics, athletics, and culture. Those are the leaders Children's Aid Society relied on to gain credibility.

"We didn't go into these schools as reformers with a solution," said Moses. "We asked everyone, 'what is your dream?' and we told them 'we're here to stay.' No one believed it but we're still there. We are powerful because we don't turn over."[28]

The Introduction to this book offered a snapshot of these schools. You may recall the doulas who assist mothers during childbirth and in the first few months afterward; the classes designed to sharpen job-seeking as well as parenting skills and give moms and dads the confidence to help educate their own children; the Early Head Start and prekindergarten classes situated in the same building as the elementary school, so that the kids can remain in familiar surroundings; the teens building a bicycle and talking with the City University professor who was teaching a writing class on the premises. Now we're going to look more closely.

"We talk about practicing 'discipline and love,' not 'discipline and fear,'" said Erica Quesada, who runs Early Head Start at P.S. 8, a Children's Aid primary school. Designed for infants and toddlers, the federally funded program combines classroom instruction with outreach to families. "Much of the learning about parenting emerges from what's happening while we're making home visits," Quesada told me during the day I spent there. There's a lot for parents to absorb, including such simple things as the fact that while a sweater is warm enough for an infant during winter in the Dominican Republic, it won't do the trick in New York.

Two teachers and seven parents sat in a circle with their infants and toddlers in the Early Head Start class that I visited. It's music time, and as one teacher, Patricia Jimenez, strummed the guitar, the other, Carmen Gonzales, shook a tambourine. Each child was singing in his or her first language, English or Spanish, and clapping to the beat. The parents followed along with the teacher, talking to their toddlers, pointing to parts of the body, colors, items of clothing, while the kids listened or squirmed.

Most of the toddlers were busily making collages during their "free time," but one boy, Joseph, was off in another world. Quesada knew him intimately. "I was the doula and I've followed Joseph ever since," she said, chronicling the family history. "He has speech issues, doesn't shift well from one activity to another. He doesn't pay attention. The parents came from Honduras; the teacher goes on home visits to do some planning with them." For babies who are progressing much more slowly than most children their age (babies with developmental delays, in the professional argot), Children's Aid runs an intensive program with a teacher for each of the babies and their parents. It looks to be worth its high cost, for after seven months, an evaluation shows, these babies begin catching up with their peers, while their parents become more knowledgeable and confident.

"We're asked to do everything," says Madelyn Gonzalez, the Children's Aid director at nearby P.S. 5, and the organization does its best to oblige. The schools have become gathering places that remain open well into the evening, on weekends, and during the summer. Children's Aid gives a teacher someone to turn to when a student needs counseling, extra help in reading, or treatment for a toothache. And when a kid messes up in class, the teacher can ask someone on the staff how she's doing in her after-school activities.

I got a fuller appreciation of what "everything" means on a visit to the Salomé Ureña School, which enrolls sixth through ninth graders. Like many schools in New York, the Salomé Ureña building has been split up into smaller schools—in this case, three of them. Two are in such demand that they have to admit students by lottery; the third is a downsized version of the former neighborhood middle school, P.S. 218. Children's Aid collaborates with all three. Within minutes of my arrival, June Barnett, the principal of P.S. 218, buttonholed Roy Laird, the social worker on the Community School staff who was showing me around. "Roberto is out of control," Barnett said. "Can you see him immediately?"

The Children's Aid staff and the teachers are so well integrated at Salomé Ureña that it can be difficult to tell who's who. Bernadette Drysdale, the principal of the academically rigorous City College Academy, one of the three schools on the premises, relies on those staffers instead of hiring assistant deans. Students who are having a rough time can see a psychologist in a Children's Aid–run clinic, which, with its comfortable sofas, feels like a family room.[29] Parents can meet there with a teacher and social worker to sort out their youngster's problems.

"Lots is happening right outside the school and we need to know about it," said Drysdale. There may have been a shooting down the block; or ICE, the apt acronym for Immigration and Customs Enforcement, may have broken up a family, deporting the parents while the kids remain behind—whatever the crisis of the moment, the Children's Aid staff is on top of it.

Jane Quinn, who runs the organization's National Technical Assistance Center, thinks about life inside the school in terms of a "developmental triangle": the core instructional program; the academic, social, cultural, and recreational enrichment offerings, which are designed to expand students' opportunities for learning; and the support services, which can remove barriers to learning. "The image of the triangle is meant to emphasize the connections among these three legs," she told me, and those connections are visible at Salomé Ureña. Children's Aid doesn't just share space in this overcrowded building; it's embedded in the quotidian life of the school. Principal Drysdale values this integration: "It's critical that the families don't have to go outside to find help for their kids."

The role played by Children's Aid in a particular school depends on which leg of the developmental triangle is most in need of strengthening. At Manhattan Center for Science and Math, a selective high school that draws 1,700 students from the five boroughs to its East Harlem campus, the aim is to keep these bright kids on track for graduation and college.

Most of them come from families that have no experience with higher education. They're the first generation to give serious thought to college, and they need help in getting there. There's a sense of urgency about those who arrive at Manhattan Center unprepared for its rigors and flunk some of their ninth-grade courses, because that makes them prime candidates for dropping out.

Together with the Manhattan Center's teachers, the Children's Aid staff developed a freshman seminar that helps students manage stress and acquire the habits of study. Because these seminars are small, the staffers evolve into mentors, keeping the youngsters from getting lost among their 1,700 fellow students. In the seminar's first year, the school's freshman failure rate dropped from 36 percent to 24 percent. It has continued to fall since, and many school systems have picked up the model. Kids are encouraged to explore college possibilities—Children's Aid pays to keep the college office open long hours and takes students on field trips to college campuses—so that the idea of earning a B.A. seems less like an impossible dream and more like a realistic possibility.

Students have a major voice in planning after-school activities at Manhattan Center. Children's Aid has made them a deal: If ten kids sign up for a club, the nonprofit pays for an adviser. That's how the hip-hop dance club came into being, as well as the knitting club. Other Children's Aid activities, like a peer tutoring venture that relies on the top students to help their classmates, emphasize the academic side.

Different secondary schools bring different concerns to the table. At Fanny Lou Hamer Freedom High School, in a bone-poor neighborhood of the Bronx, the emphasis is on getting the students and their families the medical care and social services they critically need. In Washington Heights, the High

School for Excellence and Innovation, which opened in 2009, enrolls some of the hardest-to-reach adolescents in the city— sixteen- and seventeen-year-olds who are two or three years behind academically and would almost certainly drop out if the school system didn't come up with a different approach. That's why, despite NYC Superintendent Joel Klein's stated aversion to community schools, Children's Aid was invited to participate in planning virtually every aspect of the High School for Excellence and Innovation. For its part, the nonprofit has invested heavily in counseling services, along with leadership training for the students and individual meetings with adolescents and their families to devise handcrafted roadmaps to success.

Parents and neighborhood residents are a regular and taken-for-granted presence in every Children's Aid school. "There's ten times more parent involvement than in an ordinary public school," boasted Pete Moses, the former Children's Aid CEO. Over the years the organization has offered scores of adult classes, and it helps families in many other ways as well. When parents whose first language is Spanish— or Arabic or Bengali—meet with their child's teacher, Children's Aid provides translators. It has solicited the bar association to send lawyers to counsel those with immigration woes; and when families are threatened with eviction, it has helped them stay in their apartments by taking advantage of the city's rent-to-buy program.

Indeed, Children's Aid is the second-biggest employer in Washington Heights, heavily recruiting in the neighborhood, and because it has been there for more than a generation, some of its staffers grew up in the system. Erica Quesada started as a high-school student who tutored elementary-school kids after school. She never left.

Quality doesn't come cheap. Children's Aid spends about $1,500 for each youngster during the school year and a similar amount during the summer; and the organizations it recruits to provide additional support contribute more. But, as with everything on the kids-first agenda, quality makes all the difference.

Evaluations back up the anecdotes of accomplishment. Researchers from Fordham University found that Children's Aid schools had better reading and math test results, higher attendance rates, and greater parent involvement than traditional schools in similar neighborhoods. Teachers' attendance is also better, presumably because they feel less stressed, and so are relations between students and teachers. A 2005 survey showed 25 percent fewer special-education referrals than at comparable schools, a critical measure of how children are likely to do academically. Test scores at the Children's Aid schools exceeded the citywide average by 15 percent in reading and 10 percent in math; and the more time youngsters spent in after-school activities and summer camps, the better they did academically.[30]

This research record makes the Children's Aid Society Exhibit #1 in the case for community schools nationwide. It's why Arne Duncan, not known to be a gilder of lilies, lavishes their schools with praise.

Still, much remains to be done. Because of financial constraints, lots of families who value Children's Aid services aren't being served, even in neighborhoods with established community schools. In Washington Heights, there aren't enough doulas to meet the demand; and many classes that parents would like, including cigar-making, a traditional Dominican trade, are no longer offered because the money isn't there.

Furthermore, if these schools are going to fulfill their transformative potential, what happens between 9 A.M. and 3 P.M. must get better. It's logical that students who can see the blackboard because they now have glasses, who can breathe easily because their asthma is being treated, and who aren't in constant pain because of rotting teeth will do better in class, and the research backs up this logic. But these students will do better still if learning comes to life in classrooms led by skilled teachers, and on that score, New York City's schools, like public schools in many other places, have a long way to go.[31]

CAN COMMUNITY SCHOOLS TRANSFORM THE WORST-OFF NEIGHBORHOODS?

One-stop shopping for kids, with an academically rigorous public school as the pivot, would be welcomed by any multitasking middle-class family. In communities of concentrated disadvantage, such a school comes as a godsend. In these neighborhoods, crime, poverty, unemployment, and teen pregnancy rates are sky-high, streets and parks are sites of danger, and once-vibrant institutions have been shuttered. Those who can afford to move away have long since departed, leaving a vacuum of leadership and a failure of spirit.

Beginning in the mid-1990s, the federal government conducted an experiment called Moving to Opportunity.[32] Its purpose was to test whether relocating families from such places into more stable communities would change their children's lives. The outcome was mixed, at best, but even if the results had been unequivocally positive, emptying the ghetto is no solution—it's logistically and politically inconceivable to transport to suburbia the millions of families living in broken communities.[33] The only conceivable option is to reinvent these neighborhoods by "tipping" them, reversing the outward migration of talent and encouraging "high-status" families to move in.

Although coaxing middle-class families back to the hardcore inner cities might sound as quixotic as ferrying poor families to the suburbs, the reason it might be feasible is that it takes remarkably few "role model" families to make an outsized difference. When University of Illinois sociologist Jonathan Crane used census data to test the effect that different percentages of professionals in the neighborhood had on the lives of African American teenagers, the results were entirely unexpected. Teen-pregnancy rates or school-dropout rates were similar in predominantly black neighborhoods, where between 40 percent and 5 percent of the residents were professionals, but when the figure dropped below 5 percent, the problems exploded. As the percentage of professionals fell just 2.2 percentage points—from 5.6 percent to 3.4 percent—dropout rates more than doubled, and the rate of childbearing for teenage girls nearly doubled as well.[34] Gentrification at the margin, Crane's study suggests, can have an outsized impact on youngsters' lives.

The consequences of being raised in such a neighborhood are life-changing, said Robert Sampson, who taught at the University of Chicago for many years before decamping to Harvard, where he chairs the sociology department. Sampson, who did his research on Chicago's South Side, has solid street-level knowledge of these blocks, and by analyzing precinct-by-precinct data, he has quantified his impressions.

"For a five-year-old," Sampson concluded, "coming of age in a neighborhood of concentrated disadvantage has the same effect on verbal ability as missing a school year." An entire year already lost by the time a child enters kindergarten—that's an astonishing finding, especially since Sampson isn't contrasting the effect of growing up in the ghetto with a pampered childhood on Chicago's Gold Coast. Instead he is comparing the consequences of being raised in Chicago's best-off and worst-off African American neighborhoods. "When it comes to disadvantage," he told me, "the white neighborhoods are off the charts."[35]

Social scientists frequently pinpoint a single factor, like poverty or race, to explain the achievement gap, the health gap, and other differences in kids' lives, but Sampson is interested in how all these factors interact. "It's not poverty or race that is critical by itself," he said. "Distrust, fear of violence, isolating physical landscapes—the constant stress of life affects families' mental health and leads parents to isolate themselves, so they can protect their children from harm. And because the distrust is so pervasive, there's no way to build the kinds of networks that would function as building-blocks of support, language development and social skills."

Robert Putnam, Sampson's Harvard colleague, has a slightly different take: "What's missing is social capital. The more relations a community has to draw upon to share information, assist neighbors and solve problems, the more social capital grows. That's a resource for child development and learning, fostering both parental and community engagement with the education of children."[36]

Putnam's number-crunching reveals the palpable and phenomenal impact of social capital on students' academic performance. He quantified the concept by pulling together state-level data on volunteerism, voter turnout, informal sociability, and social trust—the flip side of the pathologies that

Sampson studied—and his findings defied expectation. Social capital explained *three-quarters* of the differences in educational outcomes among students living in different states. It was a far better predictor than race, affluence, inequality, adult educational levels, educational spending, or family structure.[37]

These social scientists, looking at the achievement gap through different lenses, have reached the same conclusion—restoring the social fabric of battered neighborhoods is essential to bettering the life chances of those who grow up there. Because these places have a disproportionate number of single parents and small children, the public school makes an obvious starting point. Converting the schools from academies for failure into focal points for communities can help to reverse the spiral of decay, making those neighborhoods more appealing to the higher-status families whose presence could shift the balance. As we've seen in Washington Heights, keeping the school open longer, assuring that kids have good health care, offering them academic help and recreation—all of these things are likely to improve students' prospects. When the school offers adult classes, parents develop new skills and new confidence, and that also contributes to students' learning.

It's especially hard to create successful community schools in decimated neighborhoods, precisely because on-the-ground resources are so scarce. "Good schools depend on strong communities and strong communities require good schools," said Martin Blank, who directs the Coalition for Community Schools. But the effort has to be made, since it's in the worst-off communities that the potential payoff is greatest.

That's what the Chicago public school system is trying to do by going citywide with a slimmed-down version of the Children's Aid model. It's the most far-reaching initiative in the nation, with 150 schools, a quarter of the district, operating in 2010, and more on the drawing board. The stakes are high, for if Chicago can pull this off, then any school district in the country can do the same.

TAKING COMMUNITY SCHOOLS TO SCALE: THE CHICAGO STORY

"The worst in the nation": That's how William Bennett, secretary of education during the Reagan administration, described the Chicago public schools in 1987, and he was probably right. Drop-out rates were sky-high, the schools were falling apart, the school board bickered ceaselessly, and the system was run by hidebound civil servants.[38]

A year after Bennett's blast, a coalition of community groups and business leaders pushed through state legislation that handed over major responsibility for running the schools to locally elected councils, but the results of that reform were uneven. In about a third of the neighborhoods, mostly middle class, the schools got better; in a third there was little effect; and in the remaining third, mostly poor communities where the residents lacked experience in running anything, patronage politics made matters worse.[39]

City leaders reviewed those findings and decided that the schools weren't improving fast enough. In 1995, Mayor Richard M. Daley took charge of the system, effectively displacing the school board (this model of mayoral control has been adopted by other cities, including Boston and New York). Although local school councils remain, they have been starved financially and neutered politically. To signal the arrival of a bottom-line, business-oriented approach, the school superintendent was relabeled the chief executive officer. The shift is meant to reflect a new style of leadership, and none of the CEOs have been professional educators. In this regime, policy decisions are driven by data and benchmarks. The bottom line is fewer dropouts and better test scores.

Progress hasn't come easily in Chicago. While students' test scores have risen—in 2008, 64 percent met or exceeded Illinois standards on achievement tests, compared to 36 percent in 2000—a 2009 report by the Civic Committee of the Commercial Club of Chicago, a group of business, professional, education, and cultural leaders, concluded that those gains were largely illusory, attributable not to more effective schooling but to the state's having watered down its passing standards.[40] In a 2009 nationwide test of fourth- and eighth-graders in math achievement, Chicago recorded lower overall scores and smaller gains than many cities. It ranked thirty-first out of the fifty biggest cities in its graduation rate, with barely half of its students receiving high-school diplomas. "Chicago is not the story of an education miracle," said Chester Finn, president of the Thomas B. Fordham Institute, an education think tank. "It is, however, the story of a large urban system that has made some gains and has made some promising structural changes."[41]

Chicago's community schools initiative was promoted in the late 1990s by the Polk Brothers Foundation, a major player in the Windy City's nonprofit world. The foundation, which looks for ways to combat poverty, wanted to bring the education, housing, health, and welfare agencies together, and the public schools seemed like the right focus. When foundation staffers went looking for promising models of school reform, they were particularly impressed by the Community Schools in Washington Heights. Children's Aid represented the Cadillac model, and Polk Brothers Foundation hoped to have a comparable impact with a more modest, Kia-like, version.[42]

The foundation's initial grant, made to three schools in 1999, was regarded as a political test—would a school paired with a community-based organization be more consensus-driven than the fractious local school councils?—as well as a policy test—would the model remove obstacles to learning, leading to greater student achievement? The school district decided not to wait until the evidence was at hand before plunging ahead. In 2003 it announced the transformation of one hundred more schools into community schools and attracted more than four hundred nonprofits and corporations to work with these schools. Additional schools and partners have come on board in subsequent years. Each school receives $275,000 from the district—about half of what Children's Aid allots to each of its schools—to add staff and services, and the plan is that by 2012 every Chicago public school will be a community school.

For the past decade, Sam Whalen, an education professor at the University of Illinois and longtime school-watcher, has been monitoring the project, undertaking what he calls an "archaeology" of reform. "It's remarkable to see the talent that has come into these schools," Whalen told me, "the new ways of thinking, the mix of organizations, from the Art Institute to JPMorgan Chase, the Boys and Girls Clubs to activist neighborhood councils, that have signed on."[43]

Each community school has a lead partner that is supposed to play more or less the role that Children's Aid plays in New York, bringing its expertise to the schoolhouse and recruiting other organizations to deliver specific programs. For instance, if a Boys and Girls Club is the lead partner, it might seek a local medical clinic and a community-minded corporation as collaborators and ask LensCrafters to donate eyeglasses; if a hospital takes primary responsibility, it could link up with a nonprofit that focuses on tutoring, an after-school club, and a dance company. A school-based needs assessment drives decisions about what to offer, though lack of money has kept the worst-off schools from providing as comprehensive a network of activities and services as their students need. All the community schools stay open well past the familiar school hours, provide social services during and after school, and find ways to reach parents. Each has an onsite coordinator, often someone who lives in the community and comes with local knowledge and good connections. There is an "intentionality" to the partnering, said Whalen, "that builds layers of support for academic success, social-emotional skill-building and parent partnering."

Although Beethoven Elementary School is only a few miles south of the Loop, Chicago's pulsating downtown, its neighborhood has been one of the city's poorest and most crime-ridden.[44] In 2000, a third of the families there earned less than $10,000 a year. Until the notorious Robert Taylor Homes— twenty-eight sixteen-story towers, exemplars of everything that went wrong with the midcentury urban renewal strategy— were torn down in the late 1990s, the children who lived there attended Beethoven. So violent was this neighborhood that Educare, the model in early education that started at Beethoven in 1987, had to shut down, reopening only after the terrible towers had become history.

Against long odds, Beethoven has done reasonably well by its students, and the added resources that have come with its being a community school have led to improved student performance. In the 2007 eighth-grade class, reading and math test scores matched the citywide average and fewer students were told to repeat the grade. The percentage of the graduates who remained on track a year later for high-school graduation in 2011 was higher than the citywide average. Beethoven students give their school unusually high marks on measures that range from academic rigor to emotional support. Even after Robert Taylor was demolished and the families who had lived there moved away, many of them contrived to keep their children in the school, driving miles to drop them off in the morning and pick them up at day's end. The school promotes itself to local churches and real estate offices as "the premier school on State Street, serving all types of children," said principal Dyrice Garner Stewart.

Beethoven shows how the tenets of the community school movement can be translated into good practice. Everything pivots on the academic life of the school. Rather than being isolated in their classrooms, teachers are given the time they need to work together in planning lessons and discussing how to handle problem students. New teachers can turn to classroom veterans for support; professional development is an ongoing enterprise; and rather than treating the textbooks as gospel, the teachers use them as a jumping-off point in aligning the curriculum to the state standards. The school opens at 6:45 A.M., so that parents can drop their kids off on the way to work, and in the hour before the first class, teachers are working one-on-one with youngsters who need help.

In 1999 the Boys and Girls Club, forced out of its old building, was invited to move into the school, and it's the lead community schools partner. Together with principal Stewart, the club has sought out a host of collaborators, more than twenty in all, among them a student health clinic, a dental clinic, and counselors for mental health problems. In addition to the usual mix of tutoring and sports, the array of after-school activities includes a club for avid readers, where the students get to meet the authors of the books they're reading, entrepreneurship clubs in cosmetology and computers, and ballroom dancing. Summer camp runs full time during July and August. Although it can be hard to get parents to spend time at the school, since so many of them have moved miles away, the school does its best, remaining open until 7:30 P.M. Beethoven has organized an adult basketball league, offers parenting classes, and hosts family math and reading nights that teach mothers and fathers how they can help their kids with their homework.

Another example of how to make the vision of a community school come alive is located in the west-side slums of North Lawndale.[45] The century-old Herzl Elementary School, its white-columned exterior the grandest building in the neighborhood, is less than two blocks from where Martin Luther King Jr. lived when he brought his civil rights campaign north in the mid-1960s. Now, as then, North Lawndale is black and impoverished, a landscape of boarded-up buildings—the urban version of desertification, and the families whose children attend Herzl are the worst-off in the area. In 2000, unemployment ran 40 percent, most families were headed by a single mother, the death rate from battery was double the citywide average, and teen pregnancy rates were among the city's highest.

These ugly statistics make Herzl's recent accomplishments look all the more special. Between 2005 and 2007, the percentage of eighth-graders who met or exceeded state standards jumped from 10 percent to 62 percent, and 78 percent of seventh-graders reached that level. Although it has become easier to meet those standards, this six-fold increase, among the highest in Chicago, is an impressive feat. Attendance levels are high, tardiness almost nonexistent, and Herzl is now the safest school in the neighborhood.

Like Beethoven, Herzl has devoted a lot of energy to rethinking its approach to teaching, and the school opted to emphasize the connection between the arts and academic achievement. Columbia College of the Arts, the country's biggest private arts college, which has a long-standing commitment to inner-city education, made an ideal partner. At Herzl, art is melded into the curriculum, with classes in creative writing, painting, dance, and theater; frequently there's an artist in residence and art workshops for parents. The school's second lead partner, JP-Morgan Chase, brings both needed financial backing and a distinctive bottom-line perspective to the conversation about how to run the school more efficiently.[46]

Three-quarters of Herzl's students, well above the citywide average, participate in the after-school activities, which include classes in African dance, drama, and mural-making. Some of them rarely venture outside their neighborhood, and for them the Saturday Scholars program, which is held at the downtown Columbia campus, represents another world. Herzl, like Beethoven, has signed up a host of nonprofits to expand its reach. Mobile care vans from local hospitals make regular visits; LensCrafters supplies free glasses, and Oral Health America provides dental sealants. Among the weekend and night classes for parents is a course in the art-soaked Reggio Emilia curriculum that the school uses, and that class enables them to stay on top of what their children are learning.

"What we tried to do was to put some private sector money, some philanthropic money and some school money together," said Arne Duncan, who pushed the rapid expansion of the initiative during his tenure as Chicago's public

schools CEO, in his 2009 Children's Aid Society speech. "
We had schools compete for the right to open up schools. We
tried to make it something of value, rather than something
where we forced schools to stay open—that would be setting
ourselves up for failure. For every dollar we spent, we were
getting back five, six, seven dollars from the business community, from non-profits, from the social service agencies,
from the state, the federal government. It was easily the best
leveraged money we spent."[47]

In these redesigned schools, school officials and partner
agencies alike must make adjustments and accommodations,
for all of them are being pushed out of their comfort zones.
The partners have had to learn the norms and forms of the
school; and the schools have needed to acquire a better understanding of neighborhood dynamics. One school, for instance, joined forces with a community action organization.
That group knows how to do door-to-door canvassing and
lobbying, valuable skills in bringing parents to the schools;
but it has had to learn how to recruit and manage a nonprofit
to run the Saturday reading academy. The lead partner at
another school, a nonprofit with a long history of running
after-school clubs, has been obliged to come to terms with
the academic-achievement-oriented world of the school,
which is very different from the relaxed atmosphere of the
club. A third school made a nearby hospital its primary partner. That brought comprehensive medical, social, and mental
health services onto the campus, but the clinic then had to
figure out how to work with a host of partners that could offer
tutoring, dance, or basketball.

"There was an absolute culture change among everyone,
among the adults, the principals and among the community,"

Arne Duncan told the Children's Aid Society crowd. While this overstates the case, the introduction of outsiders into humdrum schools has exerted "useful pressure to link 'non-academic' and academic activities," said Sam Whalen. "Some school district leaders wanted narrow solutions to narrow problems. Paying greater attention to the social-emotional learning, which is what the partners brought to the table, has been a way of bridging concern about children's developmental needs and the constant academic pressures."

Not all of these partnerships have thrived—how could it be otherwise when a broad array of organizations, many of them without expertise in public education, are brought together under one roof? The challenges of corporate mergers are familiar—think of Time Warner and AOL or Quaker and Snapple—and what's happening in the schools is akin to a raft of mergers. Although all the partners have the welfare of children at heart, each of them is used to doing things its own way. Their standard operating procedures vary widely and so do their priorities. After-school programs, for example, normally concentrate on organized sports and social events, with the goal of giving kids a place to hang out or building character, but as lead partners in a community school they're obliged to expand that repertoire with a staff that usually has more enthusiasm than formal training. Partnerships with nearby hospitals pose other challenges. Doctors and nurses live by a code of confidentiality, which has led them to deny teachers valuable information, such as the names of the children who suffer from asthma. The medical staff dislikes seeing children unless their parents are there to comfort them, and although that's a commendable sentiment, the reality is that many parents can't afford to leave work for their youngsters' medical appointments.

At the same time that these partnerships are forming, with disparate worldviews bumping up against one another, the teachers and principals are being pressed to break deeply engrained habits of classroom autonomy in favor of greater collaboration, with regular student-by-student evaluation and feedback, as well as to accept far greater accountability for their students' academic performance. That's a tough task, even without the added complications that outside partners inevitably represent. What's more, most schools have kept parents at arm's-length, meeting with them once a semester at ritualized parents' nights, and when parents and teachers don't see eye to eye, a closer relationship can prove rocky.

Ron Huberman, who became CEO of Chicago's schools in 2009, is an outsider to the education world, a technology whiz who spent much of his career in the police department before being "discovered" by Mayor Daley. He's a bear for metrics-driven performance, and he insists that the fate of the community schools, like any initiative, depends on whether they can prove their worth. Taken as a whole, these schools are outperforming traditional schools in both math and reading achievement, though as you'd expect, the results have been uneven. But as you'd also expect, experience matters—most of these schools seem to be improving as they grow into their new role.

Meanwhile, the School of Social Work at the University of Chicago has started a master's program to prepare social workers for jobs in community schools, the first of its type in the country. And many Chicago public schools, although not carrying the formal "community school" designation, are behaving like community schools, staying open after dark and on weekends, reaching out to parents, and finding allies to handle some of the extracurricular work. The Community Schools Initiative kick-started this trend, and whether or not it survives Ron Huberman's bottom-line test, it has influenced the entire system—no mean feat in a school system as cumbersome and historically impervious to change as Chicago's.

Sam Whalen, who has logged hundreds of hours at these schools, chronicling their progress, has concluded that leadership—"internal imagination," he called it—distinguishes the successes from the failures. That's true in Union City and Montgomery County as well as at the Children's Aid Society schools in New York City. Nimble administrators like those at Herzl and Beethoven can capitalize on the synergies that stem from working closely with nonschool partners. Overtaxed administrators overwhelmed by a torrent of failing grades and dropouts can't deal with the added demands of the community school, since to them the potential synergies look more like burdens.

"Evaluating community schools is very hard, because there are so many moving parts," noted Whalen. How do you disentangle the pieces of this complex ecology? How do you take apart this Swiss-watch system? What's the right metric of success: Whether the schools' reading and math test scores improve and students are on track to graduate, or whether a youngster can get a needed pair of glasses or a dental filling? Whether sizable numbers of kids are staying after school to learn how to sculpt or bone up on math, or whether parents are getting more engaged in the education of their children?

Education reform in the "No Child Left Behind" era has fixated on quantitative benchmarks like "value added" (how much children's test scores improve). Though good community schools are committed to evaluation, they pay attention to broader and less tangible outcomes, like artistic development, or community service, as well as to reading and math scores. The question isn't which approach is right but how to blend them effectively in ways suited to the situation. You wouldn't dream of selecting among these criteria in deciding what's best for your own children—why should it be different for anyone else's?

COMMUNITY SCHOOLS, PROMISE NEIGHBORHOODS, AND THE FEDERAL AGENDA

The core offerings of a community school are the same everywhere—and so are the problems that accompany setting up and running such a complex organization. New schools can use help from those who've been through the process. At the Children's Aid Society, Jane Quinn heads a national technical assistance program, founded in 1994, that advises schools and their partners as they move from aspiration to implementation, distilling good practice and making it useful to others.[48]

The nature of the consulting depends on the challenges that a school district faces. In Chicago, said Quinn, Children's Aid was on the scene from the outset, helping to shape the overall plan, giving extensive how-to assistance to key partners, and training school staff on how to increase parent involvement. In Boston, which also plans to turn every school into a community school, the focus has been on building the capacity of those who are running the nonacademic activities in the schools, setting up a structure that can align all the before-school and after-school programs with the schools' academic goals. This hands-on help enables start-ups to learn what works and what doesn't without having to resort to trial-and-error, and that speeds up the learning curve.[49] In cities where community schools have been running for several years, staffers from mature schools mentor their colleagues who are opening new schools. Such help can build systems of community schools capable of adapting to circumstance—systems that can get better while getting bigger.

In 2008, the federal government doled out $2 million to a handful of community school pilot ventures. The Promise Neighborhoods initiative added $10 million to the pot in 2010, with additional funds anticipated in the coming years. But at the Education Department this is pocket change, and community schools shouldn't be seen as an afterthought. As Arne Duncan pointed out in his speech to the Children's Aid Society, it's hard to imagine a game-changing educational innovation that doesn't reach beyond the 9 A.M. to 3 P.M. world of the traditional school. School districts that receive a chunk of the Education Department's $4 *billion* Race to the Top funding are likely to have incorporated elements of the community schools strategy.

Because they do so many things, community schools have learned how to dip into multiple pots of money, including the federal government's $1.15 billion 21st Century Community Learning Centers Program, which since the mid-1990s has paid for academic enrichment activities outside regular school hours, as well as the Children's Health Insurance Program (CHIP) and Medicare, which subsidize health clinics in poor schools. The $13 billion Title I program for poor kids in low-performing schools, more widely known as the No Child Left Behind Act, has historically been spent on compensatory education, narrowly defined, but that needn't be the case. Congress is slated to review the legislation in 2011. The lawmakers should make it clear that school districts can use these funds to build layers of support for academic success.

With the growing political support as well as mounting en-thusiasm from educators, community schools have a window of opportunity—a chance to take root on a wide scale. If pub-lic dollars are scattered willy-nilly, without a strategy to pro-mote quality, the results will be predictably disappointing. But if the expansion is handled well—with a decent level of resources, sufficient time to deal with the predictable growing pains, and lots of practical help from veterans like Jane Quinn—then many more schools will resemble Salomé Ureña in Washington Heights and Beethoven in Chicago. At schools like these, students become more committed to mas-tering their courses, more likely to see the linkages between their education and opportunities in the larger world. That's why community schools can nudge public education toward greater success in its central academic mission, even as that mission expands to include the array of supports called for by the kids-first agenda.

CHAPTER 4

THE KINDNESS
OF STRANGERS
OFFERING KIDS A HELPING HAND

HALF A CENTURY AGO, when Lester Strong was a ten-year-old boy growing up in the steel mill town of Braddock, Pennsylvania, his third-grade teacher, Mrs. Shirer, sought out his parents. She had depressing news for them. "Your son is mentally retarded. Maybe he'll be able to live independently. Maybe he can become a laborer."

"Even then, I was sure that she was wrong," Strong recalled many years later, the moment still etched in his mind. So were three adults who'd known him for most of his young life—the Reverend Albert Minney, the pastor at Calvary African Methodist Episcopalian Church; Eleanor Banks, the mother of one of his friends; and Jerry Martin, who cut his hair at the barbershop on Sixth Street. "They believed in me and pushed me to work harder," he said. He listened to them, and so he started over. He repeated third grade, entered fourth grade as an honors student, and from that point on he never looked back. He was second in his high-school graduating class, won a National Merit Scholarship, graduated from Davidson College, and then spent the next quarter of a century in broadcast journalism.

"I enjoyed those years as a journalist," said Strong, but ultimately the work wasn't rewarding enough. "I wanted to give back. I wanted to stop children from being written off." In 2009, after a stint working for Building Educated Leaders for Life, generally known as BELL, a national organization offering poor kids an after-school and summer experience that has been shown to close educational gaps, he became the CEO of Experience Corps.

The 2,000 Experience Corps volunteers, age fifty-five or older, devote a considerable amount of time—at least six hours a week—to tutoring 20,000 students in twenty-three communities. These relationships begin in the first grade, with children who have already fallen behind their classmates, and continue through third grade. The model is based on solid evidence that if kids have caught up by then, they're much less likely to drop out.

The tutors help these kids become confident readers. They also pay heed to what's happening in their lives. "If a child comes to school looking hungry or embarrassed about wearing a ripped shirt, it's hard for him or her to focus on reading," Ellen Hargis, a member of the Experience Corps board who used to direct the organization's Volunteer Center of Southern Arizona, maintains. As Marc Freedman wrote in *The Kindness of Strangers*, a 1991 book that drew widespread attention to the field, "Mentoring enables us to participate in the essential but unfinished drama of reinventing community, while reaffirming that there is an important role for each of us in it."[1]

A 2009 evaluation that randomly assigned 1,000 very poor readers to an Experience Corps volunteer or a control group shows how meaningful having a mentor can be. Over the course of a single school year, the students who had been tutored by an Experience Corps volunteer made 60 percent more progress in reading comprehension than those who didn't have a tutor.[2]

"DON'T JUST TUG MY HEARTSTRINGS"

Coming of age can be a fraught journey, especially when there is no teacher or coach, no neighbor or rabbi—no one who listens, who can give a nudge at just the right moment, who can pry open the right door or maybe shut the wrong one. Parents are children's first and most influential mentors—they are children's first *everything*—but it's unrealistic to expect them to be all things to their offspring. That's why godparents, whose traditional responsibility was counseling children in spiritual matters, are often asked to assume secular commitments as well.

Ask anyone who spends a lot of time with youngsters, whatever their background, what kids need the most, and the answer is invariably the same—the presence of a caring and stable adult, a fixture in a child's life. That friendly stranger, sociologist James Coleman wrote, can promote "the norms, the social networks, and the relationships between adults and children that are of value for the child's growing up."[3] This isn't a job description—a mentor can be a teacher or a social worker, as in the Children's Aid Society's community schools; a staff member at a Boys and Girls Club; a coach; an aunt or uncle; or a neighbor. Initiatives that can effectively sustain such relationships meet the Golden Rule test, for we would surely want someone like Jerry Martin, Eleanor Banks, or Albert Minney to inhabit the lives of children we love.[4]

Efforts to "save" youngsters in trouble by uniting them with solicitous grownups have been around for a very long time. "The chief need of the poor today is not almsgiving, but the moral support of true friendship," declared the Reverend S. Humphrey Gurteen in his 1882 *Handbook of Charity Organizations*.[5] A century later, George H.W. Bush's paeans to "a thousand points of light" gave mentoring a boost. By the early 1990s, a number of Fortune 500 companies, including IBM and Proctor & Gamble, as well as powerhouses like the National Education Association and United Way, were backing mentoring projects. The Department of Labor proposed that 5,000 businesses recruit as many as 10 percent of their employees as mentors.[6]

Mentoring received the full attention of policymakers in 1995, when a random-assignment study of Big Brothers Big Sisters, the biggest and best-known program, confirmed that mentors (the "Bigs," as they are called) had a meaningful impact on their "Littles."[7] In this results-driven era, the message is, "Don't just tug at my heartstrings; prove that your social policy accomplishes something," noted Gary Walker, the former president of Public/Private Ventures, which conducted that study.[8] As we've seen, the fact that the Nurse-Family Partnership and Perry Preschool were shown in similarly designed studies to have profound effects is a critical reason why parenting support and early education, two ideas that used to command only yawns from public officials, now receive both plaudits and public dollars.

So too with mentoring.

Proponents have always had a pocketful of "feel-good" stories about children whose lives have been turned around by a solicitous adult. Although these tales move private benefactors to open their wallets, they don't always convince policymakers to do the same. With the 1995 Big Brothers Big Sisters report, a goody-two-shoes venture was turned into a plausible public investment. It enabled advocates to argue that mentoring can have a powerful impact on the lives of youth—that while it's not a cheap substitute for improving schools, reinventing communities, or sustaining families, it's part of the equation.[9]

With solid evidence on its side, mentoring gained visibility and traction. The fact that it was one of the few initiatives proven to benefit adolescents bolstered its appeal. Powerful champions signed on, among them Colin Powell and Oprah Winfrey, and a nationwide campaign was underway.[10] A 1997 conference, grandiosely entitled the President's Summit for America's Future, galvanized the movement. In a display of nonpartisanship, then-president Bill Clinton joined forces with former presidents George H.W. Bush, Jimmy Carter, and Gerald Ford (an ailing Ronald Reagan was represented by his wife, Nancy) to promote what the president called "an era of big citizenship." The exuberant conferees set a goal of providing mentors to 2 million children by 2000.[11]

Though the country has never come close to achieving that objective, mentoring did win bipartisan support in Washington. In 2002, GOP congressman Tom Osborne, a football coaching legend at the University of Nebraska before turning to politics, pushed legislation to fund mentoring projects. A year later, when most federal programs for kids were being trimmed, George W. Bush proposed a $150 million initiative that would link mentors to 100,000 children. In 2008 the Senior Corps spent $108 million, more than half its budget, to underwrite mentoring; and the 2009 Serve America Act, named for Senator Ted Kennedy, has expanded those opportunities.

In the competition for public dollars, youth have historically lost out to seniors, but at least when it comes to mentoring this antagonism may be fading. At Generations United, executive director Donna Butts has brought child advocacy groups to the table with major players like AARP. "Intergenerational activity like mentoring will explode," said Butts. "It already has, as people are looking at their later years in a different way. Elders don't want to be where the conversation is only about pain, pills and passing."[12]

As with every item on the kids-first agenda, quality is the make-or-break factor. The equation is familiar: Evidence-based programs work; ill-conceived ones are worthless, even harmful. The 1995 Big Brothers Big Sisters study concluded that the committed involvement of an adult in a youngster's life—one-on-one, for a few hours each week, week in and week out—is required to have positive effects. What's needed, according to psychologist Urie Bronfenbrenner, whose thinking has figured so prominently in our understanding of how children mature, is ample time to form "a special bond of mutual commitment and an emotional character of respect, loyalty, and identification."[13] A relationship between an adult and a youngster that falls apart within six months can be psychologically damaging because it represents yet another instance of an undependable adult drifting through a kid's life.

America is a land of joiners and doers, and across the country thousands of mentoring organizations have sprung up, many of them in the past decade, which raise an estimated $250 million a year, mainly in private funds. Most are homegrown ventures whose merits haven't been tested. During the Bush administration, Washington threw money at schemes that promised to turn around the lives of juvenile delinquents quickly and cheaply. The results from these low-quality efforts have been predictably meager.[14]

Big Brothers Big Sisters is the textbook example of the tried-and-true—the brand-name organization, known to 80 percent of Americans, which garners deservedly sky-high approval ratings. It's for all kids, not just poor kids, and there are affiliates in leafy suburbs as well as inner-city neighborhoods. When it comes to mentoring, as with every item on the kids-first agenda, poor children are often most in need of support—they're less likely to have that attentive adult paying consistent attention to them—but all children stand to gain.

A handful of other programs, such as Experience Corps, show solid evidence of accomplishment. Another captivating success story is Friends of the Children, whose mission is to reach kids who seem destined to fail and reverse that trajectory. It seeks out the hardest-case five-year-olds, those whose kindergarten teachers predict will wind up in jail, and stays with them from the time they're in kindergarten or first grade until they graduate from high school. The "I Have A Dream" Foundation takes a somewhat different approach. It links mentoring to a commitment to guaranteeing youngsters college tuition support —the fifth and final item on the kids-first agenda.

• • •

THESE INITIATIVES ARE MEANT to offset the disappearance of adults who have meaningful ties to children. The phenomenon of the childless commons is pervasive, and its cultural roots run deep. A multiplicity of factors separate the generations, including, as Gary Walker notes, "both parents working, the prevalence of one-parent families, the growth of a distinct youth culture, the reduction of local funding for recreational programs, [and] legal and practical reasons why employees in the public systems (teachers, correctional officials etc.) are discouraged from befriending youth."[15] These forces aren't new—nearly two centuries ago, in *Democracy in America*, Alexis de Tocqueville remarked on how American life "tends to isolate citizens within the solitude of their own hearts"—but they have become far more potent. Today, observes Temple University psychologist Laurence Steinberg, "few young people in America have even one significant, close relationship with a non-familial adult before reaching adulthood themselves."[16]

"It's amazing for all of us who think teenagers want more freedom, more flexibility," said Education Secretary Arne Duncan, who used to run the Chicago public school system, in a 2009 speech. "We used to survey our teens, and one of the startling findings, one of the most heartbreaking, is when their biggest request is they want to spend more time with their parents."[17] The ongoing relationship between an adult and a youngster supplies a reprieve from the social and economic forces that drive them apart in everyday life.

MENTOR, a nonprofit organization that monitors mentoring programs and lobbies for additional federal funding, estimates that 14.6 million youth between the ages of ten and eighteen who most need mentoring lack the opportunity. That figure may sound big, but it actually underestimates the need, since it does not include children younger than ten. What's more, as MENTOR acknowledges, "all youth can benefit from having a caring adult mentor." Although church youth leaders, teachers, coaches, godparents, and the like touch the lives of an uncounted number of youngsters, many children simply do not have access to an adult who is willing to make that kind of commitment to them. These estimates confirm the enormous gap between the existing number of mentors and the potential need.

"Kids need more support—in today's world, as much support as they can get," said Gary Walker at Public/Private Ventures. "Mentoring is the headline on what needs to be done in every institution that deals with young people. Youth need more nonfamily adults making intentionally positive contributions to their sense of importance, usefulness and integrity."[18]

Despite the American fervor for voluntarism and the growing numbers of new retirees, many of whom say they want to work with youth, there will never be a sufficient number of volunteers—and volunteers can't fill the gaps caused by lack of decent medical care, bad schools, and the like. Marc Freedman, the modern-day father of the movement, argued persuasively that "rather than thinking of mentoring as a sufficient solution to the problem of youth isolation—particularly a 'low cost, high-yield' one—we would do well to think of the mentoring movement as one that highlights an unmet need, goes part of the way toward redressing it, and calls out for reinforcements."[19] That's why it's essential to build a system of support from birth onward, why families and schools must be part of the story, and why it's important to populate the childless commons by encouraging lots of adults, not only those designated as mentors, to become connected to the lives of children.[20]

BIG BROTHERS
BIG SISTERS—BIG IMPACT

"When we commissioned the evaluation of Big Brothers Big Sisters we were taking a real gamble," noted Joseph Radelet, who directs the nonprofit's mentoring initiatives, when we spoke at the organization's Philadelphia headquarters. "No one had done it before. No one knew whether what we were doing really worked."

Big Brothers Big Sisters has been doing the same thing—
fostering relationships between kids and grownups—for more
than a century. It began, as successful enterprises often do,
almost by chance.

On July 4, 1903, according to *One to One*, the organization's
official history, a twenty-three-year-old Cincinnati business-
man named Irvin F. Westheimer was sitting in his office, taking advantage of the holiday to clear off his desk, when he
happened to glance out his window at the alley below.[21] There
he saw a boy rifling through a garbage can in search of food,
his mangy dog by his side. Upset, Westheimer ran into the
alley and introduced himself to the boy, who told him he was
one of five children being cared for single-handedly by their
mother. His scrounging was a matter of survival. Westheimer
took the boy out for a decent meal. Later, he took him to a
Cincinnati Reds baseball game and bought him a few things.
Mostly, though, he stayed in touch, offering understanding,
companionship, and a listening ear.

During these first years of the twentieth century, social reform was in the air. Muckrakers like Upton Sinclair were ex-
posing the seamy side of industrialization; Progressives were
becoming a political force to be reckoned with; and, much
closer to home, Rockdale Temple, the synagogue to which
Westheimer belonged, was passionate about helping the disadvantaged. Westheimer's gesture could well have wound
up as a simple and single act of kindness, but as he came to
appreciate how many children were living dead-end lives he
set out to persuade friends and business associates to look after
other youths. As he told the story, one of those boys called his
benefactor "my big brother," and the practice acquired a name.
A few years later, at a meeting held at the synagogue, an organization was born. At about the same time, volunteers from

the Men's Club of New York's Central Presbyterian Church signed up as "big brothers," and a group of women in New York City, calling themselves the Ladies of Charity, began a similar initiative to aid girls in trouble.

The story of the boy befriended by Irvin Westheimer became the emblematic tale about the power of a caring adult. The boy was no innocent—at the time they met he'd been in reform school twice—but he turned his life around. Eight years later he was supporting his family and giving time and money to charity.

Big Brothers Big Sisters is really the Irvin Westheimer story writ large. Its role is to connect adults with youngsters between the ages of six and fifteen. Here's how it works. A family hears about the program, from a teacher, a friend, or a commercial on TV. Their youngster is matched with an adult who has been carefully screened and trained. The expectation is that the two of them will get together three or four hours a week for at least a year. It's not a poverty program or a program for troubled youth—any interested youngster can sign up.

Keep it natural, simple, and fun, the Bigs are advised. "Play a board game. Hit a bucket of balls at the local driving range. Take a ride in the car with the radio on and talk about the music you like."[22] Out of such connections a friendship gradually builds. The mantra is "Length + Strength = Outcomes."

Over the course of three decades, John Barrett has been a Big Brother to four young men. He was a carpenter when he first volunteered, but his experiences as a mentor were so powerful that they led him to change careers; he went back to college and became a social worker. I met John and Philip, his fifteen-year-old Little Brother, at the San Rafael, California, office of Big Brothers Big Sisters North Bay, a comfortably worn suite of rooms tucked away on a back street of town. Philip's mother was raising her son on her own. She thought that he might benefit from having a mentor, and Philip agreed to sign on. When the relationship began two years ago, Barrett recalled, Philip was shy and reserved. Philip nodded in agreement, but the young man I was talking with was articulate and confident, with a wicked sense of humor.

When the two of them get together, as they do almost every Sunday afternoon, they sometimes go on bike trips, to the giant redwoods just a few miles away, or the Pacific coast a little farther. Some Sundays they volunteer with Habitat for Humanity, helping to build houses for immigrant families living in the gangland territory located on the wrong side of the freeway, invisible to San Rafael's well-off suburbanites.

Philip took longer to open up than the other boys he had mentored, Barrett said, but he is a patient man. "You have to build trust with your Little at their speed." Barrett is clear about his place in Philip's life—he's a trusted adult, a friend, not a surrogate teacher. "Your favorite aunt or uncle probably asked about school but didn't harass you about getting your homework done," he said. "That's an important difference."

Two years into the relationship, Philip began talking about problems he was encountering at school and asking for advice about girls. "The best part of having a Big," he said, "is getting to spend quality time with someone who's interested in me." Then he added, unprompted, "Maybe I'll be a Big Brother some day."

John Barrett is plainly not a typical mentor, and Philip doesn't bring the array of problems that can bedevil teenagers. There's no dramatic turnaround to report, just a smoother glide for Philip through the fog of adolescence. The youngsters for whom mentoring works best, said Andrea Taylor at Temple University's Center for Intergenerational Learning, "are often the kids on the edge, who got the boost they needed to make it." Whatever their particular life histories, this is the kind of relationship that Big Brothers Big Sisters aims to foster.

• • •

THE 1995 STUDY—a randomized evaluation involving over 1,000 ten- to sixteen-year-olds nationwide—showed that this model does work. The youngsters cared less about what they did during the time they spent with their mentors than about having "someone to confide in and look up to," the researchers learned, and those relationships generated positive results. After eighteen months, these youth were 46 percent less likely to begin using drugs and 27 percent less likely to start drinking than their peers. (The effect on minority youngsters was even more striking—they were 70 percent less likely to begin using drugs.) They were less aggressive and got along better with their families, did better in school, and were 52 percent less likely to skip schooldays, 37 percent less likely to cut class, and more confident about how they were doing than their peers. Their grade point averages improved as well.[23]

These effects are all connected to one another. The analysis showed that what lay behind the changes was the fact that these youngsters' relations with their parents improved. This makes sense, since parents continue to exert a powerful influence during adolescence. Getting along better with mom and dad gave youngsters a sunnier attitude toward life in general. It also led to better performance in school, which made them even more positive in their outlook.[24]

In the aftermath of the 1995 study, growth seemed like the right strategy for Big Brothers Big Sisters. "We know we have a positive impact," said then-executive director Judith Vredenberg, "and we're reaching too few children." The organization expanded rapidly, from 100,000 volunteers in 1999 to 262,000 in 2009, and increased its budget to nearly $300 million. Because Big Brothers Big Sisters relies on research, the impact of this expansion had to be assessed. The 1995 study had shown great results with John-and-Philip-type relationships. Were they the norm?

To sustain its expansion, Big Brothers Big Sisters devised a school-based model that demanded less of the grownups— a mentor meets with a child once a week for an hour or two, usually over lunch. An evaluation concluded that, while recruiting mentors was indeed easier, the results were disappointing. During the first year, youngsters who were mentored did better in science and English, but those benefits dissipated the next year. At the evaluators' suggestion, the mentors are being better trained, the relationship continues through the summer, and there's an emphasis on keeping students and mentors together for at least a year.[25]

In order to keep tabs on what is happening at each of its 391 affiliates, Big Brothers Big Sisters has devised an elaborate information system. After a Big and a Little have been together for a year, both the adult and the youngster's parents are asked how the youth is faring, and their answers can be compared with what they initially said. The national organization knows how long the average match lasts, not only for every child but also for each agency, for boys and girls, whites and nonwhites, and younger and older kids.

"We slice and dice the numbers," said Radelet. Each affiliate can see how all the other programs are doing, so when one site runs into trouble with, say, maintaining ties with older teens, it can get advice from a site with a better track record.[26]

The program doesn't cost a lot—about $1,000 for each match—but the never-ending challenge is finding enough volunteers to meet the steadily mounting demand. In many communities kids must wait months before they can be matched. It's harder to recruit men than women, and hardest to recruit men of color.[27]

A 2002 study concluded that many potential volunteers were scared away because they saw Big Brothers and Big Sisters as heroes, and when they measured themselves on the "hero" scale they fell short. The organization modified the message to downplay the Mother Teresa image, emphasizing instead that many kinds of people can be good mentors, since what's involved is mostly having a good time with a youngster.

That's not quite right, though, for relationships between adults and adolescents can be hell and the rewards hard to detect.[28] That much was certain a century ago, when, as the organization's history recounts, a Big Brother in New York who was making a home visit found himself face-to-face with a pistol-wielding mother. Not all adolescents are inclined to confide in a stranger who has been thrust into their lives; and not all grownups can find common ground with youngsters whose varied life experiences they struggle to grasp.

One reason for the success of Big Brothers Big Sisters is that the organization knows its limits. Some youngsters confront obstacles so profound that not even as psychologically sophisticated a volunteer as John Barrett can reach them, and so the organization has to turn them away. Another nonprofit, Friends of the Children, aims to help these wounded kids. It gives new meaning to the mantra of "length" and "strength" in relationships. While Big Brothers Big Sisters measures success in terms of how many months a match endures, Friends of the Children counts in *years*—twelve years, to be precise, from kindergarten to high-school graduation.

CHANGING THE SCRIPT
FOR "THROWAWAY KIDS"

It's a sorry fact of life that seasoned kindergarten teachers in downtrodden neighborhoods can predict with reasonable accuracy which of their kids are likeliest to be pregnant or in trouble with the law by the time they're teenagers. These are the five-year-olds who can't sit still and won't follow the teacher's directions, who fight with their classmates and who sometimes threaten to commit suicide. They may never have had the kind of secure relationship—the attachment—with an adult that psychologists regard as essential for normal development.[29] But there's not much that a kindergarten teacher can do to remedy that, since she has twenty or more kids on her hands and must live by rules that prohibit even the gentlest hug.

Yet life isn't always so deterministic, and the early years aren't inevitably decisive. A French study of abused and neglected children with low IQs who were adopted as four- and five-year-olds found that their IQs increased markedly after the children spent a decade with their new families. Although the researchers didn't say so, the sustained love of family likely affected not only their IQs but their emotional well-being.[30]

The odds that children will make it are markedly better if they can count on the support of adults. A study of poor black children from one-parent families in England found that "the strength and quality of the relationship may be even more important than whether the adult is a parent or even a relative. Good relationships outside the family can have a protective effect similar to that which apparently stems from the immediate family." A thirty-year examination of five hundred children raised on Kauai's sugar plantations, where poverty, alcoholism, and mental illness were rampant, concluded that those who emerged psychologically intact were able to draw on the support of stable grownups.[31]

Friends of the Children derives its approach from the psychological literature on attachment—start early, in kindergarten; be steadfast; take all the time these kids need to connect with a caring adult; and stick around until they reach eighteen, ready for the next chapter in their lives.

This formula is easy to recite but excruciatingly hard to pull off. Some years ago, a Silicon Valley entrepreneur had the same idea. He took on the entire responsibility for sustaining a class of first-graders in a barrio school, spending his spare time with them and making the commitment to finance their college education. For a while he seemed to be succeeding, but eventually most of the youngsters followed the example of their peers, quitting school and, in several cases, landing in jail. The despondent benefactor took his own life.

The contrast with Friends of the Children couldn't be starker. Almost all of these throwaway kids stay out of trouble and graduate from high school.

The program, which began in 1994 in Portland, Oregon, and now has affiliates in seven communities, is the dream of Duncan Campbell, and its inspiration comes straight from his own life history.[32] Campbell's parents were drunks, and he recalls that his earliest memories were of long nights in the local bars, watching his mother and father toss down shots. "There were police and bill collectors at the house all the time. My father was sent to prison twice. We never had a conversation." Campbell vowed that if he made enough money he'd do what he could to make sure that kids like himself got a better deal. After earning a fortune in timber investment (the roster of his firm's clients includes the John Hancock Insurance Company

and the Republic of China), he collaborated with psychologist
Orin Bolstad, who'd devoted his career to working with adolescents, to determine what kind of help would make the
biggest difference.

The Friends, as the paid staffers are called, are mostly ex-
teachers or social workers in their twenties and thirties. They
have embraced a job with low pay, great stress, long hours
(after 9 P.M., when cellphone calls are free, their phones ring
constantly)—and considerable emotional reward. Each spring
they spend six weeks in the kindergarten classrooms of dead-
end elementary schools. There they hone in on kids whose
backgrounds might involve poverty, homelessness, domestic
violence, and drug and alcohol abuse.

In making their decisions about which youngsters to mentor they consult with the principal and the teachers. Battle-
tested principals have been known to break down in tears as
these decisions are being made. "You tell me who is more at
risk," one Boston principal demanded. "Twins abandoned by
their parents, a boy whose father is a big-time drug dealer or
a girl who watched her father being stabbed to death. The
kids you pick have a chance to get out of here. What am I
going to do with the others?"

Each child is paired with a Friend, and the two of them get
together for four hours every week. Sometimes they explore
the community, visiting places to which the youth has never
been, or else they go to the Friends House, which is both a
clubhouse and a refuge for these youngsters. Because a slew
of studies have shown that children who aren't reading by third
grade are likely to fail in school, the Friends and their young
charges do a lot of reading together. They find their math puz-
zles on the streets of the city. "What's the price of two slices
of pizza?" "How much will it cost us to ride on the bus?"

Almost always, a genuine closeness emerges over time between an adult and a child who stay together for the better part of a young lifetime. Many of these kids are used to adults who suddenly and unaccountably vanish, but because Friends typically stick with the organization for four or five years, the youngsters are spared the trauma of the revolving door. If a Friend leaves, the organization assigns another adult to that child, maintaining the bond until high-school graduation.

By second grade, the children and their Friends are starting to do things with others in the group. As adolescents, much of their time is taken up with group outings, since at this point in their lives they're more interested in hanging out with their buddies than spending the day with an adult, no matter how cool he or she might be. "That's the normal course of child development," noted psychologist Bob Houck, who runs the New York program.

Over the years the kids grow extremely tight. Even if they leave the neighborhood to go to a better school, something that the program encourages, or move a few miles away, they still have their posse as well as their Friends to counter the gangs that are perpetually on the hunt for recruits.

The Friends' assignment isn't simply to boost their charges' reading and math scores (volunteer tutors help with their schoolwork) or to get them into good schools or make sure their cavities get filled. It's doing whatever it takes to build up these kids' social capital, making sure they're ready for college or good jobs and a responsible, care-for-others life. "Walk alongside the child, be consistent, show up," is how Rachel Langtry, a mentor in Portland, described what she does.[33]

• • •

THE NEW YORK CITY AFFILIATE in central Harlem opened its doors in 2001. Director Bob Houck dreams of a Friends House that fills an entire brownstone, and he has the layout planned out in his head. For now, however, it's a cramped, if comfortably furnished, basement apartment in a rundown building. The kids can do their homework there, work on the computer, try their hand at baking cupcakes, grow tomatoes in the shady yard, or shoot hoops on the cement court.

Central Park, a natural kid-magnet, is only three blocks away, but so inward-looking is the neighborhood, so bounded the horizons of the families that live here, that some of the five-year-olds had never set foot there. Programs for youth that report great results sometimes enroll the smartest kids in the community, or the nicest, or those with the most solid home lives, a practice that's called cherry-picking. Friends of the Children does its cherry-picking in reverse, taking the toughest cases. Among the youngsters in the New York program, 61 percent are being raised by a single mother and 27 percent are in foster care. Nearly half have a parent in jail or prison; 25 percent were exposed to substance abuse; 17 percent have been abused; and 20 percent are in special-education classes.[34]

No city in the world offers more enticements for youth than New York, and the program takes full advantage of those opportunities, with outings to the Museum of Natural History, Coney Island, the Staten Island ferry, Yankees games, and the ballet—even a dress-up contest for miniature French poodles (that particular youngster got to parade the pet owner's dog in front of the judges).

When the Friends go on outings with their young charges they are looking for something that evokes a spark. ("We bring them to the opera," Houck noted ruefully, "but nobody likes the opera.") "I bargained with Joey," said Pedro Resto, one of the Friends. "Let's bike across Central Park, go to the museum and then get a pretzel afterward."[35] Resto, who grew up just a few blocks from the Friends House, is a filmmaker (one of his films won an award at the Sundance Film Festival) who took a break from that career for six years, teaching film-making for troubled teens, and was chosen as one of the city's "top 5 percent educators." He became a Friend, he said, because he wants "to give something back."

The Friends get together twice a week to share their highs and lows. Davi Lakind used to work with adolescents in Ecuador and at-risk youth in her home town of Santa Fe. She joined the nonprofit as a grant-writer, she said, but "wanted to work with the kids." Her "low" was learning that Alisha, a fourth-grader, had been suspended from school for yelling at the teacher. "Alisha's a logical thinker," said Lakind. "She knows exactly what she could have done to defuse the situation, but she's bored in school." Belinda Edwards, another Friend, made a suggestion. "There's an eighth-grader from the program in Alisha's school. Let's use him to reach out to her."

Pedro Resto's "low" was much more worrying. Ramon, a second-grader, had been a handful from the outset, and things were coming to a head. Four times since the start of the school year he had threatened to commit suicide. In the classroom he sometimes punched himself—hard, in the face—and he was terrifying the other kids. "Your boy has Satan in him," a neighbor told Ramon's mother, a single parent. She wasn't willing to consider medication, having been told that it would turn her son into a zombie.

"This isn't the toughest case I've had," Resto reminded his colleagues. "I had a kid with bipolar disorder who was hospitalized for forty-five days and a second-grader who threatened a girl with a knife. His dad had come home from prison, but then he went back. You've got to care for these kids, try to stay strong, but it's devastating." He would try persuading the mother that Ramon should see a doctor, and he would push the school, which had laid all the responsibility on the mother, to devise an individual education program.

"We know that if we can break that shell, we're the right thing for that boy," said Bob Houck.

Some tales of success sound Hollywood-ish in the telling. Take Deon. He was the first child of a teenage mother, a heroin addict who was in and out of jail, and the man he believed was his father lived in the same neighborhood but was also in and out of jail and spent no time with Deon. As a boy, Deon was shuttled between his two grandmothers, never knowing whose couch he'd be sleeping on, and as a result he was tired all the time. The busywork of elementary school bored him and he began to refuse to do his homework. His grades plummeted; and while he had the potential to be a basketball star, he gave up the game. Soon enough he was in trouble, and his mentor had to sweet-talk a juvenile judge out of tossing him in jail.

The four hours a week that a Friend usually spends with his charge didn't seem enough to turn the corner with Deon. The nonprofit often places youngsters in better public schools in other neighborhoods, but because of his home life, something more dramatic made better sense. The nonprofit has developed close ties with a New England middle school designed for students like Deon, and after visiting he was eager to go. Once at his new school, Deon could push the reset button. He returned to basketball and quickly became the team's leading scorer. With new friends and a renewed passion for the game, he buckled down. He started earning A's and B's;

and with him as its star, the school won a state basketball championship. In 2011 he is slated to enroll in a private high school that guarantees its graduates, all of them from poor families, a full ride in college.

The statistics back up such stories. Since the New York City affiliate opened in 2000 not a single youth has dropped out. The promotion rate in school is 98 percent—the only exceptions are a youngster who transferred to a parochial school, where he was asked to repeat a grade, and a boy who lost a month of school because of family turmoil. The attendance record is 95.6 percent, which beats the 89 percent citywide average. The youngsters have been placed in some of the city's top charter and private schools as well as selective public schools, where they have flourished. In 2009, for the fifth straight year, their reading and math test scores were better than average in their schools. All but one has stayed out of the juvenile justice system (a boy brought a BB gun to school). The only girl who had a child decided to put her baby up for adoption and stay in school.[36]

• • •

FRIENDS OF THE CHILDREN started in Portland, and so the progress of the Portland youngsters has been monitored the longest. The statistics are mind-blowing.

Eighty-two percent of the more than 100 graduates of the Portland program have earned their diplomas—that's 13 percent higher than the national average for all American youth—and 68 percent of those who graduate are the first members of their family to do so. Forty percent have gone to college. Although 61 percent of these youngsters have at least one parent who has been incarcerated, 92 percent of them have kept clear of the juvenile justice system. The best marker for teen pregnancy is being the child of a teen mother, but although 61 percent of these kids were born to an unwed teenager, 98 percent of the girls avoided teen parenting.

In 2010, the Harvard Business School Association of Oregon translated these figures into the language of economics. The report concluded that, because of the program's impact on youngsters' educational achievement, crime rates, and teen parenting, every dollar it spent generated a greater than six-fold return. *Six-to-one:* That is light-years better than Head Start or Job Corps. It's even more impressive than some of the renowned social initiatives we've looked at, like the Nurse-Family Partnership and the Abecedarian Project—initiatives whose rates of return have prompted sizable public investments in parenting and early education.

The National Institutes of Health is sponsoring a five-year evaluation of Friends of the Children, the first long-term study of mentoring. It's too much to expect that the results will mirror the Portland figures, but given the long odds against these youngsters making it, it would be remarkable if just half of them turned their lives around.

Big Brothers Big Sisters is the giant in the field, the marquee organization that has shown that it's possible to offer something of value to a quarter of a million kids without sacrificing quality. Experience Corps is considerably smaller—it serves 20,000 children—but in the aftermath of the glowing evaluation and a $2.7 million grant from the Justice Department in 2009, it has plans to expand. Friends of the Children is tiny, just 700 youth in six cities, and while these kids are a positive influence on their own family and friends, it's only a teaspoonful in the sea of need.

Executive Director Judy Stavisky hopes that the study will prompt foundations and government agencies to take serious notice of the nonprofit. She knows the mentoring world well, since she used to be the grants officer responsible for funding a host of mentoring programs at the Robert Wood Johnson Foundation. Her ties are personal as well, since for seventeen years she has mentored a boy who is now in college. "Friends of the Children is a jewel," she said, "and its promise is second to none."

Bob Houck would like to see a Friends Place in every borough in New York City, 1,000 children potentially saved from drowning. Duncan Campbell's dreams are even bigger. "My vision is that every child in the country who needed a Friend would have one," he said. Campbell estimates that there are a million children like Deon. Consider the impact that Friends would have if it reached even one in ten of them.

THE CARING STRANGER AND THE POT OF GOLD

Eugene Lang knows an awful lot about money.[37] Described by *Forbes* magazine as "the quintessential entrepreneur," Lang spent more than six decades amassing a fortune, an estimated $300 million, in technology. As an alumnus of Swarthmore and Columbia, he also recognizes the value of a good education. The man who has become one of America's most famous philanthropists initially believed that money was the main obstacle that kept poor kids from going to college, but he has learned that, though money matters, the promise of a paid-for college education isn't sufficient to get most disadvantaged kids to make college their goal. They simply don't believe in themselves enough. The abiding presence of a caring grownup in a kid's life can make that promise seem real.

On a scorching June day in 1981, Eugene Lang returned
to P.S. 121, the East Harlem Elementary School he'd attended
half a century earlier, to give a graduation talk to sixty-one
sixth graders. For his speech he'd written out the classic Benjamin Franklin "work hard and you'll do well" homily. But
when the principal matter-of-factly told him that most of
those kids would become dropouts, he changed the content
of his speech—and the lives of those youngsters.

Lang spoke about how he had felt when he stood on the
Mall in Washington, D.C., in 1963, listening to Martin Luther
King Jr. deliver his messianic "I Have A Dream" speech. Urg-
ing the children to create their own dreams, Lang impulsively
pledged to pay the college tuition of every youngster in that
class who eventually graduated from high school. There were
shocked gasps from the audience. Then the students, parents,
and teachers cheered and mobbed him.

"Naked money can have an arrogance," Lang told a *New
York Times* reporter in 1985. As he came to know the children
he called his "Dreamers," he realized that they needed considerably more than a financial commitment that would come
true a third of a lifetime—an eon—later.

"Dropping out is what's normal," one of the students explained to the *Times* reporter. "Around here, you are big and
important if you drop out," said another.[38] To combat those
malevolent influences Lang recruited a twenty-three-year-
old from East Harlem to become a consistent presence in
these youngsters' lives, and he signed up a neighborhood
nonprofit that ran enticing after-school and summer programs. Four years later, with every one of the Dreamers still
in school, the *New York Times* article and a segment on *60
Minutes* generated a flood of inquiries.

In 1986 Lang launched the "I Have A Dream" Foundation.
Since its inception some 200 "Dreamer" cohorts have been

started in sixty-five cities, reaching 15,000 children from high-poverty schools and neighborhoods. The mentoring-plus-scholarship model has been adopted by Gaining Early Awareness and Readiness for Undergraduate Programs, popularly known as GEAR UP, a $323 million federal initiative that partners with local organizations to underwrite similar ventures.[39] Education Secretary Arne Duncan knows this terrain well, since he headed Chicago's "I Have A Dream" program before becoming the CEO of the Windy City's public schools. "My job was to take forty sixth-graders and work with them all the way through high school—to tutor them, to mentor them every day, to work with their families, to give them the opportunity to be successful," he said in a 2009 speech.[40]

"I Have A Dream" initially focused on sixth-graders, as Lang had, but because the research has shown the value of starting earlier, youngsters are now recruited in elementary school. "Every time a Dreamer Class is announced, there's lots of press coverage," said Iris Chen, the foundation's high-octane executive director, a Teach For America alum who left a lucrative consulting career at McKinsey, a premier management consulting firm, to make her mark on kids' lives. "We tell them 'we'll be with you every step of the way'—after-school and on weekends and during the summers."

Most affiliates form partnerships with public schools, but the New York City program enrolls clusters of children who live in public housing projects. In those densely packed environs, home to one schoolage youngster in nine in the city, poverty is ubiquitous, stable families are the exception, and gangs often rule. The public schools that serve these kids are inferior by New York City standards. The teachers are less experienced and less qualified, and there are fewer after-school or summer opportunities. Fewer than 40 percent of the third-graders in those schools—10 percent below the citywide average—achieve passing scores on the state's reading exam.[41]

The foundation, housed in a venerable office building in Manhattan's Garment District, has collected a raft of success stories. Juan Martinez, a member of Eugene Lang's first class of Dreamers, earned his bachelor's degree from Swarthmore and a law degree from the University of Pennsylvania and recently joined the U.S. Department of State. He devotes much of his time to two nonprofits, Do Something and Public Allies, which nurture the next generation of leaders. Another Dreamer, Emily Matos, who received her degree at the University of Miami and went to work for Hispanics for Philanthropy, was named a 2008 "Woman of the Year" by *Hispanic Business Magazine*. Several Dreamers have become scholar-athletes, including London Fletcher, a linebacker for the Washington Redskins.

The statistics back up the anecdotes. Ninety percent of Eugene Lang's original Dreamers earned high-school diplomas, and half of them went on to college. Six studies in as many cities have compared the Dreamers' high-school graduation rates with a control group or the average rate in the community, and in each instance the Dreamers have done notably better. In Chicago, three-quarters of the class of 1996 graduated, more than double the number in the control group. Graduation rates in Portland were 10 to 15 points higher than in the control group. In both cities, the rate of college enrollment was higher among the Dreamers than among their peers. What's more, these youth were considerably more likely to vote than their peers. Not only have they done better in school, they have also become better citizens.[42]

The promise that college costs will be partially covered alters the landscape of possibility. But college is so far away that it is hard for many of these youngsters to envision what that promise means, and the cost of higher education isn't a reality to their parents until their offspring start high school. The evaluations conclude that the mentoring—that constant support the youngsters receive, beginning on day one—has a bigger impact on attitudes and behavior than the pot of gold.

Although these youth are known as Dreamers, they're not always a dream. "At the beginning they're testing us all the time. They're in your face, cursing at us. They want to see if we're there for them," said Treston Lambert, who ran the program at the Chelsea-Elliott public housing project in Manhattan, when I stopped by. "The parents are skeptical too. They want to know whether it's just a tax write-off. They've seen programs come and go, but after two or three years they're convinced—and their support is critical."

At 3:30 P.M., the neighborhood school, P.S. 33, ended for the day, and in a comfortable suite of rooms on the ground floor of Chelsea-Elliott, a gaggle of fifth-graders began arriving to do their homework. Zach Menendez, a richly tattooed New School undergraduate, had been tutoring these kids for three years, leading workshops in poetry, art, and drama. He was like an older brother to them, and he wanted to make this kind of work his career.

The full-time staffers, Natalie Corujo and Terence Stokes, were former Dreamers who had recently graduated from college and returned to the neighborhood where they had grown up. They stressed that it had been the personal support, not the promise of a scholarship, that had seen them through. "They were there for us. Even when my family moved away to Rhode Island they wouldn't let go," said Stokes. Corujo's response was much the same: "It was the stability and the consistency."

A couple of times a month, these youngsters meet with their mentors. The mentors take them under their wing, arranging opportunities, like a two-week snowboarding trip or a summer arts camp that teaches furniture-making and glass-blowing, that are unimaginable to most kids living in the projects. The mentors are enacting the Golden Rule, doing for these boys and girls just what they would do for their own sons and daughters.

Still, Iris Chen wants these youngsters to do better. The big worry is that, while most Dreamers do earn high-school diplomas, still too few graduate from college. Although three-fifths of the youngsters from the first Chelsea-Elliott class, for example, graduated from high school, beating citywide expectations, only 21 percent earned a college degree. That's not uncommon for poor youth, but the Dreamers don't have to worry about paying tuition.

Some benefactors have concluded that it's unrealistic to set higher expectations—that for poor kids, "youth development" matters more than college—but Chen strongly disagrees. She has hired Lori Donoho, who headed the highly successful Washington, D.C., program, to strengthen academic programs for Dreamers nationwide. Donoho wants her charges to develop what educators call "meta-skills"—resiliency, goal orientation, and the ability to navigate.

Chen's ambitions are much broader: "The challenge is moving from 3,100 kids [the current enrollment] to systemic change—moving the needle on how kids are educated."

What's more, rather than simply handing out scholarship money, as Eugene Lang and his fellow philanthropists have done, Chen wants to galvanize parents into contributing to their child's future education by offering matching financial incentives. A government-funded version of this strategy is now being tested in several states. It's a smart idea. Because of compound interest, the money that families chip in yields a far bigger pot down the road. Even more important, the fact of making a financial contribution alters how parents, poor and middle class alike, think about their children's futures. What matters most is that it encourages youngsters to plan more confidently for their own futures. That's why the child savings account is the fifth and final big idea on the kids-first agenda.

CHAPTER 5

THE UNIVERSAL PIGGY BANK
GIVING EVERY CHILD A NEST EGG

THE KIDS-FIRST STRATEGY begins by giving parents the support they need, then expands in ever-widening circles to offer helping hands all around. There's the intimacy of the early learning center and then the excitement generated by community schools, which give youth much more than a basic education, introducing them to opportunities beyond the schoolhouse door. The consistent presence of a caring adult can ease the transitions among those universes—the public and the private; the family, the market, and the state.

Boosting social capital and human capital—competence, confidence, and connections—makes it more likely that youngsters will succeed. Each item on the agenda builds on what has gone before. Together, they form a system of supports that reaches from birth to high-school graduation and beyond. That's the *one* big idea for kids.

But a lack of dollars-and-cents capital can stop youngsters from realizing their dreams. With the economic crash having depleted their savings, middle-class as well as poor parents worry about how to pay the ever-mounting college tuition, which at some private institutions run as high as $40,000 a year. Growing numbers of parents are asking the universities their kids attend for additional financial help. Rather than attending second-tier private institutions, students are flocking to public universities, where the tuition is considerably lower (though rapidly rising), or else going to community colleges, where costs are minimal, and then transferring to four-year schools in their junior year.

As ever, the least-well-off are the hardest hit. It's difficult for kids from poor families to envision the long-term benefit of going to college when, with nothing in the bank to fall back on, they are confronted with bills to pay and looming family obligations to meet. The result, lowered expectations, translates into truncated futures and wasted opportunities, both for these youngsters and for the rest of us.

The access gap is wide. Three-quarters of the students at the most selective 160 colleges and universities come from families in the top quartile of the income bracket. Ten percent come from the bottom half; and just 3 percent are drawn from families in the lowest income quartile. Each year, about 10,000 high-achievers from poor and working-class families—students with at least a B+ average and an Advanced Placement score of 4 or 5—don't even apply to a selective college. And when poor youngsters do enroll, financial hardships make it difficult for them to stay. Just 39 percent of youth from the poorest 25 percent of families who score in the top quartile of eighth-grade math go on to earn bachelor's degrees; the college completion rate for the wealthiest quartile is almost double that. As Terry Hartle at the American Council on Education memorably put it, dumb rich students and smart poor students attend college at the same rate.[1]

A nest egg would go a long way to easing these burdens. One approach—embodied in the federal GEAR UP program and the "I Have A Dream" Foundation, which we looked at in the last chapter—assures kids from poor families that, if they graduate from high school, they will have help paying their college bills. Although that strategy directly responds to money worries, it turns students and their parents into passive recipients rather than active participants in the shaping of their lives. Another approach—the child savings account—encourages families as well as society to invest in their children. The effect is to brace up families and to make students aware that, by starting to save young, they can alter their life-scripts.

THE LEGACY

Harold Alfond was the richest man in Maine and its most generous benefactor. He made his fortune with Dexter Shoes, then sold the company to Warren Buffett and started giving away big chunks of money to support education. Health science and classroom buildings, hockey rinks, track-and-field stadiums, a middle school for troubled kids—the evidence of his generosity dots the landscape of his home state.

"Our children are our future," Alfond was fond of saying. When he was in his nineties and nearing the end of his life, the question that nagged at him was how to invest most wisely in the next generation of Mainers. In 2006, his longtime friend Greg Powell, chairman of the Alfond Foundation board, approached him with an audacious plan.

The proposal was as simple as it was bold: The Alfond Foundation would guarantee every baby born in Maine a $500 trust fund as a kick-start for higher education. This $500 would be the hook, a way to nudge parents into adding to the trust fund. Powell calculated that, through compound interest, a $500 trust fund account could grow to $2,000 in twenty years. If parents contributed $50 a month throughout that time, the account would be worth a tidy $25,000.[2]

A kick-start was certainly needed. Although Maine's high-school students shine on nationwide achievement tests, the state ranks a dismal thirty-third in the percentage of its high-school graduates who attend college. "All the attention is focused on getting sixteen-and seventeen-year-olds to en-roll," Powell pointed out, "but we should be planting the idea much earlier. Middle-class families can sign up for tax-free college savings accounts for their offspring. Let's give every family the same break."

"It's too grandiose," was Alfond's first reaction, but he de-cided to carry out the Harold Alfond College Challenge any-way, and he came to regard the universal trust fund as his most consequential legacy. On New Year's Day 2009, two years after his passing, the largesse of Harold Alfond enabled Maine to become the first state to establish trust funds for all babies born within the state.

THE LAW OF THE HAVES

Unbeknownst to Greg Powell, the universal child development account was already on the policy agenda. In 2005 Britain launched its own "baby bond" program; and the idea had also attracted some interest in Congress. More than two centuries earlier, Tom Paine had offered a similar suggestion. The pam-phleteer of the American Revolution proposed a "national fund, to pay every person, when arrived at the age of 21 years, the sum of fifteen pounds sterling, to enable him or her *to begin the world!* . . . Instead of becoming burdens on the society [they] would be put in the way of becoming useful and profitable citizens."[3]

For "useful and profitable," substitute a line from *Poor Richard's Almanac*: A universal trust fund, Ben Franklin wrote, would help to make every youngster "healthy, wealthy and wise." Indeed, it would establish every child as a stakeholder— someone who, with a welding certificate or a Berkeley B.A., could take advantage of all the social and intellectual capital acquired during youth and so "begin the world."

We're familiar with the widening income gap, but the "wealth gap" is far bigger. In 2004, the wealthiest 20 percent of Americans commanded 86 percent of the nation's assets. The poorest 25 percent of the population had *negative* assets— they owed more than they owned.[4]

The government encourages middle-class families to accumulate assets with mortgage interest tax deductions as well as tax-advantaged accounts like IRAs and 401(k) retirement plans as well as 529 plans for college savings. But those tax breaks, which add up to $400 billion a year, do not help poor families—cleaning ladies and school crossing guards rarely have 401(k) plans.[5] The conventional prescription for the poor, combining make-it-through-the-month handouts with stern admonitions to find a job, has failed to narrow the gap—and for good reason. "You can't spend your way out of poverty," noted Michael Sherraden, a professor of social work at Washington University in St. Louis, whose 1991 book, *Assets and the Poor*, led policymakers to appreciate the importance of encouraging poor people to save.[6]

The Horatio Alger legend is precisely that—a legend. The children of the wealthy learn about assets at the dinner table or the tennis court, and their families' money gives them an immense advantage. "Income bounces around, but wealth endures," Sherraden pointed out. "It can be used to nurture children for whatever success is said to require, be it tuition or orthodontia. It can buy social capital in the form of contacts, networks of protection, information, resources and so forth."[7] Youngsters without family assets have a hard time thinking straight about the long-term benefits of postsecondary education, because the short-term reality—no money—dominates their lives.[8]

LEVELING THE PLAYING FIELD

The child development account—sometimes called a baby bond, a child savings account, a stakeholder account, a college access fund, or a child trust fund—begins to level the playing field. Although the specifics vary, there is broad agreement on the underlying principles: The trust fund must be *universal, progressive, simple, and enduring.*[9]

Here's how such a plan would work. The government would open an investment account for every newborn, just as the Alfond Foundation does for the newborns in Maine. The amount of the initial deposit might be $500, as in Maine, or more, such as $6,000, as proposed by the New America Foundation.[10] Each family could decide whether to put the funds in safe money markets or to take a chance on stocks, with their allure of greater returns; and families would be able to add to the account. Most versions of the idea specify that the government would match every dollar that a poor family put into the account, up to a specified annual maximum ranging from $250 to $500. Aunts and uncles, grandparents, and godparents could chip in to a youngster's account; so could church groups, employers, or anyone else with a commitment to the child's success. Over time, the trust fund would grow, and when the youngster turned eighteen, he or she could spend it on college or job training, or, in some versions, on a first home or a retirement account.

Universal *and* progressive—though that's a tricky balancing act, it fits our sense of fairness. In *The Stakeholder Society*, Yale law professors Bruce Ackerman and Anne Alstott argued that as a matter of principle, all youngsters have a right to be stakeholders, just as they have a right to public education or health care. They advocate giving $80,000, no strings attached, to every twenty-one-year-old with a high-school diploma. Stakeholding is a "mark of citizenship," they contended, a way of "making freedom real" for all and "addressing intergenerational privilege."[11]

While one might well question the need to set up Bill Gates's offspring with a publicly subsidized trust fund, you wouldn't doubt that child's right to enroll in the local elementary school. Besides, there's no way of predicting economic futures—as the persisting high unemployment rates have shown, parents who are comfortably off when their child is born may later find themselves out of work and facing foreclosure.[12]

• • •

A GENERATION AGO, when the asset-based approach was first inserted into the national policy conversation, the rationale was that it was an effective way to reduce poverty. In *Assets and the Poor*, Michael Sherraden argued for individual development accounts, universal savings accounts, starting at birth, with a government match, which would promote saving for "life goals."

Sherraden arrived at this conclusion after interviewing scores of mothers on welfare. When he asked them what they most disliked about how welfare worked, the response was invariably the same—"You can't get anywhere." These families could never save enough to improve their lives by moving to a better neighborhood or going to school. Instead, they were penalized if they managed to save a portion of their welfare check.

To Sherraden, it seemed perverse that people receiving welfare were punished for saving, while middle-class families who put money aside for their retirement or their children's education were rewarded with tax breaks. "I went back to those women," he said, "and asked them what would happen if someone matched their savings—would they save? 'Yes,' they said, 'but it'll never happen.'"

Sherraden's proposal for individual development accounts attracted bipartisan support—Jack Kemp, George H.W. Bush's secretary of housing and urban development, was a vocal advocate—and achieved modest success. In 1998, Congress approved a five-year, $125 million demonstration project; several states funded their own pilot projects; and most states eased the asset limits that penalized welfare recipients who saved money. Meanwhile, the federal government was underwriting billions in tax write-offs for families who set up college savings accounts.

If Congress was ever going to commit billions, not millions, to asset-building, the program had to be universal—that was the takeaway message for Sherraden and his Washington-savvy ally, Ray Boshara at the New America Foundation, who had spent many years as a congressional staffer. "There would be greater political stability," said Sherraden, and the historical record backs him up. Although poverty programs like Head

Start and Medicaid are chronically underfunded—we're inclined to be stingy when policy is seen as *us* funding *them*—
initiatives like Social Security and Medicare, which include
something for everyone, have flourished. As Berkeley law
professor Gillian Lester has pointed out, people don't seem
to mind (perhaps they don't even notice) that Social Security
gives the poor relatively more than it gives the well-to-do.
What matters politically is that everyone, rich and poor alike,
emerges looking like a winner.[13]

The America Saving for Personal Investment, Retirement,
and Education (ASPIRE) Act, which codifies this universal-
and-progressive approach, has been introduced in Congress
every year since 2004, with sponsors from both sides of the
aisle.[14] The legislation would create a $500 stakeholder account
for every infant, with children in families with below-median
incomes eligible for an additional $500. The government would
also match— on a dollar-for-dollar basis—contributions up to
$500 a year made by the less-well-off families. When the trust
fund matured, at age eighteen, the accumulated funds could
go toward higher education or a first home, or else could be
socked away for retirement. The price tag would be about $38
billion over ten years. As with Social Security, the ASPIRE Act
would give something to every family, with those on the lower
rungs of the economic ladder getting the most—an estimated
80-plus percent of the public largesse.

It's the particulars that determine whether the trust-fund
plan would fulfill its promise.[15] The difference between charg-
ing 0.5 percent or 1.5 percent to manage a child savings account might not sound like much, but over time those dollars
add up. All of the proposals set a minimum on deposits to the
savings account, in order to simplify the bookkeeping, and
that amount effectively determines who can afford to chip in.

Investment firms like TIAA-CREF, which operates the Maine program, hate small deposits because it is costly to process them. But experiments conducted by Sherraden and his colleagues have shown that poor families are effectively frozen out if the minimum contribution is set above $50. These experiments also revealed that the public match is an essential element of an effective plan. It isn't the size of the match—whether it's one-to-one, say, or two-to-one—that matters. What's important is the maximum amount that the government will match.

Over the years child savings account legislation has been backed by conservative stalwarts such as South Carolina senator Jim DeMint and former Pennsylvania senator Rick Santorum, who regard it as a way of turning supplicants into investors, as well as by bedrock liberals like New York senator Chuck Schumer, who see it as an antipoverty strategy. But the idea isn't a political slam-dunk, as Hillary Clinton learned to her sorrow during the 2008 presidential primaries, when she proposed a $5,000 universal college savings account. GOP candidate Rudy Giuliani mocked the plan as big government—$20 billion to $25 billion a year big, to be precise—run amuck, and he titillated the media with a graphic of a "Hillary Baby Bond" that bore the former First Lady's likeness. Stung by the criticism, Clinton quickly backed off, declaring that health care and education were higher on her priority list.[16]

Surveys show that, while the savings account is a popular idea, it is almost no one's top priority.[17] Unlike the movement for early education, which grew out of a widely appreciated need and commands an army of supporters, the trust fund plan was dreamed up by policy intellectuals and Beltway insiders. It can gain political traction when it's seen not as a stand-alone proposition but as a component of a broader agenda.

LITTLE PURITANS

The stakeholder account vividly demonstrates the power of compound interest—a dollar invested today will almost double in eighteen years. What's ultimately more important is the fact that owning something of value can change the dynamics of a family. Money in the bank prompts parents to save more and to think more carefully about their children's future.[18] It obliges them to play an active part in deciding how to invest the funds; and so they're drawn, out of self-interest, into the world of finance. Since a quarter of all Americans don't even have a bank account, that's a good thing, and it's a reason why investment firms should regard child development accounts with modest balances as loss leaders.

Evaluations of the congressionally funded pilot projects show that parents' aspirations for their kids escalate when a savings account is opened. "When assets are present, the concept of assets becomes a meaningful schema. . . . People begin to think in terms of assets. . . . Assets *are* the future," wrote Sherraden. Those high hopes persist even when parents don't contribute a dime during the first years of a child's life. As we've repeatedly seen, parents are the biggest influence on their offspring, and their expectations for their children are tied to their assets. More assets mean higher parental expectations; which in turn affect their youngsters' grades as well as how they cogitate about the opportunities that might realistically lie ahead.[19]

Many of us regard kids as little hedonists who think only about the pleasures of the moment, yet with the right kind of encouragement they can morph into little Puritans. In Michael Sherraden's evaluation of child development accounts, 1,171

elementary-, middle-, and high-school students who were offered a dollar-for-dollar match accumulated more than $1.7
million over three years. That amounts to $1,518, nearly $50 a
month, for each of the youngsters, with half of the money coming from their own savings and the rest from family members.
The fact of having an account boosted their self-esteem and
made them smarter about money. The fourth-graders who had
been given accounts were more likely to mention savings
as one way to finance college—pretty savvy for a bunch of
ten-year-olds—and they scored significantly higher on a financial literacy test. That stands to reason, since, with their
own savings accounts to attend to, they had something to be
literate *about*.[20]

The prospect of greater financial literacy among the next
generation has made apostles out of such influential economists as Peter Orszag, the former director of the Office of
Management and Budget in the Obama administration, and
Gene Sperling, who headed the National Economic Council
during the Clinton administration and became counselor to
Treasury Secretary Timothy Geithner during the Obama administration. The College Board, that arbiter of students'
fates, has also signed on. Its 2008 report *Rethinking Student
Aid* endorses the trust fund concept as a promising way to
make college more affordable.[21]

In polls commissioned by the Corporation for Enterprise
Development (CFED), a Washington, D.C., nonprofit think
tank, voters reacted positively to the child development account
idea. The voters' perceptions coincide with the research, as
Carl Rist, who heads the asset-building project at CFED,
pointed out. Voters believed that if the legislation passed, the
incentive would encourage families to save more, children's

ambitions would expand, and children would become more knowledgeable about money. But these voters also knew that the trust fund would not be a cure-all. Good early education is necessary to improve opportunities for youngsters unprepared for school, they told the pollsters, and more financial aid is essential to increase higher education enrollments.

Will the stakeholder account turn poor families into savers? The evidence from the individual development account pilot projects is encouraging, and what happens in Maine will yield additional useful information. An ongoing experiment in Oklahoma, devised by Michael Sherraden, supplies a much more systematic test. There, 1,350 randomly selected families have each been given $1,000, set aside in a college savings plan; and until their children are four years old, contributions that poor families make to their youngsters' accounts will be matched, up to $250 a year.[22]

The Oklahoma study, largely underwritten by the Ford Foundation, which will track these families for at least eight years, poses the big questions. Will the college account alter parents' calculations, and will they put more money aside? Will their dreams for their children change? Will they get more involved in their toddlers' education, for instance, by reading to them or readying them for preschool? And what about the youngsters? Will their hopes change? Will their grades and test scores improve? Will the prospect of a nest egg reduce the stress in their lives? So far, proponents of the child savings account have had to rely on logic models and analogies drawn from studies of other strategies to promote savings. The findings from the Oklahoma project will go a long way toward determining whether the child savings account is as sensible a public investment as it appears to be.[23]

A CAPITAL IDEA:
THE BRITISH CHILD TRUST FUND

To understand how a large-scale savings account plan actually works, have a look at what's going on in Britain. In the late 1990s, when Prime Minister Tony Blair pledged, somewhat rashly, "to end poverty in a generation," that country did an about-face from Scrooge to Santa, becoming a leader in advancing a kids-first agenda. Early learning centers for infants and toddlers have been set up across the country, as have community schools, and 90 percent of the four-year-olds are going to preschool.[24]

The Child Trust Fund, begun in 2002, fit snugly into this child-friendly policy regime, and while it was operating, nearly 5 million children received a nest egg for the future. Although the newly elected British government axed the program in May 2010, as part of its massive cost-cutting, there's a lot to be learned from Britain's experience.

Here's how it worked. Every baby born in Britain between September 1, 2002, and January 1, 2011, automatically received an account of £250 pounds (about $375, calculating the value of the pound as $1.50), with babies born to families in the poorest third of the populace getting twice as much. When these youngsters were seven years old, the government made an additional £250 contribution. The annual cost was £240 million ($360 million) a year.

Parents had one year to choose among forty competing trust-fund providers, including mega-chains such as Boots and Walmart.[25] They also had to decide whether to invest in a savings account or a "mixed" portfolio of savings and stocks, or else to play the stock market. (If they didn't make a choice, the government picked the mixed portfolio as the default option.)

The account matures when the youth turns eighteen. Un-like the American versions, this money can buy anything from an Oxford education to a souped-up car.[26]

To get a feel for the program, I visited the St. George's Childcare Project, located in a genteel, slightly shabby Victorian building in the leafy Southeast England town of Tunbridge Wells. A dozen mothers of infants and toddlers—mainly mid-dle class, mostly married, in their twenties and thirties—had gathered for an afternoon's discussion of how the trust fund affected them personally. They had joined a focus group organ-ized by Children's Mutual, a major account manager, which organized such sessions to test the market. As they settled in, the women swapped stories about how having an infant had changed their lives, how they were juggling the pull and tug of having a career and raising a child, how the bills and baby toys were piling up. Taking a couple of hours out of their day to discuss such matters was a rare break from multitasking.

Martin Bellingham, a psychologist at Children's Mutual and the focus group's low-key leader, guided the discussion. "Do you know about the trust fund?" he began. As expected, all the mothers answered affirmatively; surveys done by the company show that 98 percent of new British mothers share that awareness. That's the market at work—with posters in the big grocery and pharmacy chains inviting mothers to sign up; giveaway "baby packs"; a new "Baby Channel" on TV; ads in the financial pages, aimed mainly at fathers; and a web-site, called "Emma's Diary," for the mothers, the trust fund couldn't be missed.

"Has it made a difference in your lives?" Bellingham asked the women, whose names have been changed at the request of Children's Mutual. Certainly not while they were pregnant, they agreed, since, at the time, the notion of being the parent of an eighteen-year-old seemed as far away as Jupiter. Most of these women recalled the six months after childbirth as a blur of activity and sleep-snatched nights, with no time even to glance at the trust fund material mailed to them by the Treasury Department. "It sat on the hall table for ages," Mary Palast recalled.

Sue Mason was the only woman in the room to say that she had not signed up: "It was too complicated," she said. "I didn't know how to find out the best information." She was hardly alone in her complaint. Many families were over-whelmed by the information, and the sheer number of com-petitors made the decision especially daunting.

But as infancy segues into toddler-hood, there's time to begin planning for the future. "Having that child trust focused Tom [her husband] and me on money," said Jane Luker. Sur-veys showed that in 70 percent of the families both parents were involved in deciding how to invest. "It's the vehicle we use to save for Alex, the starting point to make us think. It encourages me to see the bigger picture," added Rhea Mauldon, and others said much the same. Other women chimed in: "It's seed capital to start the ball rolling for Sara's future," "It's somewhere to put the money that the children receive in their early years," "It's a home for money for their future," "It's about some emotional security for me and know-ing Cheryl and Doug have got something for their future."

Parents are naturally keen to choose the fund that brings them the biggest return for their youngster. However, know-ing what to select can be tricky, since they must work out how much of a risk they're prepared to take with their child's cash. Individual portfolios lost as much as half of their value during the 2008 stock-market collapse, which brought critics out of the woodwork, but the parents were surprisingly unruffled. "They understand they're in it for the long haul," said David White, chief executive of Children's Mutual.

These families are saving differently than before—they're saving more, and more mindfully. "The trust fund made us stop and think about the future," said Deanne Parker. "It's changed my attitude toward my children, and not just my youngest," Naomi Salisbury chimed in. And there's a murmur of assent when Sara Doggett said that contributions were "a much better gift than clothes and dolls. We've told the grandparents, 'no more toys, please . . . please put something in Gavin's trust instead.'"

Moira Wilson, the "small d" democrat in the group, liked the fact that "those households on lower incomes get more money from the government to help them out." But Rhea Mauldon summed up the general sentiment: "It reminds you to think about your child's future and gives you a simple solution to help those dreams come true, no matter where you live and who you are."

● ● ●

DAVID WHITE, who sat in on the session, was paying close attention to these women's opinions, since they affected how he promoted his product. But White, who led the unsuccessful 2010 campaign to preserve the child trust accounts, isn't just an entrepreneur; since 2000, when Sherraden's research on child development accounts crossed the Atlantic and entered the slipstream of British politics, he has also been a policy player. The concept of a child trust fund, embellished by the Institute for Public Policy Research, a Labour-oriented London think tank, was embraced by Gordon Brown, then chancellor of the exchequer. It became law less than two years later.[27]

"The bill wasn't controversial," White recalled. "Labour saw it as a way to equalize upwards and Conservatives viewed it as promoting a nation of savers." The policy was marketed as the twenty-first-century version of the War Savings Bond, and because private providers manage the money, the trust fund doesn't carry the taint of being part of a government bureaucracy. Even though the Child Trust Fund is history, the families of the children who already have accounts can keep investing.

"In a few years the first 'baby bond' kids will be learning about how investments work," said Monica Ennis, who oversees the program at the Treasury Department. "They can watch how their fund grows"—and they're likely to prod their parents into making a bigger investment in their future.

Despite the setback in Britain, David White remains an assiduous advocate. There is baby bond legislation on the books in Singapore and Korea, and pilot projects around the globe, from Canada to Uganda. "If we had David White in the U.S.," Michael Sherraden said admiringly, "we'd already have child development accounts."

ALL TOGETHER NOW

"What I'm proudest about isn't the money," said Greg Powell at the Harold Alfond Foundation, discussing the Maine college scholarship fund. "It's the parenting education materials that every family receives in the mail along with the quarterly financial statements. That's where the real effects will be felt, in better parenting," he said. Powell's observation brings the kids-first agenda full circle, from nesting to nest egg.

"We would certainly not claim that a universal [college savings account] is a complete and sufficient solution for positive child development and educational attainment," wrote Michael Sherraden and his colleague Margaret Clancy, cautioning the overzealous. "We do think, however, that asset accumulation is a key pathway for individuals, families, and communities to formulate goals and reach their potential." In other words, the baby bond isn't a panacea, but it surely helps.[28]

The child savings account bolsters the rest of the kids-first agenda because it invites families to become more future-conscious about their children. That shift in attitude can affect more than household budgeting. It may make parents more likely to track down good early education opportunities, locate academically rigorous schools that go beyond the old-line 9 A.M. to 3 P.M. regimen, and find a reliable mentoring program like Big Brothers Big Sisters.

Each of these five ideas—helping parents to do the best they can by their offspring through parent-education initiatives; delivering high-quality early education; linking schools and communities to strengthen what both offer children; providing mentors to youngsters who need a caring, stable adult in their lives; and giving kids a nest egg—is meant to have this kind of impact.

All of them exist—somewhere—but seldom if ever are they joined. Instead of leaving gaps in kids' lives, each idea builds on and reinforces what has come before. Combine them to make children a priority and you have a Golden Rule path to maturity that all parents might well select for their own youngsters.

CHAPTER 6

THE SMART POLITICS OF THE HEART

COULD THE KIDS-FIRST AGENDA turn out to be not just a utopian scheme but the starting point for a seismic shift in policy and priorities? This agenda, as we've seen, isn't a laundry list of programs but a call to devise a system that's attentive to the constantly evolving needs of children. It's not a one-size-fits-all package but a call for policies that embrace proven ideas and keep parents in charge. Might adopting this package of evidence-tested, crib-to-college supports for America's children—this *pragmatopia*—prove a smart way for politicians to do well for themselves by doing good?

If you believe the rhetoric, the answer is yes.

In December 2009, with the health-care bill dangling, the U.S. jobless rate hovering at 10 percent, a record deficit, two unpopular wars persisting, and the Democratic Party's popularity in free-fall decline, *Newsweek* columnist Eleanor Clift asked House Speaker Nancy Pelosi about her party's priorities. Her answer was unequivocal: "The three most important issues facing Congress [are] our children, our children, our children."[1]

Words versus deeds—even as the Speaker was wrapping her arms around "our children," she was making it harder for millions of kids to get health insurance. In the first weeks of the Obama administration, Congress had expanded the Children's Health Insurance Program (CHIP) to cover most of the country's 8.1 million uninsured youngsters. For children's advocates, who had battled the Bush administration over this issue, it was a red-letter day. But the health-care reform bill that Pelosi then shepherded through the House repealed CHIP outright. Instead, parents would have to sign up their youngsters, and themselves, for private health-insurance plans that would be subsidized for families earning up to four times the federal poverty level.[2]

The proponents argued that enrolling parents and their children in the same plan would be more efficient than maintaining a separate CHIP program. But those private plans would cost families a lot more than CHIP—as much as *1,650 percent* more, for families earning $50,000—while offering stingier coverage. The Congressional Budget Office crunched the numbers and concluded that eliminating CHIP meant that millions of youngsters would lose their health insurance because their families could no longer afford it. Despite the fact that national polls show that assuring that all children have health insurance is second only to cost control as a health-reform priority among voters—and despite the fact that 616 organizations, as well as a number of Republican congressmen, petitioned Speaker Pelosi to keep CHIP intact—the impact of the health bill on youngsters went virtually undiscussed in the House.[3]

In another end-of-the-decade interview, Montana senator Max Baucus, the principal author of the Senate's health-care bill, was asked to identify the most significant development of the past ten years. Skipping over 9/11, Iraq, the election of America's first African American president, and the economic collapse, the senator singled out—wait for it—the 2009 expansion of CHIP. "I believe [everyone] should have access to quality, affordable health care, but it is most disconcerting when our youngest generations are forced to go without the care they need, because it's such a critical time for their health and development." Yet the health-reform legislation Baucus crafted for the Senate would also have terminated CHIP.[4]

The moral of this story is clear: When the topic is children, Washington is often long on love and short on cash.

THE POLITICS OF PAROCHIALISM

It should come as no surprise that Washington can't muster much enthusiasm about anything that would add to the federal budget. But the good news is that investing in youth not only promises a big payoff, it's also relatively cheap—in an entirely different league from the killer trio of budgetary behemoths, Social Security, Medicare, and the trillion-dollar-plus deficit.

The cost of underwriting the entire kids-first agenda—support for parents, early education, community schools, mentors, and children's savings accounts—amounts to about $50 billion a year, with the lion's share going to support the youngest children. In the context of a $3.518 *trillion* federal budget, that figure isn't gargantuan. It's about 15 percent more than what Washington now spends on children's programs, and just a fraction of 1 percent of the gross national product.[5] What's more, some of this money could be funneled from existing programs. (For policy mavens, the Appendix spells out how the cost of the kids-first agenda has been calculated.) Still, it's what politicians call a "big ask."

How do we get from here to there? What's required is a political strategy that capitalizes on inside-the-Beltway opportunities while also building a grassroots children's movement, mobilizing the nascent popular enthusiasm for an agenda that promises kids a brighter future. Polls show that the potential support is there—that by big majorities, and across the political divide, Americans put the needs of children high on their list of political priorities. But we're not going to get anywhere until advocates for children can get their act together.

If you ask a roomful of kids' lobby activists for their wish list, prepare yourself for cacophony, since each of the multitudinous advocacy organizations sticks, leech-like, to its own agenda. Advocates in Illinois and a handful of other states have learned how to settle their differences in private and approach lawmakers with an agreed-upon list of priorities. But with rare exceptions, such as the 2009 campaign against the elimination of the Children's Health Insurance Program, the D.C. contingent hasn't figured out how to collaborate effectively. As a consequence, it's often politically marginalized.

The Children's Leadership Council was formed in 2008 with the aim of uniting the movement. The council includes all the heavyweights—Colin Powell's America's Promise; Fight Crime/Invest in Kids, which brings sheriffs and district attorneys to the table; Docs for Tots, a pediatricians' organization; Pre-K Now and the First Five Years Fund, which promote cost-effective investments in early learning; the National Association for the Education of Young Children, which sets standards for quality early education; the National Head Start Association; Every Child Matters, which focuses on educating voters on kids' concerns—and nearly fifty other groups. "For the first time," its mission statement declares, "there is a strong, unified group of organizations speaking with one voice to achieve a singular mission—building the public awareness and creating the political will necessary to make greater federal investments in America's children and youth a reality." While that's the aspiration, it's not the reality—at least not yet.[6]

"Getting everyone in the same room was an accomplishment," said Joan Lombardi, deputy assistant secretary for early childhood at the Department of Health and Human Services, who has spent decades pushing for children's rights. Lombardi is an indefatigable optimist, and her comment speaks volumes about the state of affairs in D.C.

There's a price to be paid for this fractiousness. In February 2009, amid the debate over the economic stimulus bill, the Senate, in an effort to rein in expenditures, cut $100 billion from the proposed legislation. Nearly half of that reduction came from kids' programs—everything from school construction to Head Start. No other constituency had been so callously treated. If ever there was a moment for the council to flex its muscles, this was it, and a letter protesting the cuts was duly drafted. But so many members insisted on being wordsmiths, making sure that their particular cause got mentioned, that by the time the council could agree on the text, Congress had already cut a deal.

When House negotiators on the stimulus bill, led by House Speaker Pelosi, asked their Senate counterparts why the Senate had decimated the kids' budget, Maine senator Susan Collins queried her staff. The staffers were caught off guard, because they had only heard from each of the lobbyists about their favored cause. Since no one had made the case for kids' needs generally, the staffers had never added up all the cuts to children's programs.

A year later this sad story was repeated. The children's lobby stood by helplessly as the Early Learning Challenge Fund, a $1 billion-a-year initiative to strengthen the quality of early education and child care, was stricken from the health-care reform bill in the final hours of negotiation.

These passionate, earnest, and well-meaning advocates have been slogging in the trenches for years, fighting over scraps from the Washington table for their estimable causes, and bringing them on the same page is a herding-cats operation. That the Obama administration is attentive to kids' needs from diaper to diploma, matching that sentiment with additional dollars, makes collaboration conceivable. Yet their "comfort zone," as one insider put it, "is the annual slog to the trough. Their vision is 'more.'" The Children's Leadership Council's pointed exclusion of organizations focused on K-12 concerns, and its decision to focus entirely on health and social issues, create extraneous divisions and deprive it of the opportunity to have a voice on the biggest public investment in youth.[7] Matthew Melmed, executive director of First Three, who chairs the council, has described it as a "work in progress." It's "a tricky line to carve out a proactive investment agenda that we collectively embrace while not setting priorities and respecting the 'brands' of each group," he acknowledged when we spoke. The result is a $100+ billion wish list that's out of whack with political reality.

"As a community we're down in the weeds," Bruce Lesley, president of First Focus, a nonpartisan Washington advocacy group for children, told me. Lesley's organization, together with the Center for American Progress, the Brookings Institution, and the New America Foundation, has done much of the intellectual heavy lifting on kids' issues. He knows this field as well as anyone, having spent more than two decades on the Washington merry-go-round, including twelve years as a Senate staffer on the Finance Committee and the Health, Education, Labor and Pensions Committee. That experience, coupled with a low-key style that inspires confidence among the factions, makes him a natural peacemaker.[8]

"We need an overarching vision," Lesley said. "We need to speak in unison in presenting the needs of all children—that's so much more powerful."

The advocates aren't the only ones in the weeds. Because more than a dozen Senate and House committees have responsibility for one or another aspect of children's policy, and no one is looking at the whole picture, there's a natural tendency to fragmentation. As Cornelia Grumman, the politically astute Pulitzer Prize–winning reporter who heads the First Five Years Fund, pointed out, "to fulfill the entire kids' agenda doesn't require a single vote, but about 150 different legislative votes and administrative actions in disparate funding streams that have nothing to do with each other and no champions in common." What's more, the death of Ted Kennedy and the retirement of Senator Chris Dodd of Connecticut has left the upper chamber without a powerful champion for children.

The statute books are littered with miniature initiatives, each one the product of a legislator who can claim political credit and each one fiercely defended by its beneficiaries. In this environment it has been a tough slog for initiatives like early education or community schools that cut across these boundaries. Nearly two hundred programs for children and youth, ranging from prekindergartens run by the Defense Department to pest-eradication projects managed by the Environmental Protection Agency, are scattered across multiple federal departments and bureaus, with little coordination or communication among them. Some are of dubious worth, such as a feel-good measure that sends poor youngsters on field trips to Washington, D.C., where they can observe first hand the spectacle of lawmaking. Other measures are ideologically driven, like initiatives on sex education, abstinence-based and otherwise, as well as the teaching of "traditional American history."[9] Yet any attempt to eliminate a program, even one that's a proven failure, runs smack into a noisy constituency.

UNDER THE RADAR: SMALL VICTORIES IN D.C.

Even in the present political climate, small but significant victories can be achieved.

For starters, we need clarity about how much the government is spending on children. At present, no one knows for sure, and that's a problem. Because no official tally exists, there's no straightforward way to evaluate the level of federal investment in America's youth or to compare funding levels from one year to the next, let alone from one decade to the next. That's why it comes as such a stunner that children have fared so badly relative to other groups in the recent budget wars, and that, without the onetime boost from the stimulus spending, the share of federal dollars going to kids' programs would actually have declined between 2005 and 2010.[10]

Providing this information—in the form of a children's budget—could help to galvanize action. An easy-to-understand budget, like those being produced in Louisiana and Illinois, would enable voters to see for themselves where kids stack up on the federal priorities list; it would also make lobbying on behalf of children's programs generally more effective. It's a quick and painless launch pad for the kids-first agenda.[11]

Forming a National Commission on Children would be another modest and useful win. A generation ago, just such a commission prepared a report of 500-plus pages, *Beyond Rhetoric: A New American Agenda for Children and Families*. Reports like this are often shelved, but because of the commission's bipartisan makeup and the reasonableness of its conclusions, the document became a blueprint for action. Its key recommendations, including a health-insurance plan for children (CHIP) and child-care tax credits, were adopted during the 1990s. Conceivably, political lightning could strike twice.[12] A new Commission on Children could command substantial voter appeal, said Drew Westen, the author of the much-ballyhooed *Political Brain*, who did some polling on the concept in 2009.[13] Three out of five voters agreed that "children shouldn't be an afterthought in budget decisions. That's why we need a [commission] whose job it is to make sure we're not only investing in our children but investing wisely. That means setting targets and demanding accountability, identifying problems and proposing solutions."[14]

Bigger victories that would move the needle on the kids-first agenda may also be in store. Even with a budget freeze on discretionary programs in place, the Obama administration's 2011 budget would substantially boost the share that goes to children. More congress members are signing on to legislation that advances each item on the kids-first agenda, from parenting programs to child savings accounts. In an era when hyper-partisanship has led to gridlock, it's a positive sign that a handful of Republicans have joined Democrats among the ranks of supporters. However, the GOP's victories in the 2010 congressional elections may well bring gridlock on children's issues, or worse.

Meanwhile, beneath the radar, federal officials have advanced reforms that could, if adopted by Congress, become the building blocks for a coherent system of support for youth. The Senior Corps already spends about half its budget, more than $100 million, on cross-generational mentoring projects. The Department of Housing and Urban Development's Choice Neighborhoods initiative expands the agency's traditional bricks-and-mortar focus to include an active role in early childhood innovations and is tied to the Education Department's Promise Neighborhoods strategy for supporting community schools.[15] In 2010, Congress approved a $65 million Choice Neighborhoods pilot project. Although the legislators decided not to include early childhood funding in the health-care reform legislation, the Obama administration has pledged to continue pushing the issue.[16]

What's needed is a push, and that's where Rob Dugger and Mike Petit come in. This political odd couple is going after the politicians where it hurts—at the ballot box.

LAUNCHING A KIDS-FIRST MOVEMENT

In Washington, D.C., a city of pragmatists, Rob Dugger dreams big. An economist by training, he has been a Beltway insider for decades, starting out as a staffer with the House and Senate banking committees and the Federal Reserve Bank. After a lucrative career as a venture capitalist, Dugger dived back into the policy arena, this time with money and clout, to take up the cudgels for children. He was a major player during the 2008 campaign. "I organized fundraisers," he told me, "but

I didn't personally contribute until Obama came forward with his Children's First Agenda in late autumn 2007."[17]

Dugger has adopted a two-pronged approach to promoting a kids-first agenda—stated simply, he wants to commission the research and reshape the politics. His analysis begins with studies that detail the payoff generated by investments in young children, many of them underwritten by the Invest in Kids Working Group that he heads. "The message is that high-quality pre-k delivers a 15 percent return forever," he said, extrapolating from the Perry Preschool experiment. "But the nation has slipped into a structural trap. Pressure from interest groups has led to public investment that favors housing and consumerism over human capital, seniors over children."[18]

The only way out, Dugger argued in the course of several long conversations, is to change the spending priorities of the United States, making children's success our top concern. That's why he has turned to politics, tapping into what he calls the "visceral pull" exerted by youngsters to launch what he hopes will become a movement that officials ignore at their peril.

Over the decades, hopes for such a movement have regularly surfaced. Whole libraries'-worth of papers have been written, decades'-worth of three-day conferences held, and entire disciplines built on the unmet needs of the young. The twentieth century was destined to be *The Century of the Child*, a book published in 1901 confidently predicted, but instead, as a book published a hundred years later concluded, it turned out to be *The Failed Century of the Child*.[19] "If we could have but one generation of properly born, trained, educated, and healthy children, a thousand other problems of government would vanish. We would assure ourselves of healthier minds in more vigorous bodies, to direct the energies of our nation to yet greater heights of achievement. Moreover, one good community nurse will save a dozen future policemen." That argument, which resonates today, is taken from President Herbert Hoover's address to the 1930 White House Conference on Children.[20]

What distinguishes Rob Dugger from his predecessors isn't his invest-in-kids platform but his sense of history and his sophisticated understanding of political possibilities. Children's advocates usually take what Mike Petit, a rough-hewn ally of Dugger's and another big dreamer, derides as the "teddy-bear" approach, pleading with politicians to do what's right. Petit is a onetime Washington lobbyist who got tired of "going to congressmen's offices with detailed memos and getting shunted off to summer interns." He runs Every Child Matters, a nonprofit, as well as Vote Kids, a political entity.

"We have to get meaner," Petit insisted when we talked at his Washington office. "I'm not interested in organizing a 'kumbaya' campaign. Power rules."

Dugger, who slammed K Street lobbyists as "Gucci-shod SOBs," agreed wholeheartedly. "In times of economic crisis you want to increase your investments in kids. It's the right moment to make hard choices about allocating resources. Budgets aren't just about money. They're about civil relationships, the architecture of commitments that people make to one another over generations. Kids-first is the unifying idea in the present budget-crisis, civil-relations-shredding environment."

Consensus about the vital importance of investing in the next generation in order to rescue the American dream, combined with the economic muscle of what Dugger terms the "youth sector," would drive this sea change in political priorities. "The percentage of the gross domestic product generated by parents and what they buy, prenatal-to-eighteen, is huge—

10 percent, compared to the 7.5 percent generated by the financial sector," he said:

> Spending prenatal-to-five accounts for 2.5 percent of GDP, nearly twice the auto industry. What's more, the business sector is starting to realize that it is the biggest consumer of the products of American education, and that it will pay for the mistakes of the birth-to-eighteen human capital development system.
>
> If you could link the toy manufacturers, bus drivers, high-school teachers, pediatricians, Head Start staff, all the people who make the meals in child-care centers—if you could identify and communicate with them, you'd have the country's most potent political constituency coming together. Then, if candidates can be convinced to become "kids first" and voters perceive candidates that way, the dynamic of "kids first" politics really begins to unfold.
>
> The key to power is to organize, just like the Chamber of Commerce organizes business and AARP organizes old folks. We need to give people an emotional reason to be committed to something positive, and that visceral priority will be enough to convert affinity into political strength.

This scenario has already played out once, in one of the most conservative congressional districts in the country.

• • •

IN THE 2004 ELECTION, a Democrat named Chet Edwards beat the odds-on favorite in Texas Congressional District 17.[21] That district, which George W. Bush calls home, stretches from Waco to Lubbock. It was gerrymandered to assure a Republican victory—more than 60 percent of the voters are registered

Republicans, and George Bush received 70 percent of the vote in the 2004 election.

Edwards's opponent, veteran GOP state legislator Arlene Wohlgemuth, made budget-cutting her main message. She boasted that she'd saved the state's taxpayers a billion dollars by removing 150,000 children from the rolls of the Children's Health Insurance Program. "Children were never my primary concern," Wohlgemuth said. That was a remark she grew to regret.

A single television commercial changed the dynamics of the race by illustrating how real people were being hurt by the CHIP cuts. Staring straight into the camera, in a black-and-white image as evocative as a Walker Evans photo, a woman named Jamie Jones held her young daughter, Bailey, in her lap as she told her story. Widowed when her husband died in a house fire, she worked every day to support her child, but the state had cut off her daughter's health-care coverage. "I love my daughter more than anything in the world," she said, "and if she gets sick I don't know what I'll do."

"One TV ad, and twenty-five years of Republican talk about how 'less government is better' went out the window," Edwards told me when I interviewed him after the election. According to the exit polls, 11 percent of the voters—enough to swing the election—reported that Wohlgemuth's record on children had made up their minds.

Mike Petit's organization, Vote Kids, worked on the Edwards campaign, sending out 35,000 brochures that highlighted Wohlgemuth's dismal record on children's health insurance, early education, and child-abuse prevention. "A Is for Abandoned," went the message. "Arlene Wohlgemuth abandoned our children."

The appeal targeted women, independents, and registered Republicans alike, because focus groups had shown they were the most likely to be swayed when they learned about the impact of the CHIP cuts. "When you tell a grandmother who has always voted Republican that a Republican candidate is hurting children," Petit said, "she votes the other way."

• • •

IT REMAINS TO BE SEEN whether the strategy of Texas 17 can be used as a template for future campaigns. Ever the optimist, Rob Dugger thinks it can be done. "Texas 17 was just a first step, because we didn't have all the data we needed," he said. "Our intention is to repeat the strategy over and over—and to do it with systematic outreach. It's just the beginning—the blade of the saber has not been pulled. If elected officials want to stay in office they have to reflect what their constituents want. Our job is to make this constitutional responsibility easy by making it clear that there's an aggressive and effective constituency."

At business roundtables across the country, men in pinstripes are noodling about ideas and discussing tactics with child-care advocates in Birkenstocks.[22] They might just be onto something, for politicians are notoriously risk-averse. Immediately after Chet Edwards's victory, GOP politicians in Texas raced to restore the state's CHIP cuts that had cost Arlene Wohlgemuth the election. A few more wins like that one, and kids-first politicians will emerge from the woodwork.

Mike Petit hasn't duplicated the Chet Edwards success story yet, but he's working on it. Together with ten national children's organizations, Every Child Matters, the voter-education wing of Petit's operation, has engaged in political consciousness-raising—coordinating, for example, an annual "Step Up for Kids" day, with demonstrations on the Capitol steps in every state, demanding that lawmakers make spending on kids a priority. Vote Kids, the political wing, has launched newspaper and television ads aimed at pressuring politicians.

"Senator Vitter, look out for kids," intoned a Louisiana TV ad, "not $1,276,506 in campaign contributions from the health-care and insurance industry."[23]

For the 2010 election, Petit had staff on the ground in eight states, from Colorado to New Hampshire, where the congressional election featured candidates with opposing positions on children's services. "We're mapping all the organizations that serve children—show that to a politician and his eyes open—as well as visiting several thousand child-serving sites in a get-out-the-vote campaign, and compiling a master e-mail list of supporters. Our goal is to be the MoveOn for a kids-first movement."

"No one else is doing what we're doing on this scale," said Petit. "Rob Dugger gets it—he's taken the mapping work to Virginia—but almost all the D.C. groups are more interested in policy than politics. Going after a politician isn't in their culture. I think you have to gear up the politics first. Otherwise the policy means nothing."

This is Petit's crusade, and he's in it for the long haul. "We have a president who gets it, and that's key. The administration is trying to push kids' issues, and given the problems in the economy it's amazing that they have done so much," Petit argued. "What's more, the long-term trends are good. The immigrant population is growing. They're natural allies because they know that kids start out behind the eight ball. And it helps that more women are entering politics. Arlene Wohlgemuth is the outlier." Though the 2010 election produced a bumper crop of female Republican candidates, Petit believes that, over time, "women voters and women politicians are more likely to be supportive."

●　●　●

POLLSTERS CONFIRM THAT Dugger and Petit are on the right track, for there is widespread support, cutting across generations and ideologies, for making children a national priority.[24] By three-to-one margins, voters are convinced by the argument that "our children are our future. Investing in our children is investing in America."[25]

What's needed now, said Frank Luntz, the GOP guru who contributed "the death tax" to the political lexicon, is a "big picture" message: "When it comes to children's issues, *now* is the time when you should—*and must*—create a sense of urgency with the general public, and most importantly, with the politicians in Washington. Whether the topic is health care or education, voters need to hear that it's 'an American issue that affects us all. . . . We want tomorrow to be better . . . especially for our children. *This is the American dream.'"*[26]

When it comes to health care and education, pollsters report, four out of five voters believe in the Golden Rule standard, that every youngster deserves an equal chance. Republicans and Democrats alike support a shift in priorities to favor children. In a 2007 survey conducted by Luntz's firm, two out of three GOP voters were in favor of making children a higher priority. Tough talk works in making the political argument on behalf of kids, said Luntz—words like "action, commitment, crucial, demand, future, invest now or pay later, moral obligation, no excuses, *our* kids," not the milquetoast language of "request" and "urge" or governmentese words like "fund."

Tapping into taxpayers' self-interest also works, said Cornelia Grumman at the First Five Years Fund. "The return-on-investment argument is by far the most compelling to people," she said. "You can show them that there are short-term as well as long-term benefits to them personally—that, for example, investing in high-quality early education can lead to up to a 50 percent reduction in special education costs within just a few years."

The Edwards-Wohlgemuth campaign may not have been a fluke, since a substantial majority of voters say they would vote against a politician who scrimped on kids' health needs. That includes Republicans: 43 percent said they'd be more likely to vote against a candidate who didn't support CHIP, 11 percent more than those who'd back a politician who took that position.[27] (The remaining 46 percent said they wouldn't be affected by a candidate's stance on CHIP.) These high hopes will be tested in the coming elections.

TAX CUTS AND BUDGET DEFICITS, threats to national security, and a seemingly endless war—these have been our public preoccupations for a decade, a disheartening picture punctuated only briefly by euphoria over the election of Barack Obama. Although the kids' share of the federal budget has grown in the past few years, the ever-mounting tab for Medicare and Social Security means that, unless Congress reverses course, kids will once again get short shrift. A 2010 Brookings study, drawing on Congressional Budget Office projections, estimated that spending on children will drop as a share of the gross domestic product by 20 percent in the coming decade.[28]

It's hard at this moment to muster optimism for the transformational possibilities of politics, whether for youth or anyone else. Yet these kids-first initiatives, coupled with the possibility of a movement that puts the claims of youngsters front and center as a national priority, are reason enough to question the conventional counsel of despair. Consider the policy choices that have recently been made in Great Britian. Following the May 2010 election, the Conservative-led government cut public expenditures far more drastically than anything that's on the table in the United States. Yet amid this radical shrinkage of the public sector, kids' programs were generally spared. The new government pledged that child poverty wouldn't increase on its watch, and so it is continuing to provide child benefits (approximately $32.00 a week) for poor and middle class families. It has also maintained key initiatives like nationwide community schools and a birth-to-five neighborhood-based program. Universal preschool for three- and four-year-olds continues; what's more, the government is introducing early education for two-year-olds from poor families, one of the only new initiatives amid the cuts. Under the Conservatives, as under Labour before them, "Kids first" remains the British standard. Over the course of a generation, and because of deliberate political and policy choices emerging from the present gridlock, we could go beyond our rhetorical embrace of children, making decisions that ratify a "Golden Rule, good-enough-for-my-child," understanding of what all our youth deserve.

APPENDIX:
A KIDS-FIRST BUDGET

THE SKEPTICAL READER might well be saying: "The kids-first agenda makes sense, but surely it will cost the moon." That doesn't have to be the case. It is possible to do a lot for kids with a relatively modest infusion of dollars.

"What's the ask?" is the first question a politician is likely to pose. "A relatively modest amount" isn't the tidiest answer, but it's hard to be more precise without making a number of key assumptions. To calculate the bottom line requires specifying which children are entitled to what level of support. Take item number one on the agenda, "Teaching parents to teach their kids," as an example. Fully implementing the Nurse-Family Partnership, as laid out in chapter 1, would cost many times more than expanding the Triple P program. Similarly, when it comes to early education, the cost of providing a Perry Preschool–quality program for all three- to five-year-olds, as described in chapter 2, would be far greater than the cost of making a "good enough" Tulsa-quality prekindergarten program available.

That's hardly the only complication. The budgeter also has to estimate how many families will take up the offer. Some parents will opt to keep their three-year-olds at home rather than sending them to preschool, item number two on the agenda, but it's hard to predict how many. Some youngsters will decide to duck out of school at 3 P.M, not taking advantage of what's offered by community schools, item number three on the agenda, and some schools will opt to maintain a more traditional role, staying open from only 9A.M.–3 P.M., 180 days a year. Some teens will conclude that they already have all the adult counsel they need and so will not be interested in a mentor (item number four). In each instance, "some" has to be quantified to come up with a budget.

To further complicate matters, the rate of participation will be affected by what the government is offering. For many families, medical attention is the most important thing a community school can provide—and it's also the most expensive part of any package. (How expensive depends on what kind of medical care is available, and that adds another dimension to the puzzle.) Because every baby would receive a child savings account (agenda item number five), it's relatively easy to figure out the cost—that is, provided there's agreement on how big the initial public contribution should be, how many dollars the government should match, and on what basis, and how many births are projected for future years.

One more complexity needs to be inserted into this discussion of costs: How much should parents be asked to chip in? Throughout the book I've sought to show that *all* children, not just children from poor families, can benefit from the kind of crib-to-college support laid out in the kids-first agenda, but that doesn't necessarily mean that government should foot the entire tab. One school of thought holds that these services should be free to rich and poor alike, just like public schools and public libraries. The competing view is that, while every child should be able to take advantage of these supports, it's fair to expect parents who can afford it to pick up part of the tab. Who would pay, and how much, is another matter to be sorted out. Costs will be affected by the income level at which a parental contribution is required, and the amount of that contribution. For example, providing a free service only to families with incomes below the poverty line ($22,050 for a family of four in 2010) would cost less than making that same service free to families earning less than 150 percent of the poverty level. Which approach you'd choose and whom you'd ask to contribute is partly a disagreement about what's fair; it's also a matter of what's politically and economically doable.

A number of economists have tried their hand at calculating the cost of early education; their figures are all over the lot. Add four other initiatives to the mix and the uncertainties multiply. Nonetheless, I've dived in, not under the illusion that I can generate a definitive bottom line, but as a way of starting the necessary budget conversation.

I estimate that that the total annual cost of the kids-first agenda is between $46 billion and $67 billion. Although that is indeed a big ask, it needs to be put in context. Sixty-seven billion dollars is just a fraction of a percent of the federal budget and less than 10 percent of the 2010 Social Security tab. It would cost each taxpayer less than $300. What's more, from these totals it's necessary to subtract the money we're already spending in order to calculate the added outlay. As the following tables indicate, the government is already underwriting a considerable portion of these expenses; redirecting funds and tinkering with existing programs would reduce the tab substantially.

The most expensive item on the kids-first agenda, early education, is a good example. In 2010 the states spent almost $5 billion for preschool; and

Table A.1: Kids-First Agenda—Total Cost (in billions of dollars)

	2011	2012	2013	2014	2015	2016	Six-Year Total Cost
Parent support	1.81[1]	1.54	1.77	2.00	2.23	2.46	11.81
Early education (birth to age 2)	4.89[2]–9.32	5.87–11.18	6.85–13.04	7.82–14.90	8.80–16.77	9.78–18.63	44.01–83.84
Early education (three- and four-year-olds)	12.05[2]–17.34	14.45–20.80	16.86–24.27	19.27–27.74	21.68–31.20	24.09–34.67	108.40–156.02
Community schools	1.25–1.88	1.50–2.25	1.75–2.63	2.0–3.0	2.25–3.38	2.5–3.75[3]	11.25–16.89
Mentoring	1.67	2.0	2.33	2.66	3.0	3.33	14.99
Child savings accounts	3.75	3.75	3.75	3.75	3.75	3.75[4]	22.5
Total	**25.42–35.77**	**29.11–41.52**	**33.31–47.79**	**37.50–54.05**	**41.71–61.33**	**45.91–66.59**[5]	**212.96–306.05**

**Table A2: Kids-First Agenda—First-Year Budget Costs
(in billions of dollars)**

	Total	Current Spending	Additional Spending
Parent support	1.81	0.250	1.56
Early education	16.94–26.66	12.28[6]	4.66–14.38
Community schools	1.25–1.88	1.18[7]	.07–.70
Mentoring	1.67	.28[8]	1.39
Savings accounts	1.88	0[9]	1.88
Total	**23.74–31.14**	**13.74**	**10.01–17.41**

the budget for Head Start and Early Head Start was nearly $8 billion. As detailed below, the total cost of an adequate early education program is estimated at $34 billion; the additional cost would be about $21 billion.

Because most of these programs can't be implemented overnight, I've built in lead time. I assume that half of the total budget for the first four items on the agenda will be invested in the first year and an additional 10 percent will be invested in each of the following years. The program would be fully implemented in year six. (Because the child savings account is a cash transfer, not a social program, I assume that it will be fully implemented in year one.) Table 1 illustrates how the costs for each item on the kids-first agenda would change during the six-year ramp-up period. Table 2 sets out the total cost of each item on the kids-first agenda for the first year of its implementation; specifies what government is already spending. The difference represents the added first-year costs. For reasons laid out below, I have provided a low-end and a high-end estimate for early education and community schools.

Here's how these figures were derived: The specificity of the dollar amounts should be appreciated as an artifact of calculation (estimated costs times estimated numbers of children) and not a demonstration of precision.

PARENT SUPPORT

The Nurse-Family Partnership supports poor, first-time mothers from the second trimester of pregnancy through the first two years of a child's life. Executive director Tom Jenkins proposes to open the program to include all of the 575,000 first-time, Medicaid-eligible mothers. At just over $4,000 per family, the cost of this expansion would be about $2.5 billion per year. [10]

Triple P, a public health initiative for children from birth to age ten, is aimed at changing the behavior of entire populations. Ron Prinz, the principal investigator for the Triple P evaluation, estimates that expanding the program nationwide would require an initial investment of approximately $15 for each of the 44 million children aged birth to 10 ($660 million), plus $160 million in each subsequent year.[11] The six-year cost of implementing Triple P on this scale would be $1.46 billion. Because Triple P is a population-based program that relies on existing networks of family support, not a model like NFP, which requires the recruiting and training of new staff, I've assumed that it will be fully implemented in the first year.

The budget calculation combines the Nurse-Family Partnership for children from prenatal to age two, at an annual, fully implemented cost of $2.3 billion with Triple P for children from birth to age ten. Assuming a six-year ramp-up schedule, the first year would cost $1.91 billion, and over six years the program would cost approximately $12.7 billion.

EARLY EDUCATION

The cost of expanding early education will vary widely, depending on program eligibility and per-child expenditure. The National Institute for Early Education Research (NIERR) has proposed universal, free coverage at $8,700 per child for all three-and four-year olds. NIEER estimated that 70 to 90 percent of all children in that age range would participate; the total cost would be between $48.9 billion and $61.7 billion.[12] A less expensive alternative, with greater per-child spending but with eligibility limited to low-income three- and four-year-olds, was proposed by economists Jens Ludwig and Isabelle Sawhill. Based upon the intensive Abecedarian model, their program calls for spending $16,600 per child per year for a total cost of $40 billion.[13] A similar proposal by Jens Ludwig, Greg Duncan, and Katherine Magnuson advocates a program targeted at disadvantaged three-and four-year-olds but with a lower per-child annual expense of $12,000. The total cost of that model would be $30 billion, though the authors noted that only $20 billion in new funds would be necessary to put the program in place.[14]

Although the economists' models focus only on three- and four-year-olds, chapter 2 points out that it is just as important to offer early education to younger children. Table 1 shows the cost estimates for birth to age two and three-to four-year-olds separately. I have drawn elements from different models for birth to two (Early Head Start and Educare) and three-and four-year-olds (Brookings Institute and Perry Preschool) to determine a high- and low-end estimate for a quality early education program available to all children under age five.

In her 2007 Brookings Institution paper, "Cost-Effective Investments in Children," Julia Isaacs devised a sliding scale framework that I've borrowed here. Isaacs proposed half-day preschool for three- and four-year-olds, paid for in part by a sliding-scale fee structure. Children eligible for federally subsidized lunches (with family income below 130 percent of the poverty line) would receive free care; other children would be funded through a combination of federal, state, and local revenues and parent fees. Isaacs estimated a per-child cost of $9,200, calculated by averaging the costs of Head Start and three exemplary programs (Abecedarian, Perry Preschool, Chicago Child-Parent Centers, all of which are discussed in chapter 2). Extrapolating from kindergarten enrollment, Isaacs assumed that 75 percent of free-lunch-eligible four-year-olds and 60 percent of free-lunch-eligible three-year-olds, 1.45 million children, would participate in such a program. The total fully subsidized cost would be $13.3 billion.[15] For families with incomes greater than 130 percent of the poverty line, federal funding would cover $3,000 (30 percent) of the per-child cost. The balance would be paid by a combination of state and local funding and parental fees. Because it's likely that parents would be required to contribute, Isaacs estimated lower enrollment rates for this group—35 percent and 60 percent for three-year-olds and four-year-olds, respectively. The cost for these 2.87 million children would be $8.6 billion.[16]

Isaacs' model includes a half day of childcare for children of working parents. The estimated cost of serving 1.2 million eligible children under a sliding-scale fee structure would be $2.4 billion. The total program cost would be $24.34 billion.[17] I use this approach in calculating the low-end costs for a quality program in Table 1. The low-end cost for children from birth to age two, $10,500 per child, is derived from Early Head Start.[18] Approximately 2.1 million birth to two-year-olds and 1.04 million two-year-olds are eligible for fully subsidized Early Head Start. Using Isaacs' sliding scale formula, an additional 5.8 million birth to one-year-olds and 2.9 million two-year-olds from higher-income families would be eligible for a 30 percent subsidy.

Since infant and toddler education is far less common in the U.S. than preschool for three- and four-year-olds, I've assumed participation rates of 15 percent of birth to one-year-olds and 30 percent of two-year-olds from the lowest income families, and 10 percent of birth to one-year-olds and 15 percent of two-year-olds from higher income families. Some 626,000 children would be fully subsidized, for a cost of $6.58 billion; an additional 1 million children would receive a partial subsidy of $3000, for a cost of $3 billion. The low-end estimate for infant-toddler education is $9.58 billion in year six, when the program would be fully implemented. The total budget for the low-end birth to age five early education program, when entirely in place, is $33.92 billion.

The high end of the range birth to age three is represented by Educare, which costs $20,000 per child; the high end program for three- and four-year-olds is $15,000 per child, based on Perry Preschool and the per-pupil funding level for poor urban school districts that the New Jersey Supreme Court mandated in the *Abbott* case. Assuming take-up rates and sliding-scale fees similar to those above, the total high-end federal budget for early education is $306.05 billion.

COMMUNITY SCHOOLS

Although community schools dot the national landscape—and in some cities, such as Chicago and Portland, Oregon, such schools are a substantial presence—there is no good way to calculate the amount of money now being spent to support them. The $1.1 billion Twenty-First Century Community Learning Centers program supports after-school and summer initiatives that would be a key component of community schools. An additional infusion of federal support targeted specifically at community schools, with a required state or local matching contribution, could both increase their numbers and improve their quality.

Several such measures have been introduced in Congress in recent years. The Full-Service Community Schools Act, whose lead sponsors are Congressman Steny Hoyer and Senator Ben Nelson, would authorize $200 million a year to support partnerships between schools and community organizations. Martin Blank, the director of the Coalition for Community Schools, concluded that "the proposal could help to fund up to 2,000 community schools, based on an average federal funding investment of $100,000 per school for a community school coordinator and community outreach assistance."[19] The Developing Innovative Partnerships and Learning Opportunities that Motivate Achievement (DIPLOMA) Act would provide more generous support to many more schools, at a cost of $2.5 billion per year, enabling more communities to establish schools on the Children's Aid Society model. The Promise Neighborhoods Initiative, seeded with $10 million in 2010, is another version of community schools; it represents an additional potential source of funding. An alternative strategy, embodied in the Working to Encourage Community Action and Responsibility in Education (WE CARE) Act, would tie funding for community schools to Title I of the Elementary and Secondary Education Act, which is slated for Congressional reappraisal in 2011.[20] That $13 billion program provides funding for schools that enroll a substantial percentage of poor children.

Tying community schools to Title I, as well channeling funds from the Twenty-first Century Community Learning Centers program, makes sense. An additional $3 billion to $3.75 billion commitment would provide $100,000 to $150,000 per school (the latter figure representing the funds that Chicago makes available to each of its 150 community schools) for 25,000 high-needs schools. If a state and local match were required, the federal funds would kick-start efforts to generate additional local engagement.

MENTORING

As with community schools, there is no reliable way to estimate the level of state and local, as well as private, support for mentoring initiatives. America's Promise Alliance estimates that 3 million youth are currently being served by mentors.

The federal government provides modest backing for mentoring through the Department of Education and the Department of Justice. In 2008 the Senior Corps spent $108 million, more than half of its budget, to underwrite mentoring, and the Serve America Act has expanded on those opportunities.

The two mentoring strategies included in the kids-first agenda, Big Brothers Big Sisters and Friends of the Children, use very different approaches and focus on very different kinds of kids. Big Brothers Big Sisters relies on volunteers to work with any child who requests a "Big." Its annual per-child cost is $1,000. [21] Friends of the Children uses paid staff to help youth at greatest risk, supporting them from kindergarten through high school graduation, at an annual per-child cost of $7,000.[22]

America's Promise Alliance estimates that 10 million students are at risk of dropping out of school.[23] For the vast majority of youth, a program similar to Big Brothers Big Sisters is appropriate. I've built in a sliding scale, with full coverage for youth with family incomes below 130 percent of the poverty line, and a 1:1 match for higher-income families. Some 3,495,000 children would be eligible for full funding; assuming that half of them took advantage of the opportunity, the total cost would be about $1.75 billion.[24] Funding a like number of youth at a 1:1 match would cost an additional $875 million.

The Friends of the Children model is designed for a far smaller number of youth, essentially all of whom are likely to meet the poverty criteria. Enrolling 100,000 youngsters—considerably fewer than could benefit, but perhaps as many as such a program could handle in a six-year ramp-up period—would cost $700 million.[25] The total annual cost to fully implement the mentoring agenda is $3.325 billion.

SAVINGS ACCOUNTS

The America Saving for Personal Investment, Retirement, and Education (ASPIRE) Act offers the most detailed proposal to establish savings accounts for children nationwide. The program's per-child expense of between $500 and $1000 translates to a total program cost of $37.5 billion. Over 80 percent of that cost benefits the poorest half of the population through larger government deposits at birth and matching deposits until age eighteen. [26]

ACKNOWLEDGMENTS

MY WORK ON PRESCHOOL was the launching pad for this project. I'm grateful to Harvard University Press, the publisher of my book *The Sandbox Investment: The Preschool Movement and Kids-First Politics,* and Elizabeth Knoll, my longtime editor and confidante at Harvard, for permitting me to adapt material from that book in the chapter on early education in this one. Without the backing of the Annie E. Casey Foundation and the Smith Richardson Foundation, *Kids First* would never have gotten off the ground. Ruth Mayden at Casey and Mark Steinmeyer have been both allies and critical friends. I've been able to test some of my ideas in the pages of *The American Prospect* and *The Nation.*

In the fall of 2008 I served on the Presidential Transition Team. The experience, an eye-opener to the real world of policy and politics, led me to write this book. My colleagues in the Education Policy Working Group taught me a lot: Linda Darling-Hammond, Ann O'Leary, Geri Palast, Scott Palmer, Goodwin Liu, Bob Gordon, Bob Shireman, Steve Robinson, John Jackson, Judy Winston, Ray Mabus, Jon Vaupel, Jim Robinson, and Ian Bassin.

In framing the project, I have benefited from the good counsel of leading figures in their respective fields. Those experts whom I consulted on parenting programs include David Olds, Ann Duggan, Deborah Daro, Karen Guskin, Deanna Gomby, Ron Prinz, and Matt Sanders.

I learned a great deal about early education from Harriet Meyer, Ellen Frede, Neil Halfon, Doug Jutte, Clyde Hertzman, Jane Waldfogel, Steve Barnett, Rob Dugger, John Love, Ron Haskins, Julia Isaacs, and Art Rolnick. My special thanks to Bruce Lesley, who patiently answered my endless questions about federal policy and politics; to Libby Doggett, whose wisdom and support have made all the difference; and to Ed Zigler, mentor and mensch.

Jane Quinn, Marty Blank, and Sam Whalen took me to school on community schools. Marc Freedman, who put mentoring on the policy map, was generous with his time and kind enough to make the connection with PublicAffairs. Michael Sherraden, Ray Boshara, Reed Cramer, Carl Rist, and Lisa Mensah brought me up to speed on child savings accounts.

I spent months crisscrossing the country, searching for the most powerful examples of programs that have altered children's lives. There turned out to be far more stories worth telling than I could possibly write about. Seeing the best of what's available to youngsters, often in the most unpromising of circumstances, was genuinely thrilling and humbling. A shout-out to those in the field who gave generously of their time and energy, including Lisa Landau, Lester Strong, Geoffrey Canada, Marty Lipp, Pete Moses, Nancy Biberman, Nancy Kolben, Andrea Phillips, Adriana Birne, Sandy Sanger, Silvia Abbato, Michael Zisser, Jerry Weast, Janine Bacquie, Gordon MacInnes, David White, Ruth Eisenstadt, Monica Ennis, Pam Boyd, Tom Jenkins, Susanna Todd, Joe Hayman, Jacques Rondeau, Carey Oppenheim, Geri Cobb, Iris Chen, Lori Donoho, Erica Quezada, Bob Houck, Pete Moses, Elizabeth Vanderweide, Joe Radelet, Judy Stavisky, Duncan Campbell, Karen Guskin, Gary Mangiofico, Carol Coleman, Sue Stapleton, Sunday Gustin, Martin Bellingham, Elizabeth Vanderweide, Karen Freel, Katherine Kinsey, Adam Sonenshein, Vickie Kropenske, Cornelia Grumman, Richard Buery, Jill Morningstar, and Donna Butts. Missing from this list, but hardly forgotten, are the professionals, literally millions of them, who daily give their all to improve kids' lives. These are the unsung heroes, the individuals who keep fighting the good fight, who persevere despite meager pay and long odds—the nurses in Philadelphia, the preschool teachers in Chicago, the mentors in Portland, the teachers in Washington Heights—to whom I've dedicated this book.

I've been fortunate to have spent most of my career at Berkeley. Over the years my colleagues at the Goldman School of Public Policy and elsewhere in the university have been both whip-smart and collegial to a fault, a rare combination in higher education. My special thanks to Jane Mauldon, Steve Sugarman, Doug Jutte, Mary Ann Mason, Kristin Luker, Ann O'Leary, Bob Reich, Carolyn and Phil Cowan, Jill Berrick, Gillian Lester, Rucker Johnson, Joan Hollinger, and Norton Grubb. Members of the child and family policy faculty reading group read and commented on an earlier version of this book, and their pointed comments have made it stronger. Elsewhere in academe and thinktanks, I have turned for advice to, among others, Lynn Karoly, Larry Aber, Pedro Noguera, Henry Levin, David Cohen, Jens Ludwig, Ron Haskins, and Robert Sampson.

Over the years a number of Berkeley students have made substantial contributions to the project: Brentt Brown, Jenny Paul-Rappaport, Jeff Pertl, Chris Hebdon, Chris Schnyer, Dow-Jane Pei, Ary Amerikaner, Patrick Hazleton, Danielle Love, and Remmert Dekker. The graduate students in the spring 2010 Kids-First Policy seminar read and critiqued a draft of this book.

I've known Rhea Wilson since the mid-1980s, when both of us were working at the *Sacramento Bee*. She worked with me through multiple drafts of the manuscript, asking probing questions that extracted responses I didn't know I had it in me to generate. Without her close and repeated readings, *Kids First* would have been a succession of case studies and not a coherent narrative. At PublicAffairs, Lisa Kaufman picked up the gauntlet. Lisa describes herself as standing in for "the typical reader—someone who doesn't know a lot about parenting programs or community schools," and her editing has made for a considerably better book.

I've never had a great memory for names, and matters have only gotten worse over the years. My apologies to those of you—and I know you're out there—who in a fit of absence of mind I failed to mention.

NOTES

A NOTE FROM THE AUTHOR

1. See, for example, Abigail Thernstrom and Stephan Thernstrom, *No Excuses: Closing the Racial Gap in Learning* (New York: Simon and Schuster, 2004); David Whitman, *Sweating the Small Stuff: Inner-City Schools and the New Paternalism* (Washington, DC: Fordham Institute, 2008).

2. See, for example, Linda Darling-Hammond, *The Flat World and Education: How America's Commitment to Equity Will Determine Our Future* (New York: Teachers College Press, 2010).

INTRODUCTION

1. Claudia Goldin and Lawrence Katz, *The Race Between Education and Technology* (Cambridge: Harvard University Press, 2008).

2. *Doing Better for Children* (Paris: Organization for Economic Cooperation and Development, 2009), www.oecd.org/els/social/childwellbeing.

3. David Brooks, "The Geezers' Crusade," *New York Times*, February 1, 2010, www.nytimes.com/2010/02/02/opinion/02brooks.html?scp=1&sq=brooks%20geezers%20crusade&st=cse; Julia Isaacs, "How Much Do We Spend on Children and the Elderly?" Brookings Institution, Center on Children and Families, 2009, www.brookings.edu/~/media/Files/rc/reports/2009/1105_spending_children_isaacs/1_how_much_isaacs.pdf.

Isabel Sawhill, an economist at Brookings, has proposed a "grand deal"—a policy and political strategy to link reform of Social Security and Medicare with an increase in expenditures on youth. In "Paying for Investments in Children," in *Big Ideas for Children* (Washington, DC: First Focus, 2008), she wrote: "We need a new intergenerational contract that invests more in people when they are young, but then expects them to assume somewhat greater responsibility for their own support during their retirement years." She outlined a strategy designed to promote "generational equity," not "intergenerational conflict," while acknowledging the inevitability of bumps along the way. The analysis shows that reducing seniors' benefits by just 2 percent or tinkering with Social Security rules would pay for big improvements in preschool and public education. That's an intriguing proposition. But as Sawhill, who headed the Office of Management and Budget in the Clinton administration, knows well, the 35-million-member AARP, the seniors' leading voice in Washington, guards its constituents' priorities—Social Security, Medicare, and prescription drug coverage—

with the political equivalent of a nuclear arsenal. Anything that smacks of cutting benefits, however sensible, isn't likely to fly. As a succession of presidents have learned, to their sorrow, these priority items are untouchable—just ask George W. Bush, whose dream of privatizing Social Security went nowhere.

4. First Focus, *Children's Budget 2010*, Washington, DC, 2010, http://firstfocus.net/library/reports/childrens-budget-2010.

5. Ibid.

6. McKinsey and Co., *The Economic Impact of the Achievement Gap in America's Schools*, 2009, www.mckinsey.com/App_Media/Images/Page_Images/Offices/Social Sector/PDF/achievement_gap_report.pdf.

7. James Heckman, "Schools, Skills, and Synapses," IZA Discussion Paper 3515, Institute for the Study of Labor, Bonn, Germany, 2008, ftp.iza.org/dp3515.pdf; Coalition for Evidence-Based Policy, "Social Programs That Work: Nurse-Family Partnership," 2008, http://evidencebasedprograms.org/wordpress/?page_id=57; L. J. Schweinhart, J. Montie, Z. Xiang, W. S. Barnett, C. R. Belfield, and M. Nores, *Lifetime Effects: The High/Scope Perry Preschool Study Through Age 40* (Ypsilanti, MI: High/Scope Press, 2004).

8. *Children's Budget 2009* (Washington, DC: First Focus 2009). See, generally, Isabel Sawhill, ed., *One Percent for the Children* (Washington, DC: Brookings Institution, 2003). The concluding chapter lays out a "kids-first" budget, and further detail is provided in the appendix.

9. Annette Lareau, *Unequal Childhoods: Class, Race, and Family Life* (Berkeley: University of California Press, 2003).

10. Adrea Theodore, Jen Jen Chang, Desmond Runyan, Wanda Hunter, Shrikant Bandiwala, and Robert Agans, "Epidemiologic Features of the Physical and Sexual Maltreatment of Children in the Carolinas," *Pediatrics* 115 (2005): 331–337.

11. Childstats.gov, *America's Children: Key National Indicators of Well-Being 2009*, www.childstats.gov/americaschildren; Kaiser Commission on Medicaid and the Uninsured, *Dental Coverage and Care for Low-Income Children: The Role of Medicaid and SCHIP*, 2008, www.kff.org/medicaid/upload/7681–02.pdf; Organization for Economic Cooperation and Development, "United States: Country Highlights," in *Doing Better for Children* (Paris: OECD, 2009), www.oecd.org/document/10/0,3343,en_2649_34819_43545036_1_1_1_37419,00.html.

12. W. Steven Barnett, "Benefits and Costs of Quality Early Education," *Children's Legal Rights Journal* 27, no. 1 (2007): 7–23; Valerie Lee and David Burkam, "Inequality at the Starting Gate: Social Background Differences as Children Begin School" (Washington, DC: Economic Policy Institute, 2002), www.epi.org/publications/entry/books_starting_gate/.

13. Michelle Goyette-Ewing, "Children's After-School Arrangements: A Study of Self-Care and Developmental Outcomes," *Journal of Prevention and Intervention in the Community* 20, no. 1 (2000): 55–67; G. Petit, J. Bates, K. Dodge, and D. Meece, "The Impact of After-School Peer Contact on Early Adolescent Externalizing Problems Is Moderated by Parental Monitoring, Perceived Neighborhood Safety and Prior Adjustment," *Child Development* 70, no. 3 (1999): 768–778.

14. Philip Lovell and Julia Isaacs, *The Impact of the Mortgage Crisis on Children* (Washington, DC: First Focus, 2008), www.firstfocus.net/Download/Housingand ChildrenFINAL.pdf. See, generally, Katherine Newman, *Falling from Grace: Downward Mobility in an Age of Affluence* (Berkeley: University of California Press, 1999).

15. Suniya Luthar and Shawn Latendresse, "Children of the Affluent: Challenges to Well-Being," *Current Directions in Psychological Science* 14, no. 1 (2005): 49–53; Janet Currie and Mark Stabile, "Child Mental Health and Human Capital Accumulation: The Case of ADHD," *Journal of Health Economics* 25, no. 6 (2006): 1094–1118; Judith Warner, "Children in the Mental Health Void," *New York Times*, February 19, 2009, http://opinionator.blogs.nytimes.com/2009/02/19/is-there-no-place-on-earth/.

16. Chapter 6 and the appendix to this book provide cost estimates for a global kids-first budget and explore the political landscape to assess the possibility of government action.

17. Geoffrey Borman and Matthew Boulay, *Summer Learning: Research, Policies and Programs* (New York: Routledge, 2004), details the effects of different summer learning opportunities on school outcomes.

18. See the discussion of the Chicago public schools in Chapter 3.

19. Brenda Bianco, "Think Your Day Care Is Expensive?" *USA Today*, February 6, 2000.

20. Susan Philliber, Jackie Kaye, and Scott Herrling, *The National Evaluation of the Children's Aid Society Carrera Model Program to Prevent Teen Pregnancy*, 2001, www.childrensaidsociety.org/files/cas-full_12_site_report1.pdf. The study was sufficiently rigorous to meet the stringent standards of the Coalition for Evidence-Based Policy.

21. The Children's Aid Society schools are discussed more fully in Chapter 3.

CHAPTER ONE

1. Mary Breckinridge, *Wide Neighborhoods: A Story of the Frontier Nursing Service* (Lexington: University Press of Kentucky, 1980 [1952]), 111; Frontier Nursing Service, "History Information," www.frontiernursing.org/History/History.shtm.

2. Mary Goan, *Mary Breckinridge: The Frontier Nursing Service and Rural Health in Appalachia* (Chapel Hill: University of North Carolina Press, 2008); Breckinridge, *Wide Neighborhoods*.

3. David Kirp, *The Sandbox Investment: The Preschool Movement and Kids-First Politics* (Cambridge: Harvard University Press, 2007), 93–122.

4. Janet D. Pietro, "Baby and the Brain: Advances in Child Development," *Public Health* 21, no. 3 (2000): 455–471; John Bruer, *The Myth of the First Three Years* (New York: Free Press, 2002), 8.

5. Kirp, *Sandbox Investment*, 116–118; Richard J. Herrnstein and Charles Murray, *The Bell Curve: Intelligence and Class Structure in American Life* (New York: Free Press, 1994).

6. Michel Duyme, Louise Arsenault, and Annick-Camille Dumaret, "Discontinuity and Stability of IQs: The French Adoption Studies," in P. Lindsay Chase-Lansdale, Kathleen Kiernan, and Ruth J. Friedman, eds., *Human Development Across Lives and Generations: The Potential for Change* (New York: Cambridge University Press, 2004).

7. Eric Turkheimer, Andreana Haley, Mary Waldron, Brian D'Onofrio, and Irvin I. Gottesman, "Socioeconomic Status Modifies Heritability of IQ in Young Children," *Psychological Science* 14, no. 6 (2003): 623–630.

8. Kirp, *Sandbox Investment*, 129–134.

9. Paul Barton and Richard Coley, *The Family: America's Smallest School* (Princeton, NJ: Educational Testing Service, 2007), www.ets.org/Media/Education_Topics/pdf/5678_PERCReport_School.pdf.

10. Including race as a "risk factor" is controversial, since minority families, understandably enough, don't want to be labeled as bad parents. They do, however, have different parenting styles. On average, black and Hispanic mothers talk less with their children, read to them less, and are harsher disciplinarians—and those differences explain as much as half of the school-readiness gap. Participating in programs such as Head Start especially benefits black children, for it prompts parents to alter childrearing patterns handed down from the previous generation. Jeanne Brooks-Gunn and Lisa Markman, "The Contribution of Parenting to Ethnic and Racial Gaps in School Readiness," *Future of Children* 15, no. 1 (2005): 139–168.

11. Lawrence Aber, "Changing the Climate on Early Childhood," *American Prospect*, December 2007, http://www.prospect.org/cs/articles?article=changing_the_climate_on_early_childhood.

12. Suniya Luthar, ed., *Resilience and Vulnerability: Adaptation in the Context of Childhood Adversities* (New York: Cambridge University Press, 2003).

13. Edward Zigler, Judy C. Pfannenstie, and Victoria Seitz, "The Parents as Teachers Program and School Success: A Replication and Extension," *Journal of Primary Prevention* 29, no. 2 (2008): 103–120.

14. Katherine Boo, "Swamp Nurse," *New Yorker*, February 6, 2006, www.newyorker.com/archive/2006/02/06/060206fa_fact_boo. Science cannot supply all the answers, of course, although pseudo-experts have long pretended otherwise. Faced with mounting criticism, in 2009 the company that manufactured the "Baby Einstein" DVDs offered parents refunds. Seventy years earlier, *Parents* magazine had peddled a correspondence course called "Add Science to Love and Be a 'Perfect Mother.'" Jill Lapore, "Baby Talk: The Fuss About Parenthood," *New Yorker*, June 29, 2009.

15. Jeanne Brooks-Gunn and Greg Duncan, "The Effects of Poverty on Children and Youth," *Future of Children* 7, no. 1 (1997): 55–71; H. B. Ferguson, S. Bovaird, and M. P. Mueller, "The Impact of Poverty on Educational Outcomes for Children," *Paediatric Child Health* 12, no. 8 (2007): 701–706.

16. Erik Erikson, *Insight and Responsibility* (New York: W. W. Norton, 1972), 116.

17. T. Berry Brazleton, *Touchpoints: Birth to Three* (New York: Da Capo, 1992).

18. For thoughtful commentaries on the field, see Robert Halpern, "The Societal Context of Home Visiting and Related Services for Families in Poverty," *Future of Children* 3, no. 3 (1993): 158–171; Heather Weiss, "Home Visits: Necessary but Not Sufficient," *Future of Children* 3, no. 3 (1993): 113–128; Deborah Daro, "Home Visitation: Assessing Progress, Managing Expectations," Ounce of Prevention Fund and Chapin Hall Center for Children, Chicago, 2006, http://www.ounceofprevention.org/includes/tiny_mce/plugins/filemanager/files/Home%20Visitation.pdf.

19. David Olds, Charles Henderson, Robert Chamberlin, and Robert Tatelman, "Preventing Child Abuse and Neglect: A Randomized Trial of Nurse Home Visitation," *Pediatrics* 78, no. 1 (1986): 65–78.

20. Richard Krugman, "Universal Home Visiting: A Recommendation from the U.S. Advisory Board on Child Abuse and Neglect," *Future of Children* 3, no. 3 (1993): 184–191.

21. Kay Johnson, *State-Based Home Visiting* (New York: National Center for Children in Poverty, 2009), www.nccp.org/publications/pub_862.html.

22. Kimberly Howard and Jeanne Brooks-Gunn, "The Role of Home-Visiting Programs in Preventing Child Abuse and Neglect," *Future of Children* 19, no. 2 (2009):

119–146. See, generally, Alexandra Cawthorne and Jessica Arons, *There's No Place Like Home: Home Visiting Programs Can Support Pregnant Women and New Parents* (Washington, DC: Center for American Progress, 2010), www.americanprogress.org/issues/2010/01/home_visitation_memo.html.

23. The history of Olds's work is drawn both from interviews with Olds and the NFP staff and Andy Goodman, *The Story of David Olds and the Nurse Home Visiting Program* (Princeton, NJ: Robert Wood Johnson Foundation, 2006).

24. Urie Bronfenbrenner, *The Ecology of Human Development: Experiments by Nature and Design* (Cambridge: Harvard University Press, 1979).

25. Olds et al., "Preventing Child Abuse and Neglect," 65–78; David L. Olds, Charles R. Henderson Jr., Harriet J. Kitzman, John J. Eckenrode, Robert E. Cole, and Robert C. Tatelbaum, "Prenatal and Infancy Home Visitation by Nurses: Recent Findings," *Future of Children* 9, no. 1 (1999): 41–65. At age four there were no differences for either the full sample or the subsample of teens in the number of new reports of child abuse and neglect between months twenty-five and forty-eight. Deborah Daro, a senior researcher at Chapin Hall, University of Chicago, pointed out that the implication is that the impact of the program on child abuse faded during this period.

26. David Olds, Harriet Kitzman, Carole Hanks, Robert Cole, Elizabeth Anson, Kimberly Sidora-Arcoleo, Dennis W. Luckey, "Effects of Nurse Home Visiting on Maternal and Child Functioning: Age 9 Follow-up of a Randomized Trial," *Pediatrics* 120 (2007): E832–E837; Coalition for Evidence-Based Policy, *Social Programs That Work*, 2008, http://evidencebasedprograms.org/wordpress/?page_id=57.

27. David Olds, J. Robinson, L. Pettitt, D. W. Luckey, J. Holmberg, K. Isacks, K. Sheff, and C. R. Henderson Jr., "Effects of Home Visits by Para-Professionals and by Nurses: Age 4 Follow-up Results of a Randomized Trial," *Pediatrics* 114, no. 6 (2004): 1560–1568.

28. David Olds, C. R. Henderson Jr., R. Cole, J. Eckenrode, H. Kitzman, D. Luckey, L. Pettitt, K. Sidora, P. Morris, and J. Powers, "Long Term Effects of Nurse Home Visitation on Children's Criminal and Antisocial Behavior: 15-Year Follow-up of a Randomized, Controlled Trial," *Journal of the American Medical Association* 280, no. 14 (1998): 1238–1244. Those conclusions were qualified in a subsequent paper, Dennis W. Luckey, David L. Olds, Weiming Zhang, Charles R. Henderson Jr., Michael Knudtson, John Eckenrode, Harriet Kitzman, Robert Cole, and Lisa Pettitt, "Revised Analysis of 15-Year Outcomes in the Elmira Trial of the Nurse-Family Partnership," Prevention Research Center for Family and Child Health, Department of Pediatrics, University of Colorado Medical School (unpublished, 2008).

29. Partnership for America's Economic Success, "Long-Term Benefits of Investing in Early Childhood Programs," Issue Brief no. 5 (2008), www.partnershipforsuccess.org/docs/researchproject_dickens_bartik_200802_brief.pdf; Coalition for Evidence-Based Policy, *Social Programs That Work*. The data on abuse rates should be interpreted cautiously. Deborah Daro, at Chapin Hall, pointed out in my interview with her that the difference may partly be attributable to a "small number of cases with a very high number of reports (a common outcome in child welfare cases in which abuse begins early in a child's life), rather than a meaningful program impact on a larger proportion of participants." One objective of the program is to increase the spacing of children in families, and the fact that the women in the control group had more children "might account for a higher number of reports—the more children you have the greater the number of opportunities for abuse and neglect."

30. Throughout this chapter the names of the parents, but not the home visitors, have been changed.

31. William Rashbaum and Al Baker, "Fifty Bullets, One Dead, and Many Questions," *New York Times*, December 11, 2006, www.nytimes.com/2006/12/11/ny region/11shoot.html?_r=1.

32. In 2009 Frieden became the director of the Centers for Disease Control and Prevention.

33. Other home-visiting programs are increasingly using timely feedback systems in this way and using the data to suggest improvements and innovations.

34. The Family Development Project at the University of California at Los Angeles, which has shown highly promising results in a matched-sample study, recognizes that the needs of mothers aren't mainly medical in nature. It enrolls expectant mothers in the third trimester of pregnancy. The model includes weekly home visits for the first year and then every other week for the second year as well as a weekly mother-infant group. To encourage attendance, the FDP pays participants $10 per session. Visitors are trained in psychology or social work; their role includes simply listening to mothers' concerns and offering direct help in learning to respond to their infants' needs. A psychiatrist helps diagnose and treat difficulties such as postpartum depression. Unlike the Nurse-Family Partnership, the Family Development Project has not been expanded beyond the single site, so it is unknown how effective it would be if widely implemented. Christopher M. Heinicke, Margaret Goorsky, Monica Levine, Victoria Ponce, Gloria Ruth, Mara Silverman, and Claudia Sotelo, "Pre- and Postnatal Antecedents of a Home Visiting and Family Developmental Outcome," *Infant Mental Health Journal* 27, no. 1 (2006): 91–119.

Another initiative, First Born, is being field-tested across New Mexico. Open to all families, it provides home- and center-based weekly services utilizing registered nurses and clinical counselors as well as paraprofessionals. Ivan de la Rosa, Joanna Perry, Lisa Dalton, and Victoria Johnson, "Strengthening Families with First-Born Children: Exploratory Story of the Outcomes of a Home Visiting Intervention," *Research on Social Work Practice* 15, no. 5 (2005): 323–338, http://rsw.sagepub.com/cgi/content/abstract/15/5/323.

35. Burton White, *The First Three Years of Life* (Upper Saddle River, NJ: Prentice-Hall, 1975).

36. Urie Bronfenbrenner, *Report on Longitudinal Evaluations of Preschool Programs*, vol. 2, *Is Early Intervention Effective?* (Washington, DC: U.S. Office of Child Development, 1974).

37. Tamar Lewin, "Family Support Aims to Mend Two Generations," *New York Times*, March 3, 1988.

38. Pediatrician C. Henry Kempe, who founded the National Center for the Prevention and Treatment of Child Abuse, raised this issue in the 1970s: "Will the health visitor be seen as someone who can truly be useful and accepted like a member of the extended family, or looked on as another bureaucratic layer of busybodies who come between those who need help and those who can provide it?" I believe that, to a large extent, this will depend on whether the program is started for all people or whether it is limited, once again, to the disadvantaged or the minorities. To my mind, only a universal program will develop quality and be successful." Quoted at

Junie Svenson, Betty Kaplan, and Penny Hatcher, "Evidence That Universally-Offered Home Visiting Finds Families at Risk," Minnesota Department of Public Health (n.d.), www.health.state.mn.us/divs/fh/mch/fhv/reports/apha/evidence1.html.

The way this argument between targeting and universalism gets resolved speaks to our national character. What belongs in the commons, open to all, and what should be fenced off? Who merits our collective support and who should fend for himself? When are we our brothers' and sisters' keepers? This is an ancient American debate, one that Alexis de Tocqueville wrote about nearly two centuries ago in *Democracy in America* when he observed that when Americans come together, it isn't because of altruism but "enlightened self-interest." We take it for granted that every youngster is entitled to a free public education, at least through high school, but barely more than a century ago public high schools were regarded as "paupers' schools" and the rich paid to be tutored in rhetoric and botany. We'll revisit the "targeting versus universalism" debate in considering whether all children, or just poor children, should be able to go to free, high-quality preschool, who should be assured of having a caring and stable adult in their lives, and who should benefit from having a publicly supported child savings account.

This choice isn't necessarily an all-or-nothing one—a long-term goal of universalism can be coupled with focusing, in the here and now, on the neediest, an approach known as "targeted universalism." See Peter B. Evans, Dietrich Rueschemeyer, and Theda Skocpol, eds., *Bringing the State Back In* (New York: Cambridge University Press, 1985).

39. Healthy Families America, the third major home-visiting model—it operates in 440 communities nationwide—was initiated in the early 1990s with the aim of preventing child abuse. It has its origins in Healthy Start, a program begun in Hawaii during the 1980s that screens all families and makes sure they have access to a pediatrician; the families who are seen as most likely to abuse or neglect their infants may receive home visits during the child's first three years. Documented changes in how parents treated their children generated enthusiasm in a field hungry for answers, and though no trial had been conducted, the early evidence prompted similar ventures elsewhere. A. K. Duggan, E. C. McFarlane, A. M. Windham, C. A. Rohde, D. S. Salkever, L. Fuddy, L. A. Rosenberg, S. B. Buchbinder, and C.C.J. Sia, "Evaluation of Hawaii's Healthy Start Program," *Future of Children* 9, no. 1 (1999): 66–90; Deborah Daro, Karen McCurdy, and Kathryn Harding, *The Role of Home Visiting in Preventing Child Abuse: An Evaluation of the Hawaii Healthy Start Program* (Chicago: National Center on Child Abuse Prevention Research, 1998).

Healthy Families America draws on key features of Healthy Start while also incorporating ideas from other initiatives. Over time its sites have come to look less and less like Hawaii, with more structured materials and a professional staff. Healthy Families singles out expectant parents who, as its promotional materials state, are "overburdened"—stressed, unstable, and lacking resilience—putting their children at risk for future abuse or neglect.

In 2005 there were 899,000 substantiated child victims of substantial abuse or neglect in the United States, but that figure doesn't even hint at the scope of the problem. In a 2005 phone survey conducted in the Carolinas, mothers recounted *forty times* more physical abuse than the official reports had documented; and contrary to stereotype, the rate of harsh physical discipline does not differ significantly among poor and well-to-do households. W. Bradford Wilcox and Jeffrey Dew, "Protectors or Perpetrators: Fathers, Mothers, and Child Abuse and Neglect," Research Brief no. 7, Center for Marriage and Families, 2008, http://center.americanvalues.org/?p=70; Adrea Theodore, Jen Jen Chang, Desmond Runyan, Wanda Hunter, Shrikant Bandiwala, and Robert Agans, "Epidemiologic Features of the Physical and Sexual Maltreatment of Children in the Carolinas," *Pediatrics* 115, no. 3 (2005): 331–337.

Unlike the other leading home-visiting programs, Healthy Families has no set curriculum—each site can pick what it believes will work best—and that may be why the evaluations have been inconsistent. A recent study of the New York program showed strong positive effects. See K. Dumont, S. Mitchell-Herzfeld, R. Greene, E. Lee, A. Lowenfels, M. Rodriguez, and V. Dorabawila, "Healthy Families New York (HFNY) Randomized Trial: Effects on Early Child Abuse and Neglect," *Child Abuse and Neglect* 32, no. 3 (2009): 295–315.

40. Deanna Gomby, "Home Visitation in 2005: Outcomes for Children and Parents," Invest in Kids Working Paper no. 7 (Washington, DC: Committee for Economic Development, 2005), www.partnershipforsuccess.org/docs/ivk/report_ivk_gomby_2005.pdf. Other promising programs, such as First Born of New Mexico, are in the testing phase.

41. Zigler et al., "The Parents as Teachers Program and School Success." Other major programs, such as Healthy Families America, have also demonstrated positive outcomes. See Eunju Lee, Susan Mitchell-Herzfeld, Ann Lowenfels, Rose Green, Vajeera Dorabawila, and Kimberly Dumont, "Reducing Low Birthweight Through Home Visitation: A Randomly Controlled Trial," *Journal of Preventive Medicine* 36, no. 2 (2009): 154–160.

42. Rucker Johnson, "Health Dynamics and the Evolution of Health Inequality over the Life Course: The Importance of Neighborhood and Family Background" (unpublished paper, 2009).

43. Jude Cassidy, "The Nature of a Child's Ties," in Jude Cassidy and Philip Shaver, eds., *Handbook of Attachment: Theory, Research and Clinical Applications* (New York: Guilford Press, 1999), 3–20.

44. Jane Waldfogel, *What Children Need* (Cambridge: Harvard University Press, 2006).

45. In a reflection of the still-prevailing stereotypes about parenting, relatively little research has been carried out on stay-at-home dads.

46. Christopher Ruhm, "Parental Leave and Child Health," Working Paper no. 6554 (Washington, DC: National Bureau of Economic Research, 1998), www.nber.org/papers/w6554; Brooks-Gunn and Markman, "The Contribution of Parenting to Ethnic and Racial Gaps in School Readiness"; Pia Rebello Britto and Jeanne Brooks-Gunn, "Editors' Notes," *New Directions for Child and Adolescent Development* 92, no. 2 (2001): 73–90.

Children from poor families have it worst. *Work After Welfare Reform and the Well-being of Children*. When mothers are doing dead-end jobs where shifts change frequently and the threat of layoff looms, kids' behavior worsens; they are more likely to be left back or assigned to special education than those with stay-at-home moms. The opposite holds true for kids from middle-class homes where mothers have more stable careers and they can anticipate moving up the ladder—in those families, this research shows, babies may benefit when the mother returns to work. Rucker Johnson, Ariel Kalik, and Rachel Dunifon, *Mother's Work and Childrens' Lives: Low-Income Families after Wefare Reform* (Kalamazoo, MI: Upjohn Institute, 2010).

The baleful consequences of the 1996 welfare reform had been predicted by Harvard public policy professor Mary Jo Bane, who, as an assistant secretary in the Department of Health and Human Services during the Clinton administration, had favored a more family-friendly approach. "For some, abandonment or serious abuse or neglect will result," she wrote. "For others, the effects may show up in poor school performance and antisocial behavior." Mary Jo Bane, "Welfare as We Might Know It," *American Prospect*, January 1997, www.prospect.org/cs/articles?article=welfare_as_we_might_know_it_1197.

47. A survey of twenty-one postindustrial democracies found that the United States was least generous in supporting new parents. Rebecca Ray, *A Detailed Look at Parental Leave Policies in 21 OECD Countries* (Washington, DC: Center for Economic and Policy Research, 2008).

48. Deborah Daro and Kenneth Dodge, "Creating Community Responsibility for Child Protection: Possibilities and Challenges," *Future of Children* 19, no. 2 (2009): 67–95; Richard Barth, "Preventing Child Abuse and Neglect with Parent Training: Evidence and Opportunities," *Future of Children* 19, no. 2 (2009): 95–119. On social marketing generally, see Philip Kotler and Nancy Lee, *Social Marketing: Influencing Behaviors for Good* (Thousand Oaks, CA: Sage, 2007).

49. Parts of the model are also being used in other locales, including Cincinnati, Ohio, and Mendocino, California.

50. Ron Prinz, Matthew Sanders, Cheri Shapiro, Daniel Whitaker, and John Lutzker, "Population-Based Prevention of Child Maltreatment: The U.S. Triple P System Population Trial," *Prevention Science* 10, no. 1 (2009): 1–12. The article summarizes the substantial body of research on Triple P. A citywide trial of Triple P in Brisbane, Australia, produced comparably positive results. Matthew R. Sanders, Alan Ralph, Kate Sofronoff, Paul Gardiner, Rachel Thompson, Sarah Dwyer, and Kerry Bidwell, "Every Family: A Population Approach to Reducing Behavioral and Emotional Problems in Children Making the Transition to School," *Journal of Primary Prevention* 29, no. 3 (2008): 197–222, www.triplep-america.com/documents/Every%20Family%20A%20Population%20Approach%20to%20Reducing.pdf. For a detailed description of Triple P, see Matthew Sanders, "Triple-P Positive Parenting Program as a Public Health Approach to Strengthening Parenting," *Journal of Family Psychology* 22, no. 3 (2008): 506–517.

51. Prinz et al., "Population-Based Prevention of Child Maltreatment."

52. "Fort Mill Mother Calls Triple P 'a Blessing from Heaven,' Triple P, http://tpinfo.sc.edu/stories/padillo.html.

53. Zak Sanbor, "Prevention as Intervention," *Monitor on Psychology* 37, no. 6 (2006): 30.

54. Zigler et al., "The Parents and Teachers Program and School Success." See also Deborah Daro, "Embedding Home Visitation Programs Within a System of Early Childhood Services," Chapin Hall, University of Chicago, 2009, www.chapinhall.org/sites/default/files/publications/Issue_Brief_R3_09_09_09_0.pdf; Council on

Community Pediatrics, "The Role of Preschool Home-Visiting Programs in Improving Children's Developmental and Health Outcomes," *Pediatrics* 123, no. 2 (2009): 598–603, http://aappolicy.aappublications.org/cgi/content/abstract/pediatrics;123/2/598.

CHAPTER 2

1. The discussion of Educare is adapted from David L. Kirp and Donna Leff, "Sandbox *Cum Laude*," *Chicago Tribune Sunday Magazine*, July 16, 2006.

2. Frances Campbell, Craig Ramey, Elizabeth Pungello, Joseph Sparling, and Sheri Miller-Johnson, "Early Childhood Education: Young Adult Outcomes from the Abecedarian Project," *Applied Development Science* 6, no. 1 (2002): 42–57. Abecedarian is the only early education program model to have recorded lasting IQ gains.

3. Alex Kotlowitz, *There Are No Children Here: The Story of Two Boys Growing Up in the Other America* (New York: Anchor, 1991).

4. Noreen Yazejian and Donna Bryant, "Promising Early Returns: Educare Implementation Study Data," University of North Carolina FPG Child Development Institute, 2009, www.researchconnections.org/location/16007. Because this research does not compare Educare youngsters with a matched sample, researchers quarrel over the findings; a rigorous multiyear investigation began in 2009 to prove that the program works.

5. This section is adapted from David Kirp, *The Sandbox Investment: The Preschool Movement and Kids-First Politics* (Cambridge: Harvard University Press, 2007), 175–177, 180–186.

6. Sara Mead, "Primary Watch: Barack Obama's Early Education Agenda," *Early Ed Watch Blog*, April 10, 2008, www.newamerica.net/blog/early-ed-watch/2008/primary-watch-barack-obamas-early-education-agenda-3239; Sara Mead, "Primary Watch: Hillary Clinton's Early Education Agenda," *Early Ed Watch Blog*, April 9, 2008, www.newamerica.net/blog/early-ed-watch/2008/primary-watch-hillary-clintons-early-education-agenda-3223. Though Republican as well as Democratic governors have embraced early education, GOP candidate John McCain was silent on the topic.

7. National Institute for Early Education Research, *The State of Preschool 2008*, http://nieer.org/yearbook/pdf/execsummary.pdf (updated version). In his successful 2006 Virginia gubernatorial race, Democrat Tim Kaine ran successfully on a platform that called for new highways and preschool for all. The enrollment of three- and four-year-old children in some form of preschool increased from 9 percent in 1964 to over 55 percent in 2007.

8. Gregory Camilli, Sadako Vargas, Sharon Ryan, and W. Steven Barnett, "Meta-Analysis of the Effects of Early Education Interventions on Cognitive and Social Development," *Teachers College Record* 112, no. 3 (2010): 579–620; W. Steven Barnett, "Research on Preschool Education and Its Lasting Effects: What Are the Implications for Policy?" (Rutgers: National Institute for Early Education Research, 2008), http://nieer.org/resources/research/PreschoolLastingEffects.pdf. The Milwaukee Project, in which both mothers and children were given high-quality support, generated strong positive outcomes. Howard Garber, *The Milwaukee Project: Preventing Mental Retardation in Children at Risk* (Washington, DC: American Association on Mental Retardation, 1988).

9. This section is adapted from Kirp, *Sandbox Investment*, 50–66.

10. David Weikart, *How High/Scope Grew: A Memoir* (Ypsilanti, MI: High/Scope Educational Research Foundation, 1994), 37.

11. Westinghouse Learning Corporation, *The Impact of Head Start* (Washington, DC: U.S. Department of Commerce, 1969).

12. John Beruetta-Clement, Lawrence J. Schweinhart, W. Steven Barnett, Ann S. Epstein, and David P. Weikart, *Changed Lives: The Effects of the Perry Preschool Program Through Age 19* (Ypsilanti, MI: High/Scope Educational Research Foundation, 1984).

13. W. Steven Barnett, *Lives in the Balance: Age-27 Benefit-Cost Analysis of the High/Scope Perry Preschool Program* (Ypsilanti, MI: High/Scope Educational Research Foundation, 1996); John Donohue and Peter Siegelman, "Allocating Resources Among Prisons and Social Programs in the Battle Against Crime," *Journal of Legal Studies* 27, no. 1 (1998): 1–43. See, generally, "Special Report. Life Chances. The Case for Early Investment in Our Kids," *American Prospect*, December 2007, www.prospect.org/cs/archive/view_report?reportId=15; Albert Wat, "Dollars and Sense: A Review of Economic Analyses of Pre-K" (Washington, DC: Pre-K Now, 2007), www.pewcenteronthestates.org/uploadedFiles/DollarsandSense_May2007.pdf.

14. L. J. Schweinhart, J. Montie, Z. Xiang, W. S. Barnett, C. R. Belfield, and M. Nores, *Lifetime Effects: The High/Scope Perry Preschool Study Through Age 40* (Ypsilanti, MI: High/Scope Press, 2004).

15. A review of research examining which factors most influenced children's learning found that the home and community environment contributed significantly to students' success. Margaret C. Wang, Geneva D. Haertel, and Herbert J. Walberg, "What Helps Students Learn?" *Educational Leadership* 51, no. 4 (1993): 71–79.

16. A benefit cost analysis of the Abecedarian Project also yielded impressive results, as did an assessment of a third early education model, the Child-Parent Centers in Chicago. Arthur Reynolds, *Success in Early Intervention: The Chicago Child-Parent Centers* (Lincoln: University of Nebraska Press, 2000).

17. James Heckman, "Policies to Foster Human Capital," *Research in Economics* 54, no. 1 (2000): 3–56; Flavio Cunha, James Heckman, Lance Lochner, and Dimitriy Masterov, "Interpreting the Evidence on Life Cycle Skill Formation," National Bureau of Economic Research, 2005, www.nber.org/papers/w11331.pdf.

18. Robert Lynch, *Exceptional Returns: Economic, Fiscal and Social Benefits of Investment in Early Childhood Development* (Washington, DC: Economic Policy Institute, 2004).

19. In 2009, Heckman reanalyzed the Perry Preschool data and concluded that the previous estimates of the rate of return were inflated because of "compromises" in how the children were randomized. James Heckman, Seong Moon, Rodrigo Pinto, Peter Savelyer, and Adam Yavitz, "The Rate of Return to the High/Scope Perry Preschool Program," National Bureau of Economic Research, 2005, www.nber.org/papers/w15471.pdf.

20. Bruce Fuller, *Standardized Education: The Political and Cultural Struggle over Early Education* (Palo Alto: Stanford University Press, 2007).

21. "Policies, program development and professional development efforts that improve teacher-child interactions can facilitate children's school readiness." A. J. Mashburn, R. C. Pianta, B. K. Hamre, J. T. Downer, O. A. Barbarin, D. Bryant, M. Burchinal, D. M. Early, and C. Howes, "Measures of Classroom Quality in Prekindergarten and

Children's Development of Academic, Language, and Social Skills," *Child Development* 79, no. 3 (2008): 732–749 at 732; NIEER, *State of Preschool 2008.*

22. Kirp, *Sandbox Investment,* 186–198.

23. For an insightful critique of the conventional wisdom, see Diane Ravitch, *The Death and Life of the Great American School System: How Testing and Choice Are Undermining Education* (New York: Basic Books, 2010).

24. Montgomery County, Maryland, has also done remarkably well in educating poor youngsters, many of whom come from homes where English is not the first language. Students in what is termed the "red zone" graduate from high school at rates comparable to the national average, and they graduate from college at a rate that exceeds the national average. Stacey M. Childress, Denis P. Doyle, and David A. Thomas, *Leading for Equity: The Pursuit of Excellence in the Montgomery County Public Schools* (Cambridge: Harvard Education Press, 2009).

25. Much of the material in this section comes from my visits to Union City, interviews with key staffers, and unpublished reports.

26. Union City, which reengineered its public schools from the bottom up, is applying to its high schools the same one-step-at-a-time approach that has transformed the elementary and middle schools.

27. Alison Gopnik, *The Philosophical Baby* (New York: Farrar, Straus and Giroux, 2009).

28. Between 1983 and 2009, the *Abbott* litigation spawned twenty decisions by the state's high court. See, generally, "Symposium on School Finance Litigation: Emerging Trends or New Dead Ends," *Yale Law and Policy Review* 22, no. 2 (2004).

29. The Sanger response appears on the Union City school district website, www .union-city-nj.org/modules/mxdirectory/singlelink.php?cid.

30. This section draws on Kirp, *Sandbox Investment,* 207–219.

31. Carol Copple and Sue Bredekamp, *Developmentally Appropriate Practice in Early Childhood Programs* (Washington, DC: National Association for the Education of Young Children, 2009); Sharon Kagan, "American Early Childhood Education: Preventing or Perpetuating Inequity?" (unpublished draft, November 12, 2008), www .policyforchildren.org/pdf/Kagan%20Equity%20Symposium%20Paper.pdf.

32. Smart Start, a North Carolina zero-to-five program, illustrates this migration to quality. Donna Bryant, Kelly Maxwell, Karen Taylor, Michele Poe, Ellen Peisner-Feinberg, and Kathleen Bernier, "Smart Start and Preschool Child Care Quality in N.C.: Change Over Time and Relation to Children's Readiness, A Report by the FPG-UNC Smart Start Evaluation Team," University of North Carolina FPG Child Development Institute, 2003, http://www.fpg.unc.edu/smartstart/reports/Child_Care_ Quality_2003.pdf.

33. The center is just one of a host of programs run by Para Los Niños, a settlement house that has repositioned itself for the twenty-first century. Established thirty years ago, it grew from a single child-care center to a $24 million operation serving 4,600 kids and almost as many families. The myriad offerings include home visiting for the families of infants and toddlers, after-school activities, and a charter school as well as job training for poor teenagers who, like almost half of all LA youth, have dropped out of high school.

34. Carolyn Edwards, ed., *The Hundred Languages of Children: The Reggio Emilia Approach to Early Childhood Education* (Norwood, NJ: Ablex, 1993).

35. On child-care generally, see Edward Zigler, Katherine Marsland, and Heather Lord, *The Tragedy of Child Care in America* (New Haven, CT: Yale University Press, 2009); Jane Waldfogel, *What Children Need* (Cambridge: Harvard University Press, 2006); Joan Lombardi, *Time to Care* (Philadelphia: Temple University Press, 2001); Deborah Vandell and Barbara Wolfe, "Child Care Quality: Does It Matter and Does It Need to Be Improved?" (Madison: Institute for Research on Poverty, University of Wisconsin, 2001).

36. On a budget of $10,000 (half coming from LAUP), Montes converted her backyard into a playground with a fancy sandbox, a swing set on steroids, and a racetrack for tricycles with signs reading "alto" and "stop."

37. Gordon MacInnes, *In Plain Sight: Simple, Difficult Lessons from New Jersey's Expensive Effort to Close the Achievement Gap* (New York: Century Foundation Press, 2009), 50–55.

38. U.S. Department of Health and Human Services, Administration for Children and Families, "Head Start Impact Study and Follow-up, 2000–2010," www.acf.hhs.gov/programs/opre/hs/impact_study/.

39. J. M. Love, E. E. Kisker, C. Ross, H. Raikes, J. Constantine, K. Boller, J. Brooks-Gunn, et al., "The Effectiveness of Early Head Start for 3-Year-Old Children and Their Parents: Lessons for Policy and Programs," *Developmental Psychology* 41, no. 6 (2005): 885–901. There is evidence to suggest that the positive impact of Head Start only becomes apparent years after the program ends. In a seminal article, "Does Head Start Make a Difference?" *American Economic Review* 85, no. 3 (1995), 341–364, economists Janet Currie and Duncan Thomas compared the life histories of siblings who were of Head Start age in the mid-1970s in cases where one of the siblings participated in Head Start but the other one did not. They found that the children who had been in Head Start were more likely to have graduated from high school and attended college than their brothers or sisters who were not in Head Start. A 2009 follow-up carried out by Harvard public policy Ph.D. candidate David Deming tracked these youngsters into their early twenties, and by then the impact of Head Start looked impressive indeed. The Head Start alumni were significantly less likely to have been left back or assigned to special education, more likely to have graduated from high school or earned a high-school equivalency diploma, more likely to have enrolled in college, and more likely to have had some work experience and stayed healthy. Deming calculated that Head Start's long-term impact was about 80 percent that of Perry Preschool or the Abecedarian Project, and that every dollar invested in Head Start had generated a return of $3.50. David Deming, "Early Childhood Intervention and Life-Cycle Skill Development: Evidence from Head Start," *American Economic Journal: Applied Economics* 1, no. 3 (2009): 111–134. See also Eliana Garces, Duncan Thomas, and Janet Currie, "Longer-Term Effects of Head Start," *American Economic Review* 92, no. 4 (2002): 999–1012.

For more on the long-term effects of Head Start, see Jens Ludwig and Douglas Miller, "Does Head Start Improve Children's Life Chances? Evidence from a Regression Discontinuity Design," *Quarterly Journal of Economics* 122, no. 1 (2007): 159–208; Valerie E. Lee, J. Brooks-Gunn, Elizabeth Schnur, and Fong-Ruey Liaw, "Are Head Start Effects Sustained? A Longitudinal Follow-up Comparison of Disadvantaged Children Attending Head Start, No Preschool, and Other Preschool Programs," *Child*

Development 61 (1991): 495–507; Martha Abbott-Shim, Richard Lambert, and Frances McCarty, "A Comparison of School Readiness Outcomes for Children Randomly Assigned to a Head Start Program and the Program's Wait List," *Journal of Education for Students Placed at Risk* 8, no. 2 (2009): 191–214.

40. Quoted in Mary Ann Zehr, "Head Start Study Finds Brief Learning Gains," *Education Week*, January 14, 2010, www.edweek.org/ew/articles/2010/01/14/18 headstart.h29.html.

41. Ibid.

42. Three percent of the Head Start budget is reserved for "quality improvement" grants, though there is little evidence that these have led to systemic improvement.

43. Theda Skocpol, "Targeting Within Universalism: Politically Viable Policies to Combat Poverty in the United States," in Paul Peterson and Christopher Jencks, eds., *The Urban Underclass* (Washington, DC: Brookings Institution, 1991).

44. Quoted in Paul Krugman, "Why Americans Hate Single-Payer Insurance," *New York Times*, July 28, 2009, http://krugman.blogs.nytimes.com/2009/07/28/why -americans-hate-single-payer-insurance/.

45. Jerome Corsi and Kenneth Blackwell, "Democrats' War on Poverty Has Failed," *Human Events*, September 6, 2006, www.humanevents.com/article.php?id=16860.

46. Lisa Guernsey, "A Mother's Myriad Questions Point to Need for Connected System of Early Education," New America Foundation, 2009, http://earlyed.new america.net/blogposts/2009/a_mothers_myriad_questions_point_to_need_for_ connected_system_of_early education-18488.

47. Compare W. Steven Barnett, "Benefits and Costs of Quality Early Education," *Children's Legal Rights Journal* 27, no. 1 (2007): 7–23 (arguing, on economic grounds, for universal preschool) with Douglas Clement, "Interview with James Heckman," Federal Reserve Bank of Minneapolis, June 2005, www.minneapolisfed.org/publica tions_papers/pub_display.cfm?id=3278 (arguing for targeted preschool).

48. This section draws on Kirp, *Sandbox Investment*, 87–91.

49. James Heckman, "Catch 'Em Young," *Wall Street Journal*, January 13, 2006.

50. Ibid.

51. Edward Zigler, Walter Gilliam, and Stephanie Jones, *A Vision for Universal Preschool* (New York: Cambridge University Press, 2006), offers a careful distillation of the arguments. In 1985, after completing the first Perry Preschool study, Barnett argued against universal preschool on familiar economic grounds: The social return was likely to be small, and parents were already investing in their children's education. What he has learned since then, both about social benefits and politics, has led him to change his mind. See W. Steven Barnett, *The Perry Preschool Program and Its Long-Term Effects: A Benefit-Cost Analysis* (Ypsilanti, MI: High/Scope Educational Research Foundation, 1983), 102.

52. Jonah B. Gelbach and Lant Pritchett, "Is More for the Poor Less for the Poor? The Politics of Means-Tested Targeting," *Topics in Economic Analysis and Policy* 2, no. 1 (2002), http://www.bepress.com/bejeap/topics/vol2/iss1/art6/.

53. James Coleman et al., *Equality of Educational Opportunity Survey* (Washington, DC: Government Printing Office, 1966).

54. K. Sylva, E. Melhuish, P. Sammons, I. Siraj-Blatchford, and B. Taggart, "The Effective Provision of Preschool Education (EPPE) Project," in J. J. van Kuyk, ed., *The*

Quality of Early Education (Arnhem, Netherlands: Cito, 2006), 4556; Gary Henry, Bentley Ponder, Dana Rickman, Andrew Mashburn, Laura Henderson, and Craig Gordon, "An Evaluation of the Implementation of Georgia's Pre-K Program," Andrew Young School of Policy Studies, Georgia State University, 2004, aysps.gsu.edu/publications/2005/GAPreK2004.pdf. See also Zigler et al., *A Vision for Universal Preschool*, 99–101. This research is far from the last word, as neither the Georgia nor the British studies were experiments. What made the critical difference may not have been the fact of integration but the initial differences between the poor kids going to economically isolated schools and those going to economically integrated schools, or the effect of the resources that economically mixed schools can attract. Still, for the policymaker, based on what we know about preschoolers from the landmark 1966 *Equal Education Opportunity Survey*, integration is a better bet than class-based segregation.

55. Karen Schulman and W. Steven Barnett, *The Benefits of Prekindergarten for Middle-Income Children* (New Brunswick, NJ: National Institute for Early Education Research, 2005), nieer.org/resources/policyreports/report3.pdf.

56. Norman Brosterman, *Inventing Kindergarten* (New York: Harry N. Abrams, 1997).

57. Much of the material in this section comes from my visit to the Rosemount Center and interviews with key staffers.

58. Valerie Lee and Suzanna Loeb, "Where Do Head Start Attendees End Up? One Reason that Preschool Effects Fade Out," *Educational Evaluation and Policy Analysis* 17, no. 1 (1995): 62–82.

59. Stacey Childress and Geoff Marietta, "Investing in Early Learning as Economic Development at the Minneapolis Federal Reserve Bank" (Cambridge: Harvard Business Publishing, 2009), http://harvardbusiness.org/product/investing-in-early-learning-as-economic-development/an/309090-PDF-ENG; Erika Gaylor, Donna Spiker, Kate Ferguson, Cyndi Williamson, and Annie Georges, "Pre-kindergarten Allowances Project: Final Evaluation Report" (Menlo Park, CA: SRI International, 2009), http://policyweb.sri.com/cehs/publications/MELF_Pre-KAlllowancesFinalEvaluation Report.pdf.

60. The Minnesota Early Learning Foundation has established a research consortium, which includes the Center for Early Education at the University of Minnesota, Child Trends, SRI International, and Wilder Research. Evaluations are to be completed by the time the initiative ends in 2011.

61. Isabel Sawhill and Jens Ludwig, "Success by Ten: Intervening Early, Often and Effectively in the Education of Young Children" (Washington, DC: Hamilton Project, Brookings Institution, 2007). According to this study, "what's required is to intervene early, often, and effectively."

62. Rucker Johnson, "School Quality and the Long-Run Effects of Head Start," Goldman School of Public Policy, working paper, 2010.

CHAPTER 3

1. Arne Duncan, "Education Reform's Moon Shot," *Washington Post*, July 23, 2009, www.washingtonpost.com/wp-dyn/content/article/2009/07/23/AR2009072302634.html.

2. Arne Duncan, "Every School a Community School: A Vision Implant," keynote address, Children's Aid Society National Center for Community Schools, October 22, 2009 (unpublished).

3. See, generally, Rudy Crew, *Only Connect: The Way to Save Our Schools* (New York: Farrar, Straus and Giroux, 2007); Anthony Bryk and Mary Driscoll, *The School as Community: Theoretical Foundations, Contextual Influences, and Consequences for Students and Teachers* (Madison, WI: National Center on Effective Secondary Schools, 1988); Karen Pittman, Nicole Yohalem, and Joel Tolman, eds., "When Where, What and How Youth Learn: Blurring School and Community Boundaries," special issue, *New Directions for Youth Development* 97, no. 1 (2003). The idea of linking school and community dates to John Dewey, America's most influential education philosopher. See John Dewey, *The School and Society* (Chicago: University of Chicago Press, 1900).

In "The School Rural Community Center," *Annals of the American Academy of Political and Social Science* 67, no. 1 (1916): 140–148, L. J. Hanifan, West Virginia's supervisor of rural schools, describes one such effort that engaged a poor community in improving its schools. The result was the creation of school libraries, the establishment of evening classes for adults who couldn't read—and, most significantly, an increase in school attendance, prompted by a new interschool baseball program. The community later voted for a bond that would underwrite a much-needed road. Hanifan describes these developments as "social capital . . . that in life which tends to make these tangible substances [money, real estate, etc.] count for most in the daily lives of a people, namely, good-will, fellowship, mutual sympathy and social intercourse among a group of individuals and families who make up a social unit . . . whose logical center is the school." The result is "a social potentiality sufficient to the substantial improvement of living conditions in the whole community." Hanifan, "School Rural Community Center," 130.

Beginning in the 1930s, Flint, Michigan, with support from the Charles Stewart Mott Foundation, pioneered a community school model that anticipated the contemporary model. See Larry Decker, *The Evolution of the Community School Concept* (Fairfax, VA: National Community Education Association, 1999).

4. Robert Putnam, *Bowling Alone: The Collapse and Revival of American Community* (New York: Simon and Schuster, 2000), 290. "The embeddedness of young persons in the enclaves of adults most proximate to them, first the family and second, a surrounding community of adults," shapes their futures, concluded University of Chicago sociologist James Coleman, summing up decades' worth of research. James Coleman, "Social Capital in the Creation of Human Capital," *American Journal of Sociology* 94, supplement (1988): S95–S120.

5. The typology of social capital is developed in Michael Woolcock, "The Place of Social Capital in Understanding Social and Economic Outcomes," *Isuma: Canadian Journal of Policy Research* 2, no. 1 (2001): 1–17.

6. Milbrey McLaughlin, *Community Counts* (Washington, DC: Public Education Network, 2000), www.publiceducation.org/pdf/Publications/support_services/communitycounts.pdf. See also Richard Elmore, *School Reform from the Inside Out* (Cambridge: Harvard University Press, 2004), 166: "[The community school movement is] an intentional response to assembling the necessary developmental assets for school success, dealing with the dogged prevalence of conditions that stymie school readiness and sap the energy of most reform-minded schools."

7. Some school districts run community schools themselves rather than seeking partners as site coordinators.

8. Rita Axelroth, *Raising Graduation and College Going Rates: Community School Case Studies* (Washington, DC: Coalition for Community Schools and National Association of Secondary School Principals, 2009); Saba Bireda, *A Look at Community Schools* (Washington, DC: Center for American Progress, 2009), www.americanprogress.org/issues/2009/10/community_schools.html; Martin Blank, Sheri DeBoe Johnson, and Bela Shah, "Community as Text: Using the Community as a Resource for Learning in Community Schools," *New Directions in Youth Development* 97, no. 1 (2003): 107–121. Changing the culture of the school is always a daunting task. See Seymour Sarason, *Revisiting the Culture of the School and the Problem of Change* (New York: Teachers College Press, 1996).

9. Edward Zigler and Matia Finn-Stevenson, "From Research to Practice: The School of the 21st Century," *American Journal of Orthopsychiatry* 77, no. 2 (2007): 175–181; Matia Finn-Stevenson and Edward Zigler, *Schools of the 21st Century: Linking Child Care and Education* (Boulder: Westview Press, 1999); Matia Finn-Stevenson, Laura Desimone, and An-Me Chung, "Linking Child Care and Support Services with the School: Pilot Evaluation of the School of the 21st Century," *Children and Youth Services Review* 20, no. 3 (1998): 177–205; Christopher Heinrich, Misty Ginacola, and Matia Finn-Stevenson, *The School of the 21st Century Is Making a Difference: Findings from Two Research Studies* (New Haven, CT: Zigler Center in Child Development and Social Policy, Yale University, 2006), www.yale.edu/21C/documents/2006_IssueBrief_WebVersion.pdf; Matia Finn-Stevenson, "Evaluation of the Arkansas School of the 21st Century Program, 2006–2007" (New Haven, CT: Zigler Center in Child Development and Social Policy, Yale University, 2007), www.yale.edu/21C/documents/2007ARExecSum_001.pdf. Schools of the 21st Century should not be confused with 21st Century Community Learning Centers, a federally funded after-school program.

10. Joel Klein, "Urban Schools Need Better Teachers, Not Excuses, to Close the Education Gap," *U.S. News & World Report*, May 4, 2009, www.usnews.com/articles/opinion/2009/05/04/urban-schools-need-better-teachers-not-excuses-to-close-the-education-gap.html.

11. Diane Ravitch, *The Death and Life of the Great American School System: How Testing and Choice Are Undermining Education* (New York: Basic Books, 2010); Claus von Zastrow, "Diane Ravitch on the Broader, Bolder Approach to Accountability," *Public School Insights*, June 26, 2009. See also "A Broader, Bolder Approach to Education: Main BBA Statement," www.boldapproach.org/statement.html. I am on record as endorsing the Broader, Bolder Approach to Education.

12. Stacey M. Childress, Denis P. Doyle, and David A. Thomas, *Leading for Equity: The Pursuit of Excellence in the Montgomery County Public Schools* (Cambridge: Harvard Education Press, 2009). My summary of Montgomery County's initiative is informed by a day-long visit to the district and an interview with Superintendent Jerry Weast. See also David Kirp, in "Book Reviews," *Journal of Policy and Management* 29, no. 1 (2009), www3.interscience.wiley.com/cgi-bin/fulltext/123195123/PDFSTART.

13. Gordon MacInnes, *In Plain Sight: Simple, Difficult Lessons from New Jersey's Expensive Effort to Close the Achievement Gap* (New York: Century Press, 2009). The summary of Union County's initiative is informed by several visits to the district and an interview with Superintendent Sandy Sanger. See also David Kirp, in "Book Reviews," *Journal of Public Policy and Management* 29, no. 1 (2009).

14. Heinrich et al., *School of the 21st Century*. A study of high-implementing community schools found that, as compared with a matched sample of schools, eighth-graders in the program scored 6 percent higher in math and 5.1 percent higher in reading. *Research Brief 09*.

15. Patricia Lauer, Motoko Akiba, Stephanie B. Wilkerson, Helen S. Apthorp, David Snow, and Mya L. Martin-Glenn, "Out-of-School-Time Programs: A Meta-Analysis of Effects for At-Risk Students," *Review of Educational Research* 76, no. 2 (2006): 275–313; Geoffrey Borman and N. Maritza Dowling, "Longitudinal Achievement Effects of Multiyear Summer School: Evidence from the Teach Baltimore Randomized Field Trial," *Educational Evaluation and Policy Analysis* 28, no. 1 (2006): 25–48; Barbara Heyns, "Schooling and Cognitive Development: Is There a Season for Learning?" *Child Development* 58, no. 5 (1987): 1151–1160.

16. In the typical community school, about a third of the students participate in after-school activities, said Jane Quinn, of the New York City Children's Aid Society, in my interview with her. Such participation can be seen as a measure of student attachment to the school. Students who participate in such activities are likely to do better academically than those who choose not to get involved, making it difficult to parse the distinctive effects of after-school programs. However, the fact that overall academic performance in community schools is better than in comparable traditional schools indicates that these extra programs have a value-added effect. See Joy Dryfoos, *Evaluation of Community Schools: Findings to Date* (Washington, DC: Coalition for Community Schools, 2000), www.communityschools.org/Resources/evalcontents .html.

17. Annette Lareau, *Unequal Childhoods: Class, Race, and Family Life* (Berkeley: University of California Press, 2003); Laura Desimone, "Linking Parent Involvement with Student Achievement: Do Race and Income Matter?" *Journal of Educational Research* 93, no. 1 (1999); Eric Dearing, Kathleen McCartney, Heather Weiss, Holly Kreider, and Sandra Simpkins, "The Promotive Effects of Family Educational Involvement for Low-Income Children's Literacy," *Journal of School Psychology* 42, no. 6 (2004): 445–460; Joel Erion, "Parent Tutoring: A Meta-Analysis," *Education and Treatment of Children* 29, no. 1 (2006): 79–106; William Jeynes, "The Relationship Between Parental Involvement and Urban Secondary School Student Academic Success: A Meta-Analysis," *Urban Education* 42, no. 1 (2007): 82–110; William Jeynes, *Parental Involvement and Academic Success* (New York: Taylor and Francis, 2010); Joanne D'Agostino, "Title I Parent-Involvement Programs: Effects on Parenting Practices and Student Achievement," in Geoffrey Borman, Sam Stringfield, and Robert Slavin, eds., *Title I: Compensatory Education at the Crossroads* (Mahwah, NJ: Lawrence Erlbaum Associates, 2001), 117–136; Milbrey McLaughlin and Patrick Shields, "Involving Low-Income Parents in the Schools: A Role for Policy?" *Phi Delta Kappan* 69, no. 2 (1987): 56–60; *Strong Families, Strong Schools: Building Community Partnerships for Learning* (Washington, DC: U.S. Department of Education, 1994), www.eric.ed.gov/ERICDocs/data/ ericdocs2sql/content_storage_01/0000019b/80/15/bc/13.pdf. It's far easier to conscript parents than to end poverty.

18. Esther Ho Sui-Chu and J. Douglas Willms, "Effects of Parental Involvement on Eighth-Grade Achievement," *Sociology of Education* 69, no. 1 (1996): 126–141 at 138.

19. Anthony Bryk and Barbara Schneider, *Trust in Schools: A Core Resource for Reform* (New York: Russell Sage, 2001); A. T. Henderson and K. L. Mapp, *A New Wave of Evidence: The Impact of School, Family and Community Connections on Student Achievement* (Austin: Southwest Educational Laboratory, 2002).

20. Dryfoos, *Evaluation of Community Schools*. See also ICF International, *Communities in Schools National Evaluation School-Level Report* (Fairfax, VA: ICF International, 2008). Communities in Schools (CIS), a community school model designed to reduce dropouts by bringing community services and mentors into the schools, had the desired effect—but only when schools fully implemented the model.

21. See, for example, S. A. Weissman and D. C. Gottfredson, "Attrition from After-School Programs: Characteristics of Students Who Drop Out," *Prevention Science* 2, no. 2 (2002): 202–205; American Youth Policy Forum, "Helping Youth Succeed Through Out of School Programs," 2006, www.aypf.org/publications/HelpingYouthOST2006.pdf.

22. Paul Tough, *Whatever It Takes: Geoffrey Canada's Quest to Change Harlem and America* (New York: Houghton Mifflin Harcourt, 2008). But see also Helen Zelon, "Is the Promise Real?" *City Limits* 34, no. 1 (2010).

23. Arne Duncan, "The Promise of Promise Neighborhoods: Beyond Good Intentions," 2009, www2.ed.gov/news/speeches/2009/11/11102009.html.

24. Susanne James-Budumy, Mary Moore, Linda Rosenberg, John Deke, and Wendy Mansfield, *When Schools Stay Open Late: The National Evaluation of the 21st Century Community Learning Centers Program* (New York: Mathematica, 2005). Efforts to eliminate this program on the basis of the unfavorable evaluation have failed.

25. Duncan, "Every School a Community School." Duncan referenced the $4.35 billion "race to the top" fund as well as the $650 million innovation fund for "districts and nonprofits that are partnering in two ways—to close the achievement gap and raise the bar" as potential sources of funding for community schools.

26. In Britain, all 23,000 public schools are now "extended schools." The transformation began with a carefully monitored pilot project a decade ago. The pilot program was expanded gradually. The "core offer," which all schools must deliver, includes child care for primary school students from 8 A.M. to 6 P.M.; a variety of activities, such as tutoring and sport and music clubs; "swift and easy access" to specialized services such as speech therapy and counseling; family support services; and adult and family learning. The extended schools have received generally high marks. Colleen Cummings, Alan Dyson, Daniel Muijs, Ivy Papps, Diana Pearson, Carlo Raffo, Lucy Tiplady, and Liz Todd, with Deanne Crowther, *Evaluation of the Full Service Extended Schools Initiative* (Manchester: University of Manchester, 2007), www.dcsf.gov.uk/research/data/uploadfiles/RR852.pdf. My impression, based on visits to communities across Britain with different socioeconomic and ethnic demographics, is consistent with that conclusion. Where it is fully applied, the extended-day approach has radically changed how these schools are run.

27. Philip Coltoff, *The Crusade for Children: The Children's Aid Society's Early Years to Present* (New York: Children's Aid Society, 2008).

28. Jane Quinn and Joy Dryfoos, *Community Schools: A Strategy for Integrating Youth Development and School Reform* (New York: Wiley, 2005).

29. Children's Aid brought in Mt. Sinai Hospital, located nearby, to run a health center.

30. Kira Krenichyn, Helene Clark, Nicole Schaefer-McDaniel, and Lymari Benitez, *21st Century Community Learning Centers at Children's Aid Community Schools* (New York: ActKnowledge, 2008), www.aypf.org/documents/CASCommunitySchools EvaluationSummary.pdf; Anthony Cancelli, Ellen Brickman, Arturo Sanchez, and Glenda Rivera, "The Children's Aid Society/Board of Education Community Schools: Third-Year Evaluation Report" (New York: Fordham University Graduate School of Education, 1999); Ellen Brickman and Anthony Cancelli, "Washington Heights Community Schools Evaluation: First-Year Findings" (New York: Fordham University Graduate School of Education, 1997); Helene Clark and Robert Engle, "The Children's Aid Society Community Schools: Summary of Research Findings, 1992–1999" (New York: Center for Human Environments, City University of New York Graduate Center), www.communityschools.org/CCSFullReport.pdf.

Children's Aid runs an adolescent pregnancy prevention program for eleven- and twelve-year-olds that focuses on helping youth develop personal goals and desires for a productive future as well as on sexual literacy and education about the consequences of sexual activity. The elaborate program includes academic tutoring, SAT prep, college trips, a job club, and family life and sex education as well as weekly music, dance, writing, and theater workshops and full medical and dental care. An evaluation found that girls in the program were two-thirds less likely to become pregnant and significantly more likely to graduate from high school and enroll in college. Susan Philliber, Jacqueline Kay, Scott Herrling, and Emily West, "Preventing Pregnancy and Improving Health Care Access Among Teenagers: An Evaluation of the Children's Aid Society-Carrera Program," *Perspectives on Sexual and Reproductive Health* 34, no. 5 (2002): 244–251. The study met the top tier evidentiary standard of the Coalition for Evidence-Based Policy. See Social Programs That Work, "Carrera Adolescent Pregnancy Prevention Program," Coalition for Evidence-Based Policy, http://evidencebasedprograms.org/wordpress/?page_id=114.

31. Ravitch, *The Death and Life of the Great American School System*.

32. John Goering and Judith Feins, eds., *Choosing a Better Life? Evaluating the Moving to Opportunity Social Experiment* (Washington, DC: Urban Institute Press, 2003); Tami Leventhal and Jeanne Brooks-Gunn, "Moving to Opportunity: What About the Kids?" Center for Children and Families, Teachers College, Columbia University, 2001, www.nber.org/mtopublic/NY/ny_mto_kids.pdf.

33. Lisa Sanbonmatsu, Jeffrey Kling, Greg Duncan, and Jeanne Brooks-Gunn, "Neighborhoods and Academic Achievement: Results from the Moving to Opportunity Experiment," *Journal of Human Resources* 41, no. 4 (2007): 644–691.

34. Jonathan Crane, "The Epidemic Theory of Ghettos and Neighborhood Effects of Dropping Out and Teenage Childbearing," *American Journal of Sociology* 96, no. 5 (1991): 1226–1259.

35. Robert Sampson, Patrick Sharkey, and Steven Raudenbush, "Durable Effects of Concentrated Disadvantage on Verbal Ability Among African-American Children," *Proceedings of the National Academy of Sciences* 105, no. 3 (2008): 845–852.

36. Robert Putnam, "Community-Based Social Capital and Educational Performance," in Diane Ravitch and Joseph Viteritti, eds., *Making Good Citizens: Education and Civil Society* (New Haven, CT: Yale University Press), 58–96. See also

Ricardo Stanton-Salazar and Stephanie Urso Spina, "The Network Orientations of Highly Resistant Urban Minority Youth: A Network-Analytic Account of Minority Socialization and Its Educational Implications," *Urban Review* 32, no. 3 (2000): 227–261.

37. As Putnam has pointed out, the next step is to test the proposition with more localized data.

38. Associated Press, "Schools in Chicago Are Called the Worst in the Nation by Education Chief," *New York Times*, November 8, 1987.

39. Anthony Bryk, Penney Bender Sebring, Elaine Allensworth, Stuart Luppeseu, and John Easton, *Organizing Schools for Improvement: Lessons from Chicago* (Chicago: University of Chicago Press, 2010).

40. Civic Committee of the Commercial Club of Chicago, "Still Left Behind: Student Learning in Chicago's Schools," June 2009, www.civiccommittee.org/Still%20Left%20Behind%20v2.pdf.

41. Nick Anderson, "Education Secretary Arne Duncan's Legacy as Chicago's School Chief Questioned," *Washington Post*, December 29, 2009.

42. The Polk Brothers Foundation staff and educators and civic organizations elsewhere were introduced to the idea of community schools by Joy Dryfoos in *Full-Service Schools: A Revolution in Health and Social Services for Children, Youth and Families* (San Francisco: Jossey-Bass, 1998).

43. Sam Whalen, "Three Years into Chicago's Community Schools Initiative (CSI): Progress, Challenges, and Emerging Lessons" (unpublished paper, 2007).

44. Sam Whalen, Elizabeth Duffrin, and Joanne Howard, "Sustaining Community in a Changing Neighborhood: Beethoven Elementary School and the Boys and Girls Clubs of Chicago" (unpublished paper, 2008).

45. Sam Whalen, "Corporate Partnership Goes to Community School: P Herzl Elementary, the Center for Community Arts Partnerships at Columbia College Chicago, and J. P. Morgan Chase" (unpublished paper, 2008).

46. Chase's involvement in Chicago's community schools can be traced directly to the Children's Aid schools in New York. Judy Dimon, the wife of Chase CEO Jamie Dimon, has long been a passionate supporter of those schools, and when they moved to Chicago she became a leading advocate for community schools in her new hometown.

47. Duncan, "Every School a Community School."

48. National Center for Community Schools website, http://nationalcenterfor communityschools.org/.

49. Joy Dryfoos, "Full-Service Community Schools: A Strategy, Not a Program," *New Directions for Youth Development* 107 (2005): 7–14. The Children's Aid Society helped Portland, Oregon, establish the Schools Uniting Neighborhoods (SUN) system. Dianne Iverson, "Schools Uniting Neighborhoods: The SUN Initiative in Portland, Oregon," *New Directions for Youth Development* 107 (2003): 81–87; Claire Goss and Suzanne Bouffard, "Complementary Learning in Action: The SUN Service System," Harvard Family Research Project, 2007, www.hfrp.org/publications-resources/browse-our-publications/ complementary-learning-in-action-the-sun-service-system; Chris Hebdon, "Community Schools Uniting Neighborhoods in Portland, Oregon" (unpublished paper, 2009).

CHAPTER 4

1. Marc Freedman, *The Kindness of Strangers* (San Francisco: Jossey-Bass, 1991), 24.

2. Nancy Morrow-Howell, James Hinterlong, and Michael Sherraden, "Experience Corps: Effects on Student Reading" (St. Louis: Center for Social Development, Washington University, 2009), http://csd.wustl.edu/Publications/Documents/RB09–03.pdf. Half of the students scored in the bottom 16th percentile; one in eight scored in the bottom 3 percent. The evaluation generated considerable popular attention and led directly to the multimillion-dollar Justice Department grant. Jay Mathews, "Class Struggle," *Washington Post*, June 6, 2009. See also G. W. Rebok, M. Carlson, and T. A. Glass, "Short-Term Impact of Experience Corps Participation on Children and Schools: Results from a Pilot Randomized Trial," *Journal of Urban Health* 81, no. 1 (2004): 79–93. Other articles in that issue of the journal assess different facets of Experience Corps, including its positive impact on seniors who participate. Experience Corps uses two tutoring models: one-on-one tutoring and in-class group tutoring. Group tutoring costs $500 per student; one-on-one tutoring costs as much as $1,200.

3. James Coleman, *Foundations of Social Theory* (Cambridge: Harvard University Press, 1990), 334.

4. On mentoring generally, see Irene Wielawski, "Mentoring Young People," *Robert Wood Johnson Health Care Foundation Anthology*, vol. 9 (Princeton, NJ: Robert Wood Johnson Foundation, 2008), www.rwjf.org/files/research/022208weilawskianthology.pdf. The fact that the mentor isn't a family member may be beneficial, since he or she doesn't carry the personal baggage that comes with propinquity. Jean Rhodes, "A Theoretical Model of Youth Mentoring," in David L. Dubois and Michael J. Karcher, eds., *Handbook of Youth Mentoring* (Thousand Oaks, CA: Sage, 2005), 30–43. The handbook is a trove of research on all aspects of the field.

5. Cited in Harriet Bartlett, "The Social Survey and the Charity Organization Movement," *American Journal of Sociology* 32, no. 2 (1928).

6. David Baker and Colleen Maguire, "Mentoring in Historical Perspective," in David L. Dubois and Michael J. Karcher, eds., *Handbook of Mentoring* (Thousand Oaks, CA: Sage, 2005), 14–29.

7. Joseph Tierney and Jean Grossman, with Nancy Resch, "Making a Difference: An Impact Study of Big Brothers/Big Sisters" (Philadelphia: Public/Private Ventures, 1995).

8. Gary Walker, "Youth Mentoring and Public Policy," in David L. Dubois and Michael J. Karcher, eds., *Handbook of Youth Mentoring* (Thousand Oaks, CA: Sage, 2005).

9. MENTOR, "Statistics and Research" (n.d.), www.mentoring.org/mentors/about_mentoring/statistics_and_research/.

10. Gary Walker, "Mentoring, Policy and Politics," Public/Private Ventures Brief, October 2007, www.ppv.org/ppv/publications/assets/224_publication.pdf.

11. "Seeking to Turn Summit Promises into Service," *Education Week*, May 7, 2007, www.edweek.org/ew/articles/1997/05/07/32.

12. In a letter to the Obama Presidential Transition Team, Butts laid out intergenerational policy priorities. See http://otrans.3cdn.net/ec7b7a70cfee2cbf28_z3m6b9chg.pdf.

13. Urie Bronfenbrenner, *The Ecology of Human Development* (Cambridge: Harvard University Press, 1979), 5.

14. Walker, "Youth Mentoring and Public Policy."

15. Ibid.

16. Laurence Steinberg, "The Logic of Adolescence," in Peter Edelman and Joyce Ladner, eds., *Adolescence and Poverty* (Washington, DC: Center for National Policy Press, 1991), 19–36.

17. Keynote address by U.S. Secretary of Education Arne Duncan, "Community Schools Practicum 2009—October 22, 2009" (unpublished).

18. Walker, "Youth Mentoring and Public Policy."

19. Freedman, *Kindness of Strangers*, 187. In identifying the pool of potential mentors, advocates point out that 10,000 Americans turn sixty every day. As they enter retirement, many seniors say they want to get involved in youth-oriented programs, and they have the time available to do so. However, only a small number of adults are interested in being mentors. The demands are great: once a week for several hours each time adds up to a 100-hour yearly commitment—more than two work weeks. Peter Scales, *Other People's Kids: Social Expectations and American Adults' Involvement with Children and Adolescents* (New York: Springer, 2003).

20. By building housing adjacent to a campus for foster-care youth and a public school, San Diego has pioneered a program that places adults and children in full-time proximity to one another. In Hope Meadows, Illinois, fifty neglected and abused children were given permanent homes with adopted parents and "honorary grandparents." Both models look to intergenerational relationships as a solution to the perpetual shuffling of young discards from one foster home to the next. See Wes Smith, *Hope Meadows: Real Life Stories of Healing and Caring from an Inspiring Community* (New York: Berkley, 2001). Though anecdotal accounts and, in the case of San Diego, small-scale evaluations have shown that these programs have positive effects, few communities have tried to emulate either approach. At each site a charismatic leader has been largely responsible for the success of the initiative, and that isn't a recipe easily replicated.

21. George Beiswinger, *One to One—The Story of the Big Brothers/Big Sisters Movement in America* (Philadelphia: Big Brothers/Big Sisters of America, 1985). There are several Big Brothers "founding" stories—mentoring is an idea that fit the moment, and the idea was likely "discovered" independently in a number of cities.

22. Big Brothers Big Sisters, "FAQ" (n.d.), www.bbbs.org/site/c.diJKKYPLJvH/b.1539785/.

23. Tierney et al., *Making a Difference*. The effect on minority youngsters was especially striking. Those who had a Big Brother were 70 percent less likely to use drugs. The array of benefits from mentoring is detailed in Keoki Hansen, *One-to-One Mentoring: Literature Review* (Philadelphia: Big Brothers Big Sisters, 2007), http://oregonmentors.org/files/library/BBBS%201-to-1%20Mentoring%20Literature%20Review%20_Mar%202007_.pdf.

24. Jean Rhodes, Jean Grossman, and Nancy Resche, "Agents of Change: Pathways Through Which Mentoring Relationships Influence Adolescents' Academic Adjustment," *Child Development* 71, no. 6 (2000): 1662–1671.

25. Carla Herrera, Jean Grossman, Tina Kauh, and Amy Feldman, with Linda Jucovy, "Making a Difference in Schools: The Big Brothers Big Sisters School-Based Mentoring Study" (Philadelphia: Public/Private Ventures, 2007).

26. This shift in practice coincides with "best practice" research. See Timothy Cavell and Anne-Marie Smith, "Mentoring Children," in David Dubois and Michael Karcher,

eds., *Handbook of Youth Mentoring* (Thousand Oaks, CA: Sage, 2005), 160–176. Another excellent review of the literature is David Dubois, Bruce Halloway, Jeffrey Valentine, and Harris Cooper, "Effectiveness of Mentoring Programs for Youth: A Meta-Analytic Review," *American Journal of Community Psychology* 30, no. 2 (2002): 157–197.

Big Brothers Big Sisters has also developed a mentoring model using high-school students. The results have been decidedly mixed. Carla Herrera, Tina Kauh, Siobhan Cooney, Jean Grossman, and Jennifer McMaken, "High School Students as Mentors" (Philadelphia: Public/Private Ventures, 2008). The report recommended changes in the program that, consistent with its commitment to research-based practice, the organization has put in place.

27. Amachi, a program developed by Big Brothers Big Sisters and Public/Private Ventures that provides mentoring for the children of prisoners, has recruited substantial numbers of African American male mentors, something that other programs have been unable to do. In Philadelphia, Amachi's first site, 82 percent of the mentors were African American and 34 percent were African American males. The program now operates in thirty-four cities. W. Wilson Goode and Thomas Smith, "Building from the Ground Up: Creating Effective Programs to Mentor Children of Prisoners" (Philadelphia: Public/Private Ventures, 2005).

28. The 1995 study found that one in four adult volunteers was not doing a very good job. Tierney et al., *Making a Difference*.

29. John Bowlby, *Child Care and the Growth of Love* (London: Penguin, 1953), is the classic work in the field.

30. Michel Duyme, "Discontinuity and Stability of IQs: The French Adoption Studies," in P. L. Chase-Lansdale, K. E. Kiernan, and R. J. Friedman, eds., *Human Development Across Lives and Generations: The Potential for Change* (New York: Cambridge University Press, 2004), 111–119.

31. Michael Rutter, "Protective Factors in Children's Responses to Stress and Disadvantage," in M. W. Kent and J. E. Rolf, eds., *Primary Prevention in Pathology*, vol. 3, *Social Competence in Children* (Hanover, NH: University Press of New England), 49–74; Emily Werner and Ruth Smith, *Journeys from Childhood to Midlife: Risk, Resilience and Recovery* (Ithaca, NY: Cornell University Press, 2001).

32. In 2009 Campbell received the Purpose Prize, which is awarded annually by Civic Ventures to "social innovators in their encore careers." See "Duncan Campbell: 2009 Purpose Prize Winner," www.youtube.com/watch?v=mhtQz7YGs_g.

33. Friends of the Children, "2007 Annual Report for Friends of the Children—Portland" (2008).

34. Friends of the Children, "Our Children," www.friendsofthechildrenny.org/Our_Children.

35. The names of the youngsters, as well as some personal details, have been changed to protect their privacy.

36. Metis Associates, "Friends of the Children New York: 2005–2006 Evaluation Report" (unpublished, 2007).

37. The discussion of Eugene Lang's career draws on Peter Henley and Mark Drajem, "Where Have You Gone, Andrew Carnegie?" www.thefreelibrary.com/Where+have+you+gone,+Andrew+Carnegie%3F-a018285113; Rachel Breitman and Del Jones, "Should Kids Be Left Fortunes, or Be Left Out?" *USA Today*, July 26, 2006, www.usatoday.com/money/2006-07-25-heirs-usat_x.htm.

38. William Geist, "One Man's Gift: College for 52 in Harlem," *New York Times*, October 19, 1985, www.nytimes.com/1985/10/19/nyregion/about-new-york-one-man-s-gift-college-for-52-in-harlem.html?scp=10&sq=eugene%20lang%20+%20dropping%20out%20+%201985&st=cse.

39. The impact of GEAR UP on college enrollment is described in N. C. Aizenman, "Mentoring Helps Immigrants' Children Aim for College," *Washington Post*, December 13, 2009, www.washingtonpost.com/wp-dyn/content/article/2009/12/12/AR2009121201305.html.

40. Duncan, "Community Schools Practicum 2009."

41. "Public Housing and Public Schools: How Do Students Living in NYC Public Housing Fare in School?" New York University, Furman Center for Real Estate and Urban Policy (n.d.), FurmanCenterandIESPPolicyBriefPublicHousingand-PublicSchools_000.pdf.

42. Arthur Levine and Jane Nidiffer, *Beating the Odds: How the Poor Get to College* (San Francisco: Jossey-Bass, 1996), 147–178; Christopher Coons and Elizabeth Petrick, "A Decade of Making Dreams into Reality: Lessons from the I Have a Dream Program," *Yale Law and Policy Review* 10, no. 1 (1994); Joseph Kahne and Kim Bailey, "The Role of Social Capital in Youth Development: The Case of 'I Have a Dream'" (unpublished, 1997); Laudan Aron and Burt Barnow, "Evaluation of New York City's Class of 1992 'I Have a Dream' Program" (unpublished, 1994); Beth Manke and Susan Haggard, "I Have a Dream Houston: Program Evaluation 2000–2001 (unpublished, 2001). The studies are summarized in "'I Have a Dream': The Impacts," Abete Corporation, 2001, www.ihaveadreamfoundation.org/images/downloads/Arete Summary_2003.pdf.

CHAPTER 5

1. David Kirp, "Our Two-Class System," *American Prospect*, November 2009, www.prospect.org/cs/articles?article=our_two_class_system.

2. This section draws on interviews with Greg Powell, chairman of the board of the Alfond Foundation, and Elizabeth Vanderweide, program manager at Finance Authority of Maine, who directs the Harold Alfond College Challenge. See also Matthew Stone, "Harold Alfond's College Fund for Babies Expands," *Kennebec (Maine) Journal and Morning Sentinel*, December 12, 2008, http://morningsentinel.maine today.com/news/local/5702592.html.

3. Thomas Paine, *Agrarian Justice* (New York: Penguin, 1987 [1795]). Emphasis in original.

4. Corporation for Enterprise Development, "Assets and Opportunity Scorecard" (n.d.), http://scorecard.cfed.org/.

5. Corporation for Enterprise Development, "Hidden in Plain Sight: A Look at the $335 Billion Federal Asset-Building Budget," Spring 2004, www.cfed.org/knowledge _center/publications/savings_financial_security/hidden_in_plain_sight_a_look_at_the _335_billion_federal_asset-building_budget_long_version/. Since the publication of this report, the asset-building budget is estimated to have grown to more than $400 billion. The gap is even more extreme for African American families. Dalton Conley, *Being Black, Living in the Red: Race, Wealth, and Social Policy in America* (Berkeley: University of California Press, 1999).

6. Michael Sherraden, *Assets and the Poor: A New American Welfare Policy* (New York: M. E. Sharpe, 1991). See also Robert Haveman, *Starting Even: An Equal Opportunity Program to Combat the Nation's New Poverty* (New York: Simon and Schuster, 1988).

7. Sherraden, *Assets and the Poor*, 164. A best-selling advice book, Robert Kiyosaki, *Rich Dad, Poor Dad: What the Rich Teach Their Kids About Money—That the Poor and Middle Class Do Not* (New York: Running Press, 2009), gives fathers some pointers about how to overcome the "advice gap."

There is a debate among researchers as to the extent and nature of the "asset effect" on life outcomes. Compare John Brynner, "Effect of Assets on Life Chances," in John Brynner and Will Paxton, eds., *The Asset Effect* (London: Institute for Public Policy Research, 2001) (showing an effect), and Ruth Lister, "Poverty, Material Insecurity and Income Vulnerability: The Role of Savings," in Sonia Sodha and Ruth Lister, eds., *Saving Gateway: From Principles to Practice* (London: Institute for Public Policy Research, 2006) (showing that assets increase resilience to shocks), with Stephen McKay and Elaine Kempson, *Savings and Life Events* (London: Department of Work and Pensions, 2003) (finding no evidence of an effect). This research focuses on adult savings plans, however, not child savings accounts.

8. Kirp, "Our Two-Class System."

9. Reid Cramer, "Net Worth at Birth: A Proposal to Improve Life Chances Through a National System of Children's Savings Accounts," in Duncan Lindsey and Aron Shlonsky, *Child Welfare Research: Advances for Practice and Policy* (New York: Oxford University Press, 2008); Reid Cramer, "The Big Lift: Federal Policy Efforts to Create Child Development Accounts," CSD Working Paper no. 09-43, 2009, csd.wustl.edu/Publications/Documents/WP09-43.pdf; Katie Campbell and Jason Newman, "A Springboard to the Ownership Society," in *Big Ideas for Children* (Washington, DC: First Focus, 2008).

10. Ray Boshara, "The $6000 Solution," New America Foundation, 2003, http://newamerica.net/publications/articles/2003/the_6_000_solution.

11. Bruce Ackerman and Anne Alstott, *The Stakeholder Society* (New Haven, CT: Yale University Press, 1999), 88.

12. In 2009, the National Alliance to End Homelessness estimated that the recession could force an additional 1.5 million families into homelessness. *Homelessness Looms as Potential Outcome of Recession* (Washington, DC: National Alliance to End Homelessness, 2009), www.endhomelessness.org/content/general/detail/2161. Children have been disproportionately affected: It is estimated that the recession will make 2 million youngsters homeless. Philip Lovell and Julia Isaacs, "The Impact of the Mortgage Crisis on Children" (Washington, DC: First Focus, 2009), www.firstfocus.net/Download/HousingandChildrenFINAL.pdf.

13. Gillian Lester, "Means Testing, Universalism, and the Formation of Social Preferences" (unpublished paper, 2009).

14. Cramer, "The Big Lift."

15. Fred Goldberg, "The Universal Piggy Bank: Designing and Implementing a System of Savings Accounts for Children," in Michael Sherraden, ed., *Inclusion in the American Dream: Assets, Poverty, and Public Policy* (New York: Oxford University Press, 2005); Barbara A. Butrica, Adam Carasso, C. Eugene Steuerle, and Desmond J. Toohey, *Children's Savings Accounts: Why Design Matters* (Washington, DC: Urban Institute, 2008), www.urban.org/UploadedPDF/411677_childrens_savings.pdf.

16. Ann Kornblut, "Clinton Floats Baby Bonds," *Washington Post*, September 29, 2007. The $5,000 figure may have been a slip of the tongue, since Clinton had previously spoken of a *$500* baby bond at birth, with an additional $500 government contribution at age ten. A bipartisan proposal to establish a $500 child savings account in California, which ran into a buzzsaw of opposition when introduced into the state legislature in 2007, was quickly shelved.

17. Peter D. Hart Research Associates, "Public Opinion Poll on Children's Savings Accounts: Public Support for Children's Savings Accounts," Corporation for Enterprise Development, 2007, http://cfed.org/knowledge_center/publications/savings_financial_security/public_opinion_poll_on_childrens_savings_accounts_public_support_for_childrens_savings_accounts/; DeQuendre Neeley-Bertrand, "Making the Connection: Messages That Advance Children's Development Accounts," Corporation for Enterprise Development, 2008, http://preview.cfed.org/assets/pdfs/Growing_Knowledge_August_08.pdf

18. Min Zhan and Michael Sherraden, "Assets and Liabilities, Educational Expectations, and Children's College Degree Attainment," Working Paper no. 09-60, Center for Social Development, George Warren Brown School of Social Work, Washington University, St. Louis, Missouri, 2009.

19. Sherraden, *Assets and the Poor*, 150–155.

20. Edward Scanlon, Jennifer Wheeler Brooks, and Deborah Adams, "How Young People Save Money: Findings from Interviews with SEED Participants" (St. Louis: Center for Social Development, 2006); Edward Scanlon and Deborah Adams, "Do Assets Affect Well-Being? Perceptions of Youth in a Matched Savings Program" (St. Louis: Center for Social Development, 2006); William Elliott III, Margaret Sherraden, Lissa Johnson, Susan Johnson, and Signe Peterson, "College Expectations Among Young Children: The Potential Role of Savings" (St. Louis: Center for Social Development, 2007); Lewis Mandell, "Teaching Young Dogs Old Tricks: The Effectiveness of Financial Literacy Intervention in Pre–High School Grades," in Thomas Lucey and Kathleen Cooter, *Financial Literacy for Children and Youth* (Athens, GA: Digitaltext books.biz, 2008); Min Zhan and Michael Sherraden, "Assets, Expectations, and Children's Educational Achievement in Female-Headed Households," *Social Service Review* 77, no. 2 (2003): 190–211; Stuart White, "What's the Point of (Something Like) the Child Trust Fund," presentation for seminar on Asset-Based Welfare in Ireland: Lessons from the UK Child Trust Fund, 2008, www.policyinstitute.tcd.ie/White_CTFseminar_28MarchTCD.pdf.

21. College Board, http://professionals.collegeboard.com/policy-advocacy/affordability/student-aid.

22. Michael Sherraden and Margaret Clancy, *SEED for Oklahoma Kids: Demonstration Child Development Accounts for All Newborns* (St. Louis: Center for Social Development, 2008), www.ok.gov/treasurer/documents/SEED%20OK%20CSD%20Backgrounder.pdf.

23. In Maine and Oklahoma, simply convincing parents to sign up has proven to be more arduous than expected. Elizabeth Vanderweide, the state official who directs Maine's baby bond program, said that "it's hard to bring people who have never had a bank account into the financial system. They don't believe the trust fund is real. 'There must be a catch,' they say, 'It's too good to be true.'" Every initiative aimed at helping poor people runs into the same problem—those who need the help the most are least likely to take advantage of it. The Earned Income Tax Credit is a good illustration.

Though it puts money into the pockets of individuals who don't have enough income to benefit from tax credits, fully a fifth of the $36 billion credit goes unclaimed. Federal Reserve Bank of Boston, "Earned Income Tax Credit," www.bos.frb.org/consumer/eitc/index.htm.

24. David L. Kirp, *The Sandbox Investment: The Preschool Movement and Kids-First Politics* (Cambridge: Harvard University Press, 2007), 226–240. Several other countries have established child development accounts. See Vernon Loke and Michael Sherraden, "Building Assets from Birth: A Global Comparison of Child Development Account Policies," CSD Working Paper no. 08-03, Center for Social Development, 2008, http://www.treasurer.il.gov/programs/childsavings/pdf/Building%20Assets%20from%20Birth.pdf.

25. The U.S. models do not take the British "leave it to the market" approach but instead rely on account managers or a model of government-managed accounts.

26. Reid Cramer, "Asset-Based Welfare Policy in the UK: Findings from the Child Trust Fund and Saving Gateway Initiatives" (Washington, DC: New America Foundation, 2007), www.newamerica.net/publications/policy/asset_based_welfare_policy_uk; Jim Bennett, Elena Chavez Quezada, Kayte Lawton, and Pamela Perun, "The UK Child Trust Fund: A Successful Launch" (Washington, DC: Institute for Public Policy Research, 2008).

27. Rajiv Prabhakar, *The Assets Agenda* (Basingstoke, UK: Palgrave, 2008); Gavin Kelly and Ravin Likssauer, *Ownership for All* (London: Institute for Public Policy Research, 2000); David Nissan and Julian Le Grand, *Capital Idea: Start-Up Grants for Young People* (London: Fabian Society, 2000); Tony Blair, "The Saving Grace of the Baby Bond," *The Guardian*, April 10, 2003.

28. Sherraden and Clancy, *SEED for Oklahoma Kids*.

CHAPTER 6

1. Eleanor Clift, "The Target," *Newsweek*, December 21, 2009, www.newsweek.com/id/227756.

2. In 2008–2009, the federal poverty level was $22,050 for a family of four.

3. Lake Research Partners, "Partnership for America's Economic Success/Invest in Kids Working Group," January 28, 2008, www.partnershipforsuccess.org/docs/ivk/iikmeeting_slides200801lake.pdf.

4. Mike Lillis, "Baucus: CHIP Expansion Was Highlight of the Decade," *Washington Independent*, January 4, 2010, http://washingtonindependent.com/73097/baucus-chip-expansion-was-highlight-of-the-decade. Baucus wound up voting for an amendment that salvaged CHIP in the Senate proposal. On dollars versus rhetoric in congressional budgeting, see Aaron Wildavsky and Naomi Kaiden, *The New Politics of the Budgetary Process* (New York: Longman, 2002).

5. The children's budget is estimated differently by different researchers. By one calculation, federal expenses on children totaled $295 billion in 2008, with an additional $72.7 billion in tax savings. Julia Isaacs, Tracy Vericker, Jennifer Macomber, and Adam Kent, *Kids' Share: An Analysis of Federal Expenditures on Children Through 2008* (Washington, DC: Brookings Institution and Urban Institute, 2009), 13, http://www.firstfocus.net/library/reports/kids-share-analysis-federal-expenditures-children-through-2008. First Focus calculates the children's budget at $265.9 billion, making somewhat different assumptions about what to include. First Focus, *Chil-*

dren's Budget 2009, www.firstfocus.net/Download/CB2009.pdf. Missing from both estimates are programs run by the Departments of Defense, State, Agriculture, and Housing and Urban Development as well as the Environmental Protection Agency.

6. The mission statement can be found at www.leadershipcouncil.org. In May 2007, House Speaker Nancy Pelosi organized a National Summit on America's Children, which brought together experts on early education, child care, and health. The intention was to set a policy agenda based on the best scientific evidence. The children's advocacy groups were excited by the prospect, but there was no follow-through and the initiative died.

7. The 2009 stimulus bill doubled the budget of the Education Department, and several billions of dollars are earmarked for early education, after-school programs, and other items on the advocates' wish list.

8. First Focus is a member of the Leadership Council but has not been able to play a unifying role.

9. First Focus, *Children's Budget 2009*.

10. First Focus, *Children's Budget 2010*. The Annie E. Casey Foundation compiles a trove of valuable information on numerous indicators of child well-being, including federal, state, and community-level data. See www.kidscount.org.

11. A Children's Budget Act introduced in recent years has drawn bipartisan support. See www.ffcampaignforchildren.org/fact_sheets/ChildrensBudgetAct.pdf.

12. *Beyond Rhetoric: A New American Agenda for Children and Families. Final Report of the National Commission on Children* (Washington, DC: Government Printing Office, 1991), http://www.eric.ed.gov/PDFS/ED336201.pdf; Westen Strategies, "Making Children a National Priority" (research conducted for First Focus, unpublished, 2009).

13. Drew Westen, *The Political Brain: The Role of Emotion in Deciding the Fate of the Nation* (New York: PublicAffairs, 2007).

14. Westen Strategies, "Making Children a National Priority." The report noted: "A White House Convening would focus the nation's attention, . . . encourage leadership, . . . [and] generate substantive recommendations." First Focus, "First in Ten: A National Commission on Children," (2009) (unpublished).

15. Prepared Remarks for Secretary of Housing and Urban Development Shaun Donovan at the Brookings Institution Metropolitan Policy Program's Discussion— "From Despair to Hope: Two HUD Secretaries on Urban Revitalization and Opportunity," National Press Club, July 14, 2009, www.hud.gov/news/speeches/2009 -07-14.cfm. The mechanism is ingenious: cities seeking Choice Neighborhood funds are favored if they include provision for early education in their applications.

16. As a member of the Presidential Transition Team in 2008–2009, I helped to craft the Early Learning Challenge Fund proposal.

17. "Remarks of Senator Barack Obama: Our Kids, Our Future," November 20, 2007, www.barackobama.com/2007/11/20/remarks_of_senator_barack_obam_34.php. Obama also recorded a "kids first" video for YouTube.

18. Dugger's analysis draws on several of the papers he commissioned. See, for example, Jagadeesh Gokhale, "The Public Finance Value of Today's Children (and Future Generations)," Working Paper no. 1, Invest in Kids Working Group, May 2003, www.ced.org/docs/report/report_ivk_gokhale10_2003.pdf.

19. Ellen Key, *The Century of the Child* (New York: G. P. Putnam's Sons, 1901); Judith Sealander, *The Failed Century of the Child* (New York: Cambridge University Press,

2003). See also William Koops and Michael Zuckerman, eds., *Beyond the Century of the Child* (Philadelphia: University of Pennsylvania Press, 2003).

20. *Official Proceedings of the White House Conference on Child Health and Protection* (Washington, DC: United States Daily Publishing Corporation, 1930).

21. This section is adapted from David Kirp, *The Sandbox Investment: The Preschool Movement and Kids-First Politics* (Cambridge: Harvard University Press, 2007), 251–258.

22. Dugger isn't the only one who has been able to enlist the business community. The First Five Years Fund has linked the billionaire backers of Educare centers across the United States with members of Congress, including Republicans and Blue Dog Democrats. See Chapter 2.

23. Vote Kids, "Louisiana," www.votekids.org/?page_id=1461.

24. These reports use instant-response dial sessions with "opinion influencers" and voter samples. Luntz, Maslansky Strategic Research, "The Language of First Focus," 2007 (unpublished); Westen Strategies, "Making Children a National Priority." Though the methodologies differ, the conclusions of the two reports are consistent.

25. Westen Strategies, "Making Children a National Priority."

26. Luntz, Maslansky, "The Language of First Focus."

27. "Memo from Tony Fabrizio and David Lee to First Focus," September 24, 2007 (unpublished).

28. Julia Isaacs, C. Eugene Steuerle, Stephanie Rennane, and Jennifer Macomber, *Kids' Share 2010: Report on Federal Expenditures on Children Through 2009* (Washington, DC: Urban Institute and Brookings Institution, 2010), www.urban.org/publications/412140.html.

APPENDIX

1. This calculation includes initial set-up cost of $500 million. Consistent with what has happened in other countries that have adopted Triple P, the calculation assumes that Triple P will be fully implemented in the first year of funding.

1. The estimate assumes a sliding-fee scale with some costs borne by parents and enrollment rates varying from 10 to 30 percent, as detailed in the Early Education section of the Appendix.

2. The range is based on costs per child varying from $9,200 to $12,000 per child per year, and assumes a sliding fee scale, with some costs borne by parents and enrollment rates varying as detailed in the Early Education section of this Appendix.

3. See "Hoyer, Nelson reintroduce community schools bill," *Ed Daily*, September 11, 2009.

4. The full annual cost of $3.75 billion is based upon the annual average cost of $3.75 billion proposed in the ASPIRE Act of 2009. See The New America Foundation, "The ASPIRE Act of 2009," *www.newamerica.net/publications/policy/aspire_act_2009*.

5. Some of these funds could come through Race to the Top, the Education Department initiative, funded at $4 billion in 2010; the Obama Administration is requesting a similar amount for 2011. First Focus offers alternative routes for identifying relevant funds in their annual Children's Budget report. See "Children's Budget 2009," *www.firstfocus.net/pages/3631*.

6. This number draws on data from the Child Welfare League of America's (CWLA) 2010 "Funding for Selected Children's Programs Chart." It includes $5.04 billion in

Child Care and Development Block Grant funds (both mandatory and discretionary) and $7.23 billion in Head Start funding.

7. CWLA 2010 Funding Chart. This figure includes $1.166 billion in funding for two Education Department programs, Twenty-First Century Community Learning Centers (mainly used for after-school programs) and $10 million for Promise Neighborhoods, the 2010 down payment for that initiative to link schools and communities. In 2010 the Obama Administration requested $250 million to implement that program.

8. This number includes $100 million in Fiscal Year 2011 for youth mentoring programs at the Office of Juvenile Justice Delinquency Prevention (OJJDP). Other funding sources include $50 million at Health and Human Services to fund community-based organizations that provide mentors for children with an incarcerated parent, $25 million in Fiscal Year 2011 for youth mentoring grants at OJJDP to serve Native American communities, and $100 million from the 2009 Serve America Act.

9. Though there is currently no federal spending on college savings accounts, Maine projects spending $7 million to $9 million annually on state-funded college savings accounts for all newborns in the state.

10. The Parents as Teachers (PAT) program, which costs $3500 per child, is open to all parents of young children regardless of how much they earn or the number of children in the family. If PAT were to serve 9 million children (20 percent of the children in the United States below age ten), the annual cost would be $3.15 billion. I have not included this program in the cost estimate.

11. Ron Prinz. "Re: Triple P—Fully-Funded Cost," e-mail to author, December 14, 2009.

12. National Institute for Early Education Research, "Cost of Providing Quality Preschool Education to America's 3-and 4-year olds, " http://nieer.org/resources/facts/index.php?FastFactID=5.

13. Jens Ludwig and Isabelle Sawhill, "Success by Ten: Intervening Early, Often, and Effectively in the Education of Young Children," *The Hamilton Project*, February 2007, 1–8.

14. Greg Duncan, Jens Ludwig, and Katherine A. Magnuson, "Reducing Poverty Through Preschool Interventions," *The Future of Children* 17, no. 2 (Fall 2007): 143–160.

15. Julia Isaacs, "Cost Effective Investments in Children," *Budgeting for National Priorities*, January 2007, 10.

16. Ibid., 11.

17. Isaacs also proposed investing $20 million in "research and demonstrations to continue studying and refining the key dimensions of program quality."

18. Julia Isaacs, "Impacts of Early Childhood Programs: Early Head Start," *First Focus*, September 2008.

19. "Hoyer, Nelson Reintroduce Community Schools Bill," *Ed Daily*, September 11, 2009.

20. See "S.1411—Keeping Parents and Communities Engaged Act," Open Congress, www.opencongress.org/bill/111-s1411/show, and "H.R.3762—Working to Encourage Community Action and Responsibility in Education Act," Open Congress, www.opencongress.org/bill/110-h3762/show.

21. Joseph Radelet. "Re: Mentoring—Fully-funded cost," e-mail to author, January 16, 2009. Public/Private Ventures has also performed a cost-analysis study of mentoring

programs. See "Making A Difference in Schools," Public/Private Ventures, www
.ppv.org/ppv/publications/assets/220_publication.pdf.

22. Although Friends of the Children currently projects a $9500 per-child cost, we
derive the lower $7000 per-child estimate from to-scale cost savings the organization
would achieve through the use of AmeriCorps volunteers (an approach currently
being tested in Boston) and other efficiencies.

23. America's Promise Alliance, *Dropouts Diplomas and Dollars* (2007) www.google
.com/search?q=america%27s+promise+%2B+dropouts&ie=utf-8&oe=utf-8
&aq=t&rls=org.mozilla:en-US:official&client=firefox-a

24. The U.S. Census estimates that 23.3 percent of children under the age of eighteen live below 130 percent of the poverty line. See U.S. Census Bureau, "Annual
Demographic Survey," http://pubdb3.census.gov/macro/032005/pov/new02_130_0
.htm.

25. As noted in Chapter 4, establishing a quality mentoring program is not just a
problem of funding—any mentoring program will also be restricted by the number
of available volunteer mentors. The numbers of children used for calculations in this
section do not reflect the total number of children who could benefit from a mentor.
Rather, they represent a realistic estimate of the number of available mentors.

26. See New America Foundation, "The ASPIRE Act of 2009," www.newamerica
.net/publications/policy/aspire_act_2009

INDEX

David L. Kirp is a professor and former acting dean at the Goldman School of Public Policy at the University of California at Berkeley. In 2008 he served on President Obama's Transition Team. He previously taught at the Harvard Graduate School of Education and was the founding director of the Harvard Center on Law and Education, where he helped shape landmark litigation expanding the rights of poor and minority students, English-language learners, and special needs children. He has been a consultant to public agencies, foundations, and nonprofit organizations, among them the U.S. Department of Education, the New Zealand Ministry of Education, the Victoria (Australia) Premier's Department, the California Public Utilities Commission, and the Hewlett and Packard foundations. A former associate editor of the *Sacramento Bee* and a syndicated columnist, he now writes for publications including the *New York Times*, the *Los Angeles Times*, *The American Prospect*, and *The Nation*. He is the author most recently of *The Sandbox Investment: The Preschool Movement and Kids-First Politics*, a *San Francisco Chronicle* "best book" and winner of the Association of American Publishers Award for Excellence, and of *Shakespeare, Einstein, and the Bottom Line: The Marketing of Higher Education*, which received the best book award from the Council for the Advancement and Support of Education. A graduate of Amherst College and Harvard Law School, and a former trustee of Amherst College, he is currently a member of the board of Experience Corps, which sends adult volunteers to tutor elementary school students; Friends of the Children, which provides twelve years of mentoring to children who are at greatest risk; and the San Francisco Coro Center for Civic Leadership, which trains future leaders.

PublicAffairs is a publishing house founded in 1997. It is a tribute to the standards, values, and flair of three persons who have served as mentors to countless reporters, writers, editors, and book people of all kinds, including me.

I. F. STONE, proprietor of *I. F. Stone's Weekly*, combined a commitment to the First Amendment with entrepreneurial zeal and reporting skill and became one of the great independent journalists in American history. At the age of eighty, Izzy published *The Trial of Socrates*, which was a national bestseller. He wrote the book after he taught himself ancient Greek.

BENJAMIN C. BRADLEE was for nearly thirty years the charismatic editorial leader of *The Washington Post*. It was Ben who gave the *Post* the range and courage to pursue such historic issues as Watergate. He supported his reporters with a tenacity that made them fearless and it is no accident that so many became authors of influential, best-selling books.

ROBERT L. BERNSTEIN, the chief executive of Random House for more than a quarter century, guided one of the nation's premier publishing houses. Bob was personally responsible for many books of political dissent and argument that challenged tyranny around the globe. He is also the founder and longtime chair of Human Rights Watch, one of the most respected human rights organizations in the world.

·　·　·

For fifty years, the banner of Public Affairs Press was carried by its owner Morris B. Schnapper, who published Gandhi, Nasser, Toynbee, Truman, and about 1,500 other authors. In 1983, Schnapper was described by *The Washington Post* as "a redoubtable gadfly." His legacy will endure in the books to come.

Peter Osnos, *Founder and Editor-at-Large*